Breaking the
Cycle of Abuse

Breaking the Cycle of Abuse

How to Move beyond Your Past to Create an Abuse-Free Future

Beverly Engel

WILEY

John Wiley & Sons, Inc.

Published by John Wiley & Sons, Inc., Hoboken, New Jersey
Published simultaneously in Canada

For general information about our other products and services, please contact our Customer Care Department within the United States at (800) 762-2974, outside the United States at (317) 572-3993 or fax (317) 572-4002.

Wiley also publishes its books in a variety of electronic formats. Some content that appears in print may not be available in electronic books. For more information about Wiley products, visit our web site at www.wiley.com.

Library of Congress Cataloging-in-Publication Data:

Engel, Beverly.
    Breaking the cycle of abuse : how to move beyond your past to create an
abuse-free future / Beverly Engel.
        p.   cm.
    Includes bibliographical references and index.
    ISBN-13 978-0-471-65775-0 (cloth)
    ISBN-10 0-471-65775-1 (cloth)
    ISBN-13 978-0-471-74059-9 (pbk.)
    ISBN-10 0-471-74059-4 (pbk.)
    1. Family violence.   2. Victims of family violence.   3. Sexual abuse
victims.   4. Psychological abuse.   I. Title.
    HV6626.E54 2004
    362.82'924—dc22

                                                            2004006065

Printed in the United States of America

10 9 8 7 6 5 4 3 2 1

I dedicate this book to every person

who continues to struggle to break

the cycle of abuse. I commend you

on your courage and determination

and offer you my deepest respect.

Contents

Part Four Long-Term Strategies to Help You Break the Cycle

Acknowledgments

Once again I wish to thank my fantastic support team: Tom Miller, my editor at John Wiley & Sons, and Stedman Mays and Mary Tahan, my wonderful agents. Tom, thank you so much for your expert guidance, your continued support, your unwavering faith in me, and your incredible patience as I continue to turn in manuscripts that are too long. Sted and Mary, aside from being the best agents anyone could ask for, you are incredible human beings. Thank you for all your hard work and for treating me with dignity, kindness, and generosity. I especially want to thank you, Mary, for all your hard work on my foreign rights sales. Also, thanks for all your fabulous title and subtitle suggestions—including the subtitle to this book!

I would also like to thank all the clients I have worked with over the years who so bravely endeavored to heal from their abuse and break the cycle. I learned much of what I know from you. Even though the case examples presented are composites of clients (in order to protect each client's identity), your stories created the backbone of this book. Thank you for your stories, the insights about yourselves that you shared with me, and most especially for your courage and determination to heal and to stop passing on the legacy of abuse.

I called upoon my many years of experience working with abused and abusive clients for much of what I wrote in this book, as well as my own experiences in healing. I also relied on research conducted by other professionals to round out my own knowledge and experience. I wish to thank the following researchers for their contributions to the field of abuse and trauma recovery: Judith Herman, M.D., author of *Trauma and Recovery: The Aftermath of Violence—from Domestic Abuse to Political Terror,* and Lenore Terr, M.D., author of *Too Scared to Cry: How Trauma Affects Children . . . and Ultimately Us All.*

I would also to thank the following authors for adding to my knowledge about the emotion of shame: Gershen Kaufman, author of *Shame: The Power of Caring,* Herbert E. Thomas, M.D., author of *The Shame Response to Rejection,* and Lewis B. Smedes, author of *Shame and Grace.*

Introduction

You decide to do something, perform one small action, and suddenly it's a tide, the momentum is going, and there's no possibility of turning back. Somehow, even though you thought you foresaw all that would happen, you didn't know the pace would pick up so.

AMANDA CROSS

I've written many books on abuse, but none are more important than this book. If you think about it, breaking the cycle of neglect and abuse is one of the most significant endeavors any of us will ever embark on in our lifetime. This is especially true for those who were emotionally, physically, or sexually abused as children, and for those who have been emotionally or physically abused as adults. There is no greater gift to give to oneself, one's intimate partners, or one's children than to stop passing on to others the abuse or neglect that we have experienced.

The Legacy of Abuse and Neglect

A child who is deprived of the necessary emotional bonding, love, and support grows up with severe emotional and even physical disadvantages. A child who is verbally or physically abused grows up angry and often violent, and suffers from crippling low self-esteem. And children who are sexually abused suffer from severe psychological damage that will follow them for the rest of their lives.

Abuse and neglect never occur in a vacuum. When a child is emotionally, physically, or sexually abused it not only damages the child but it damages the offspring of that child. It damages other members of the child's family—particularly his or her siblings. The same holds

1

true of spousal abuse. When a man beats his wife he is also damaging his children—and his children's children. The same is true when one partner emotionally abuses his or her spouse in front of their children.

Domestic violence and emotional abuse in adult relationships damage more relationships and more lives than anyone can imagine. Domestic violence is a national tragedy of staggering proportions: up to six million women are believed to be beaten in their homes each year; four million incidents are reported.

If we ever hope to bring more peace into our world, we must start by ending the emotional and physical violence that occurs in our homes. Having made the connection between childhood abuse and adult abuse and violence, we need only expand this knowledge to help us understand the violence that occurs in our communities. Children who are neglected or abused are far more likely to become either bullies in school or the victims of bullies. Many of the students discovered with guns at school were found to have been the target of vicious bullying by their classmates. And we know that a majority of those in prison for violent crimes were either emotionally, physically, or sexually abused as children. Those who are mistreated perpetuate a culture of violence that affects us all. Therefore the work we do to break the cycle of abuse in our own families will have even greater ramifications for society at large.

Not Enough Is Being Done

Even though many people recognize the cyclical aspect of neglect and abuse, not enough is being done to break the cycle. Those who come from abusive or neglectful backgrounds are generally not offered courses or therapeutic programs that would help them to clear up the debris of their childhood before embarking on a new life with a husband or wife. Neither are there such programs for potential parents. Most programs are offered only to those who have already begun to abuse their spouses or their children. This book will help partners and parents to avoid becoming abusive in the first place, as well as offer assistance to those who have already begun to abuse.

Abuse prevention should be taught in grammar school and continue through high school, at which time young people can be taught how to choose intimate partners who will treat them with respect, how to prevent emotional and physical abuse in their relationships, and how to avoid becoming an abusive parent.

Those who perpetuate the cycle of neglect and abuse do so because they are out of control and feel they have no other options. This book provides strategies to help you gain control over your emotions and offers alternatives to your old way of reacting to stress, anger, fear, and shame.

Shame is a significant factor in the continuation of the cycle of abuse. It is not only one of the emotions that cause the cycle to continue, but it often prevents people from getting help. In this book I talk a lot about shame and how to overcome its deadly legacy. It is time to stop blaming and shaming those who do to others what was done to them. It does no good to make monsters out of those who continue the cycle of violence by abusing their children or their partners. This negative reaction only serves to harden them even more and make them less inclined to reach out for help.

This book offers the kind of help people need but are usually afraid to admit to other people. There is such a negative stigma attached to physical abuse that those who begin to batter their spouses or children are usually too ashamed to reach out for help. The negative stigma attached to child sexual abuse is even more profound, preventing those who have the impulse or who have actually crossed the line from getting the help they so desperately need. Current laws requiring professionals to report to authorities any suspicion or knowledge of child abuse (although an important step in the protection of children) has also discouraged many from seeking help. This book offers you the opportunity in the privacy of your own home, and at your own pace, to complete an entire therapeutic program designed to help prevent you from crossing the line or from continuing to do so.

Another Legacy: Victimhood

In addition to preventing you from becoming abusive or continuing abusive behavior, this book will help you avoid repeated victimization in adult life. Very few programs are offered for people who have established a pattern of being continually victimized. Those who tend to become victims of emotional, physical, or sexual abuse as adults usually do not realize they have established a pattern until it is well engrained. Even though they may have experienced abuse at the hands of various partners, friends, or coworkers, they often do not recognize the connection between what is currently happening to them and their previous history of abuse. This book will help those of you who have a history of being abused or neglected as adults to understand that unless you take immediate action, you are at great risk of being revictimized or of passing your victim mentality on to your children. It explains why these patterns are established and presents both short-term and long-term strategies that will enable you to break the cycle.

Who Will Benefit from This Book

Nearly every person who was abused or neglected as a child has some concern that they will pass this legacy of pain on to those they love, including their children. If you share this concern, this book will be of great benefit to you. The book will be especially helpful to those who:

- Have already seen signs of abusive or neglectful behavior in themselves. This book offers strategies that will help you short-circuit your negative behavior before it becomes habitual and before you have caused significant harm to your loved ones or to your relationships.
- Have already established a pattern of being a victim in their adult life (i.e., they continually get involved with unavailable, rejecting, or abusive partners). This book offers advice and strategies that will help you realize that there is a way out of the seemingly endless cycle of victimization.
- Are afraid of getting married or becoming a parent out of fear that they will continue the cycle of abuse and neglect.
- Are survivors of childhood sexual abuse and are afraid they will sexually abuse their own children. This book addresses the sensitive topic of how to avoid sexually abusing your own or other people's children if you were sexually abused yourself.

The Time Is Right and the Time Is Now

I have wanted to write this book for a long time, but have never felt the time was right. Now, more than any time in the past twenty-five years, the American public seems to be open to realizing that they are responsible for passing on the legacy of abuse, and that there are things they can do to change this negative pattern. It is within everyone's power to ensure that we do not continue to pass on the neglect and abuse that we experienced.

Twenty years ago, when child abuse was first exposed on a broad basis, people became overwhelmed with the information. Talk show after talk show, article after article, told us about the atrocities that were being visited upon women and children in our culture. We were bombarded with stories about domestic violence, the physical abuse of children, child sexual abuse, and severe child neglect. After several years of this, we just couldn't take in any more. There were no real solutions being presented, and so we were left feeling raw and impotent. We shut down. Because of court cases like the one involving the Menendez brothers, we became tired of "the abuse excuse" and became cynical when anyone talked about his or her abusive childhood. We took on a "get over it" attitude.

Now, after years of people not wanting to talk about any type of child abuse, there seems to be a renewed interest. It has become overwhelmingly clear that people don't just get over child abuse. They continue to suffer, and even more important, they pass on the abuse to other people. This time around we aren't just talking about the subject but about solutions.

Who Am I?

Many of you know me from my previous books on abuse, but some of you may be unaware of my background. Because trust is such an important issue for survivors, I will take this time to tell you a little about myself. There are three factors that make me uniquely qualified to write this book:

1. For nearly thirty years I have worked with clients who were emotionally, physically, or sexually abused as children or adults and am considered one of the world's leading experts in these fields.
2. Through years of study, training, and experience working with clients I have put together a unique program that has proven effective in breaking the cycle of neglect and abuse.
3. I was emotionally, physically, and sexually abused as a child and have struggled against repeating the cycle of abuse for a

great deal of my life. Therefore, I can offer not only important information but compassion and true understanding.

This book will arm you with the kind of information you can use to take positive and powerful action to prevent child abuse, domestic violence, and emotional abuse, as well as teach you how to repair damage that has already occurred to important relationships. The book focuses on both short-term strategies and long-term recovery. Short-term strategies provide ways to short-circuit abusive or victim-like behavior. Long-term recovery focuses on helping you to heal from the damage you experienced from being abused or neglected. Until victims of abuse and neglect experience their own healing, they have a tendency to continue old behaviors and to suffer from deficits in their personality that cause them to repeat the cycle of abuse.

Throughout the book I pose challenging questions meant to confront denial and complacency. I also encourage each of you to revisit your own personal childhood experiences because these experiences shape our behavior and our beliefs concerning abuse. For example, many people have been sexually abused without realizing it and are today suffering from the negative effects without knowing it. Some are actually passing on the legacy of abuse without realizing it. By providing questionnaires, exercises, and writing assignments I encourage each reader to face some important truths about their own childhoods, their denial systems, and their parenting practices.

The Legacy of Hope

The experiences of our childhood directly—consciously or unconsciously—affect our intimate relationships with partners, our parenting styles and thus the self-worth and character of our children, and the way we treat those in our work environment. Although those who were abused or neglected tend to either become abusive or continue being victims in their adult life, this does not mean that there is no hope for change.

Instead of a survivor's legacy being the passing down of abusive or victimlike behaviors, survivors of abuse can offer a legacy of hope to their children and their family in general. This book offers specific strategies that you can begin to use right away, strategies that will produce immediate, tangible results.

PART ONE

UNDERSTANDING THE LEGACY OF ABUSE

CHAPTER 1

What Will Be Your Legacy?

Nicole had wanted a baby for so long, and now here she was holding her newborn daughter, Samantha. She looked down at her beautiful baby and was full of pride. As she began nursing she anticipated feeling love well up inside her. But instead all she felt was impatience. Why isn't she sucking? I don't have all day, Nicole thought to herself. She pushed her nipple inside Samantha's mouth but the baby wouldn't take hold. "What's wrong with this baby? Why is she rejecting me like this?" Unfortunately, this was only the beginning of the problems between Nicole and Samantha, problems that mirrored those Nicole had with her own mother as she was growing up.

Peggy couldn't believe it. Once more she'd chosen a man who turned out to be emotionally abusive toward her. "I don't know why this keeps happening to me; they always seem so nice at the beginning but they all turn out to be monsters. I feel like I'm some kind of 'abuser magnet' or something."

Janice couldn't believe the words that came out of her mouth. "You selfish little bitch. You think the world revolves around you, don't you?" As much as she'd vowed it would never happen, Janice said the exact words to her daughter that her mother had so often said to her when she was growing up.

Marianne was trying to watch her favorite TV program but her two-year-old son kept screeching at the top of his lungs. Marianne had warned the boy to keep quiet but he just wasn't listening. Now she'd had it. She got up, picked up her son, and shook him hard. "What's wrong with you? Why don't you listen?" she yelled. When she finally stopped shaking her son she was horrified to discover that he was unconscious.

Robert couldn't control himself. How dare his wife speak to him like that! He shoved her against a wall and began hitting her over and over again. Then he dragged her near lifeless body through the house and dumped her on the bed. He went back into the kitchen, poured himself another drink and sat down. He was still shaking inside with rage. "That'll teach her to talk back to me," he told himself. But several minutes later another voice inside him whispered, "You're no better than your father—you're a monster just like he was."

Jack was horrified the first time he felt a sexual attraction toward his daughter. "What kind of scumbag am I?" he asked himself. Then he found himself getting angry with her for no apparent reason and pushing her away whenever she wanted to sit on his lap. He criticized the way she dressed and accused her of being a little tramp. Even though he had blocked out the memory of his own molestation as a child on a subconscious level, Jack was deathly afraid that he would do to his daughter what had been done to him.

Karen could hardly breathe. A voice in her head kept saying, "It isn't true, it isn't true." The social worker was telling her that her daughter Heather had accused her stepfather of sexually molesting her. "That's impossible," she found herself saying to the social worker. "He's been a wonderful father to Heather. Heather lies. She always has. You can't believe anything she says. She's just trying to get attention." But deep inside Karen knew the truth. And she knew the horror that her daughter must be going through. She knew because she had been molested when she was a child.

If you relate to any of these examples, you are not alone. There are thousands of others like yourself who are reenacting the abuse or neglect that they experienced as a child, adolescent, or adult. Some, like Janice, Marianne, and Robert, find themselves acting out their frustration and anger in the same ways that their own parents did, in spite of their best efforts to the contrary. Others, like Nicole and Jack, blocked out the memory of their own abuse but are forced to revisit it when they find themselves thinking or behaving in ways that upset or even repulse them. Still others, like Peggy and Karen, repeat the cycle of abuse not by becoming abusive themselves but by continually being victimized or by marrying an abuser and becoming a silent partner in the abuse of their own children.

If you were emotionally, physically, or sexually abused as a child or adolescent, or if you experienced neglect or abandonment, it isn't a question of whether you will continue the cycle of abuse or neglect, it is a question of how you will do so—whether you will become an abuser or continue to be a victim. The sad truth is that no one gets through an abusive or neglectful childhood unscathed, and an even sadder truth that no one escapes without perpetuating the cycle of violence in some way. In many cases, those who were abused or neglected become both abusers and victims throughout their lifetimes. Although this may sound unnecessarily negative to you, it is the truth. Research clearly shows that those who have been abused either absorb abuse or pass it on. In the past twenty-five years studies on abuse and family assaults strongly suggest that abused children become abusers themselves, and that child victims of violence become violent adults. Individuals with a history of childhood abuse are four times more likely to assault family members or sexual partners than are individuals without such a history. Women who have a history of being abused in childhood are far more likely to continue being victimized as adults.

We don't need research to tell us what we know intuitively. If abuse and neglect were not passed down from generation to generation we simply would not have the epidemic of childhood abuse and neglect we are experiencing today. "But I know plenty of people who were abused or neglected as children who did not grow up to be abusers or victims," you might counter. Even though I'm sure there are any number of survivors you can think of who seem, on the surface, to be leading normal, healthy lives, I can assure you that there are many things that go on behind closed doors that the average bystander never knows about. If you could be a fly on the wall in the home of the average couple where one or both were abused or neglected as children I can guarantee that you would see history repeating itself every day in a multitude of ways.

You might see it in the way the husband talks to his wife in the same dismissive, condescending tone in which his father spoke to his mother. Or you'd notice the way his wife passively concedes to her husband's demands, just as her mother did to her father's. You might see it in the way one or both parents has an inordinate need to dominate and control their children. Or both parents may repeat the cycle by neglecting their children in much the same way they were neglected by their parents—putting their own needs before those of their children; not taking an interest in their children's school work, hobbies, or friends; or being emotionally unavailable to their children because they are abusing alcohol.

If one spouse was physically abused as a child you would likely see that kind of abuse repeated as well. Even the most well-meaning person will find himself exploding in the same kind of rage he witnessed or experienced as a child. His rage is likely to surface when he drinks too much, when he feels provoked, or when he is reminded of or "triggered" by memories of his own abuse. Or, the reverse may be true; if a woman was battered as a child or witnessed her mother being abused she may have grown up to marry a man who physically abuses her or her children. Like her mother, she will be rendered helpless— unable to defend herself or to leave.

If one or both spouses was sexually abused you would have to be a fly on the wall in order to discover how the cycle is repeated in the family because it is done in such secrecy. All too often a sexually abused male (and less often, a female) will sexually abuse his or her own children. If he married a woman who was also sexually abused (which happens more times than not) she will often become what is called a silent partner—someone who is in such denial about her own abuse that she stands by while her own children are being molested. Although not all victims of childhood sexual abuse molest their own or other people's children, sometimes they are so afraid of repeating the cycle that they cannot be physically affectionate toward their own children. Others raise their children to believe their genitals and their sexual feelings are dirty and shameful.

There are also many other ways that abuse gets passed down to the next generation that are even more difficult to spot, at least initially. Charlene couldn't wait to have a baby. She wanted someone she could call her own, someone she could shower with love. Much to her surprise, Charlene discovered that she was unable to bond emotionally with her son no matter how much she tried. "I love him, of course, and I'd do anything for him. But somehow I just can't bring myself to be affectionate toward him. And I always feel guarded with him—like I can't allow myself to feel the love I know I have for him."

When Charlene and I explored her history the reason for her inability to bond with her son became evident. Charlene's mother was unable to emotionally bond with her when she was a baby, and her mother remained emotionally distant from her as she was growing up. "I used to question whether she was even really my mother. I always felt like maybe I'd been adopted or something. She just didn't treat me like a mother should treat her own child. My gosh, is that the way I'm treating my son?"

Todd's mother was just the opposite. She had lavished him with affection and emotionally smothered him from the time he was a baby. As Todd got older his mother became very possessive of him, not wanting him to leave her side for very long, not even to go outside to play with friends. This possessiveness continued well into his teens when she would feign sickness to keep him from going out on dates. When Todd did manage to have a girlfriend his mother always found things wrong with her and insinuated that the girl wasn't good enough for him.

Surprisingly, Todd finally did manage to get married, and he and his wife had two children. On the surface, it looked like Todd had escaped unscathed from his emotionally smothering mother. But the truth was that Todd was an extremely angry man. He felt trapped by his wife and kids, just as he had with his mother, and he verbally abused them mercilessly. He also acted out his anger against his mother by compulsively seeing prostitutes and subjecting his wife to venereal disease and AIDS.

Tracey tried all her childhood and into her adulthood to get her father's love and approval. But her father was very remote and distant, and she found she could never get his attention, no matter how hard she tried. When Tracey was eighteen she left home. Although she never gained her father's love, it appeared that Tracey was a normal young woman. She moved to a nearby city and got a good job and her own apartment. Shortly thereafter she met a young man named Randy who swept her off her feet. He lavished her with affection and praise and told her he was madly in love with her. She agreed to marry Randy after knowing him for only two months.

Initially, because Tracey had been so love starved, the fact that Randy didn't like being away from her made her feel good. But gradually Randy became more and more possessive and jealous. He didn't like Tracey going out with her girlfriends because he was convinced she would flirt with other men. Tracey understood this—she was afraid other women would flirt with Randy, too—so she stayed home with him. Then Randy started getting upset when Tracey wanted to go visit her parents. He'd start a fight every time she wanted to go, and she would end up staying home. Gradually, Tracey became isolated from all her friends and family. This was to be the first step in what was to become an extremely violent relationship. In Tracey's attempt to marry someone who was different from her father, someone who would give her the attention she so desperately needed, she had fallen for a man who was so insecure that he had to have complete control over his wife.

As you can see, someone who may seem like they have adjusted quite well to an abusive or neglectful childhood may look entirely different in the privacy of his own home when he is interacting with his partner or his children. But I'm preaching to the choir here. Most of you who are reading this book are aware that there is a risk that you will repeat what was done to you in some way. And for many of you, that risk has already become a reality. You've already begun to abuse your partner, neglect or abuse your children or other people's children, or abuse your employees or coworkers. You've already been emotionally or physically abused by at least one partner and perhaps already established a pattern of being revictimized in the same ways you were as a child.

The cycle of violence is manifested in other ways as well. Those who were raised by alcoholic parents often become alcoholic parents themselves. Those who were raised by parents who suffer from a personality disorder sometimes end up having the same personality disorder. (It can be argued that alcoholism and some personality disorders may have a genetic component, but the truth is that the environmental influence cannot be denied. When many of these individuals enter therapy and begin to work on their unfinished business from childhood, many are able to recover from their disorders.) Our parents also pass on negative beliefs that not only influence us but can cause us to become abusive or victimlike in our behavior.

From a Legacy of Pain to a Legacy of Hope

If we are honest, most of us remember moments when we heard or saw ourselves interacting with our partner, our children, or someone else close to us in ways that are far too reminiscent of the way we ourselves were treated as children. We usually react to these moments with disbelief and horror: "Oh, my God, I sound just like my mother," or "I can't believe I'm acting just like my father." We simply cannot believe that we have repeated the very behaviors we despised in our parents.

The truth is we all carry with us the legacy of our childhoods—whether it is security and nurturing or abandonment and neglect, guidance and respect, or abuse and disdain. In fact, we carry the legacy of not only our own childhoods but also the childhoods of our parents and their parents before them. Unfortunately, often times this legacy is a legacy of pain. Although many parents try to treat their children better than they themselves were treated, generation after generation of people continue to pass down emotional, physical, and sexual abuse to their children and their children's children.

We also repeat the legacy of pain by reenacting the abuse we experienced at the hands of those other than our parents. Those who were sexually abused as children—whether it was by parents, other caretakers or authority figures, siblings, or older children—tend to either reenact the abuse they experienced by introducing younger children to sex, by becoming child molesters when they become adults, or by being continually revictimized as adults. Research shows that children who are sexually abused tend to act out their anger and rage by becoming bullies, torturing animals, and abusing other children. Women often reenact their abuse by becoming strippers and prostitutes, whereas adult males often become sex addicts who make unreasonable demands on their female partners.

The Less Obvious Legacies of Abuse and Neglect

Most people already understand that someone who was neglected; abandoned; or emotionally, physically, or sexually abused as a child is far more likely to repeat the abuse or neglect as an adult than anyone else. They know that many will become abusive themselves unless they take definite steps to prevent it. Those who do not become abusive will likely continue to be victimized throughout their lifetime. But not everyone knows the more subtle legacies of abuse and neglect. For example, those with such a history are often unable to see their partners, children, and even their coworkers clearly. Instead they see them through a distorted lens of fear, distrust, anger, pain, and shame. They see ridicule, rejection, betrayal, and abandonment when it really isn't there. Their low self-esteem will cause them to be hypersensitive and to take things far too personally. And they will likely have control issues causing them to either have a need to dominate others or to be far too easily dominated by others.

Those with a history of neglect or abuse are often unable to trust their partners. Instead they repeat the past dramas of their parents and perceive their partners as enemies instead of allies. Those who become parents find that it is difficult to see their own children's needs and pain without being reminded of their own. They also find it difficult to allow their children to make a mistake without taking it as a personal affront or a sign that they are not a good parent. In work environments past dramas with their parents and siblings get reenacted with bosses and coworkers.

Think about the effect the neglect or abuse you experienced has had on you. How has it affected the way you view yourself and the way you view others? What kind of a legacy are you going to pass on to your children and your children's children? Although these may be depressing or even frightening thoughts, there is a way out of the seemingly endless cycle of abuse and neglect. There are coping skills that can be adopted, positive ways of dealing with anger and shame that can be learned, and ways to make up for the personality deficits that usually accompany experiences of neglect and abuse. There are ways for you to confront your pain, anger, fear, and shame directly so you do not have to transfer it to your partner, your children, your friends, or your coworkers.

Last, but certainly not least, there are ways to break into an abusive or neglectful family system, expose it for what it is, and repair the damage so that one more generation of children does not grow up to either become abusers or victims.

My Story

As a psychotherapist specializing in emotional, physical, and sexual abuse I was able to help each person described in the beginning of this chapter, as well as hundreds of others, to break the cycle of abuse and neglect. But instead of acting as an impersonal expert, throughout the book I will also tell you my own story—and my triumph over my own abusive and victimlike tendencies.

As many of you know from reading my previous books, *The Emotionally Abusive Relationship, The Emotionally Abused Woman,* and *Encouragements for the Emotionally Abused Woman,* I was severely emotionally abused by my mother when I was a child and even into my adulthood. This abuse seriously damaged my self-esteem and created intense shame and rage in me. It also set me up to be in relationships with emotionally abusive partners, as well as becoming emotionally abusive myself.

I was also sexually abused. When I was nine years old the husband of one of my mother's friends molested me for about six months. The molestation included being forced to orally copulate my abuser. This experience changed me forever. I was so shamed by the abuse and sexualized at such an inappropriately early age that I began acting out sexually shortly after the abuse stopped. I introduced sexual play to nearly every child in my neighborhood and came on to a young man who, out of kindness, had volunteered to teach basketball to the neighborhood children. These experiences filled me with incredible shame and added to my belief that I was a horrible person.

But nothing that had been done to me or that I had done to others at that point in my life compared with what came next. It happened one day when I was babysitting for a one-year-old boy. I was twelve years old. As I was changing his diaper I felt overwhelmed with an intense impulse to suck his penis. I was filled with a tremendous desire to feel the power of doing to someone weaker than myself what had been done to me. Fortunately, this impulse was followed by an overwhelming feeling of shame and revulsion. I was horrified at what I was thinking of doing—so horrified that it stopped me in my tracks. Because of the experience I decided to never babysit for the little boy again and avoided babysitting other young boys.

Those experiences gave me a keen understanding of exactly how abuse gets passed from one person to another. They also gave me tremendous empathy for anyone who has experienced the impulse to do to others what was done to them.

How Do You Break the Cycle?

There isn't just one way to break the cycle, there are many. In this book I offer you a program of healing and prevention that encompasses many aspects, including:

- Making the connection between your current behavior and your childhood history of neglect or abuse. This will require many of you to come out of denial once and for all about exactly what was done to you as a child and the effect it has had on your life.

- Placing what was done to you in the context of your family history. As you explore your family history many of you will be shocked to learn that such things as alcoholism, child abuse, child abandonment, domestic violence, depression, and other emotional problems and criminal behaviors have been in your family going back many decades.

- Learning to manage your emotions—especially the emotions of shame, anger, and fear.

- Changing the negative attitudes and beliefs that create a victim or abuser mentality.

- Choosing intimate partners who are capable of having an equal relationship.

- Learning healthy ways of resolving conflicts in your intimate relationships.

- Deciding whether you are a good candidate to become a parent.

- Learning parenting skills that will ensure that you will not become an abusive parent and pass on neglectful or abusive family patterns.

- Continuing to work on healing from the abuse or neglect you experienced.

- Working on gaining independence from your parents and other caretakers.

- Breaking into your dysfunctional family system to ensure that other family members do not harm your children or continue to treat you in damaging ways.

Your "Empowering Tools" for Breaking the Cycle

As you can see, this is a lot of work, and much of it will be difficult, confusing, and even painful. But throughout the process, I want you to know that you are not alone. I'd like you to imagine that I am working right alongside you, supporting you, encouraging you through the rough times. Each chapter will offer you vitally important information that will take time to process, and questionnaires and exercises that will help move you further along on your journey. You may wish to think of each chapter as a separate therapy session. This will encourage you to take it slow and to take the time to process the material in each chapter.

I encourage therapists, group leaders, and teachers to use this book as a guide and teaching aid. If you do use it as a guide for group therapy, for group discussions, or as a teaching tool, you may find it helpful to focus on one chapter for several meetings.

I offer you seven empowering tools that will help you along the way:

1. Support and compassion
2. Education
3. Ongoing strategies
4. Abuse prevention strategies
5. Strategies to help you stop abusing
6. Long-term recovery strategies
7. Information and resources for further help

Support and compassion. It is going to take tremendous courage and determination for you to break the cycle of abuse and neglect. The rewards will be incredible, and that's what will keep you going. But you'll also need support. It is my hope that you will find that support in this book.

There is one message that I want to send you above all others: your tendency to be abusive or to be a victim is not your fault. When you were abused or neglected as a child you experienced tremendous shame. You blamed yourself, thinking that it must be your fault. You may have even been told that it was your fault. Instead of being further shamed because you've had a tendency to repeat the cycle, in this book you will be treated with respect and admiration for having the courage to admit you have a problem. And because I will share my own struggles with breaking the cycle of abuse, you will receive empathy and compassion from someone who not only understands but who has actually been in your shoes.

If we are to truly break the cycle of abuse we must remove the stigma that is attached to being a victim or a victimizer. No one consciously sets out to become an abusive person. Neither does anyone set out to become a victim. We are propelled into these patterns by our upbringing, by our own experiences of trauma and neglect, and by our inability to work through this trauma and neglect. Getting stuck in blame and shame will only hamper your progress in breaking the cycle and will serve no positive function.

Given the right amount of support, education, and strategies, anyone can break the cycle, but without these things we have no choice but to continue blindly repeating what has been done to us.

Education. Another one of the goals of this book will be to educate you about the effects of abuse and neglect. Until you completely understand exactly how you were affected by your past experiences, you will not be in the position to spot the ways you are repeating certain destructive behaviors, and you will not be able to forgive yourself for your actions.

Ongoing strategies. Those who become abusive and those who develop a pattern of victimization have certain behaviors and perceptions in common that tend to set them up for unhealthy, negative ways of relating to others. These include:

- A tendency to suppress or push down their feelings

- Poor communication skills

- The lack of opportunity to learn good coping skills (i.e., solve problems, make decisions, compromise, resolve conflict, take personal responsibility)

- Low self-esteem and shame (i.e., lack of power and control over their own lives, feelings of inadequacy)

- Unrealistic or inappropriate expectations and beliefs (i.e., lessons learned from culture concerning male privilege, promotion of violence)

- Poor habits formed while growing up (i.e., violence is a viable and perhaps only option for resolving problems)

- A self-destructive path (i.e., substance abuse, alcohol abuse, suicidal thoughts)

- Poor health (i.e., poor diet, lack of sleep, low energy)

I offer a program that includes suggestions on how to fully connect with your emotions (perhaps for the first time) and how to heal your shame so that you are not constantly triggered by the behavior of others or constantly surrounding yourself with those who shame you. I'll provide suggestions on how to build up your self-esteem so that you are not as inclined to tear down the self-esteem of those around you or to allow others to treat you in ways that will further damage your self-esteem or self-image. You'll learn how to communicate your needs and desires in an assertive rather than an aggressive, passive, or passive-aggressive manner. You'll learn constructive ways of dealing with stress and ways to communicate your anger instead of erupting in a rage, projecting your anger onto other people, or attracting angry people into your life.

Abuse prevention strategies. You will learn how to prevent becoming abusive or being a victim in your intimate relationships. You'll learn how to spot an abuser or a victim and how to avoid the most common pitfalls of emotionally and physically abusive relationships. You'll also learn how to prevent child abuse, either at your own hands or the hands of your spouse.

Strategies to help you stop abusing or being a victim. The chances are high that many of you reading this book have already begun to repeat the cycle. Because of this I offer specific strategies to help you, no matter what your particular circumstances are: emotional abuse, domestic violence, or childhood sexual abuse.

Long-term recovery strategies. The long-term program will focus on helping you to heal the dysfunctional or traumatic treatment you experienced in childhood. This will include continuing to come out of denial about what actually happened to you, and grieving your neglectful or abusive childhood so you can give up the false hope that you can now get what you didn't receive as a child. It will also include the process of emotionally separating from your family and completing your unfinished business with your abuser and other family members.

Information and resources for further help. At the end of the book I offer resources for finding further help and assistance that goes beyond the scope of this book.

Whether you are afraid of becoming abusive or you have already begun to abuse, afraid of being victimized or have already established a pattern of being a victim, this book will offer you the support, information, and strategies that will not only help you break the cycle of abuse, but change your life. Instead of living a life in which you are stuck in the past, constantly reliving the experience of being emotionally, physically, or sexually abused, you will be able to break free from your past and create a future of your own choosing. Instead of your life being like a broken record, in which you constantly replay the same old refrain over and over, you will be free to write your own song.

This book will also help you change the lives of others. There is nothing more loving or more important than actively working on breaking the cycle of abuse or neglect in one's family. Instead of repeating what was done to you and passing on the legacy of pain to your own children, you will be able to break the cycle and offer your offspring the legacy of hope. Instead of doing to your partners, friends, and coworkers what was done to you, or allowing these people to abuse you, you can begin to treat others with respect and demand respect in return. Instead of blindly passing on the emotional, physical, or sexual abuse that has plagued your family for generations, you can be the first one to expose it and to break the cycle once and for all.

Unless you commit yourself to breaking the cycle of abuse, chances are very high that you will, in fact, do to your children or to your partner the very things that were done to you. Your own healing from the devastating damage you no doubt experienced is obviously important, but making sure you don't inflict damage on others is an important aspect of that healing. If you end up treating others the way you were treated you will not only damage that person's life but further damage your own by adding more shame, humiliation, and guilt to your already shame-bound psyche. By following the steps outlined in the book you can be successful at the biggest undertaking of your life, and by doing so offer your loved ones, your family, and all those with whom you have contact a tremendous gift.

CHAPTER 2

Assessing Your Risk Factors

The events of childhood do not pass, but repeat themselves like seasons of the year.

ELEANOR FARJEON

Jennifer came to see me because she was afraid she was going to lose control and abuse her son Kyle. "I vowed I would never hit my children, but when Kyle talks back to me I just lose it. I've slapped him in the face a few times and I feel horrible about it. I apologize and tell him I'm not going to do it anymore, but I can't seem to control myself. Slapping him is bad enough, but I'm afraid I'm going to hurt him even worse one day."

As I was to learn, Jennifer had good reason to be worried. Her mother had beaten her mercilessly when she was a child, and even though she had promised herself she would never do to her own children what was done to her, there were signs that her son Kyle was indeed in danger. In addition to the fact that she was a victim of physical abuse herself, Jennifer had some other risk factors making her a prime candidate for becoming a child abuser.

In this chapter I offer you information and questionnaires to help you determine the likelihood that you will either become an abuser or develop a victim pattern based on your personal and family history. This will also help you come out of denial and help determine what you will need to do in order to break the cycle. While your past and present behavior is certainly a good barometer, there are many other predictors as well. For example, those studying child abuse and battered women have found that a child who watches his father batter his mother is seven hundred times more likely to use violence in his own life than a child who has no abuse in his home. If that child is also

23

abused himself, the risk for his learning to use violence is raised to one thousand times the norm.

Risk Factor #1: If You Were Abused or Neglected As a Child

Let's start with what we've been alluding to all along: the fact that those who were abused or neglected as children are most at risk of either becoming abusive themselves or of continually being revictimized as adults. Research to date indicates that maltreatment in childhood is associated with aggressive and criminal behavior and a wide range of clinical syndromes and personality disorders in adulthood. For example, in a sample of people seeking medical attention for intravenous drug use, it was found that individuals with a history of childhood abuse were four times more likely to assault family members or sexual partners than were individuals without such a history.

Convened in May 1994, the American Psychological Association's (APA) Presidential Task Force on Violence and the Family spent two years examining the psychological research and clinical experience of practitioners to explore the psychological factors influencing victims or perpetrators of child abuse, dating violence, partner abuse, and elder abuse. Here are some of their findings:

- Children who are neglected or experience harsh, excessive physical punishment and who do not receive support outside the home are the most likely to be violent as adults.

- The likelihood of marital violence increases when one partner had experienced physical abuse and observed violence between the parents.

- Children who experience multiple acts of violence, or violence of more than one variety, appear to be at a greater risk of continuing the cycle of violence.

Adult survivors of childhood abuse are also at great risk of establishing a pattern of repeated victimization in adult life. This is especially true of female victims. The risk of rape, sexual harassment, or battering, although high for all women, is approximately doubled for survivors of childhood sexual abuse. Diana Russell, author of *The*

Secret Trauma, interviewed 930 women and found that of those who had been incestuously abused as children, two-thirds were subsequently raped.

In general, trauma appears to amplify the common gender stereotypes: men with histories of childhood abuse are more likely to take out their aggression on others, whereas women are more likely to be victimized by others or to injure themselves. In fact, the "cycle of violence" theory suggests that physically abused boys are more likely to grow into physically abusive and violent men than their nonabused counterparts and that physically abused girls are more likely to become victims of abuse as adults.

According to many experts, including Judith Herman, M.D., author of *Trauma and Recovery,* most survivors have great difficulty protecting themselves in relationships. According to Dr. Herman, their often unconscious habits of obedience make them vulnerable to anyone in a position of power or authority. Their dissociative defensive style makes it difficult for them to form accurate assessments of danger. Their desperate longing for nurturing and care makes it difficult to establish safe and appropriate boundaries. Their tendency to idealize those to whom they become attached clouds their judgment. And their wish to relive the dangerous situation and make it come out right (repetition compulsion) may lead them into reenactments of the abuse.

If you have clear memories of being abused or neglected as a child then you know you are at risk. But many people's memories are not so clear, and many more question the memories they do have. Even more people have not labeled their experiences as abuse or neglect even though it is clearly what they experienced. For this reason I have provided a brief overview of exactly what constitutes childhood abuse and neglect.

Neglect. Neglect of a child is when a caretaker fails to provide for the child's basic physical needs (food, water, shelter, attention to personal hygiene) as well as his or her emotional, social, educational, and medical needs. It also includes failure to provide adequate supervision.

Emotional Abuse. Emotional abuse of a child includes acts or omissions by the parents or caretakers that can cause serious behavioral, cognitive, emotional, or mental disorders in the child. This form of maltreatment includes verbal abuse (including constant criticism, belittling, insulting, rejecting, and teasing); placing excessive, aggressive, or unreasonable demands on a child that are beyond his or her capabilities; and failure to provide the emotional and psychological nurturing and positive support necessary for a child's emotional and psychological growth and development—providing little or no love, support, or guidance (National Committee for the Prevention of Child Abuse, 1987).

Psychological maltreatment. While sometimes coming under the heading of emotional abuse, this term is often used by professionals to describe a concerted attack by an adult on a child's development of self and social competence, a pattern of psychically destructive behavior. Under this definition, psychological maltreatment is classified into eleven behavioral forms:

1. Rejecting—behaviors that communicate or constitute abandonment of the child, such as a refusal to show affection

2. Isolating—preventing the child from participating in normal opportunities for social interaction

3. Terrorizing—threatening the child with severe or sinister punishment, or deliberately developing a climate of fear or threat

4. Ignoring—where the caregiver is psychologically unavailable to the child and fails to respond to the child's behavior

5. Corrupting—caregiver behavior that encourages the child to develop false social values that reinforce antisocial or deviant behavioral patterns, such as aggression, criminal acts, or substance abuse

6. The denial of emotional responsiveness

7. Acts or behaviors that degrade children

8. Stimulus deprivation

9. Influence by negative or inhibiting role models

10. Forcing children to live in dangerous and unstable environments (e.g., exposure to domestic violence or parental conflict)

11. The sexual exploitation of children by adults and parents who provide inadequate care while under the influence of drugs or alcohol

Physical abuse. The physical abuse of a child includes any nonaccidental physical injury or pattern of injuries inflicted upon a child (under the age of eighteen) that may include beatings, burns, bites, bruises, fractures, shaking, or other physical harm.

Child sexual abuse. Child sexual abuse means any exploitation of a child for the sexual gratification of an adult. It includes any contact between an adult and a child or an older child and a younger child for the purposes of sexual stimulation that results in sexual gratification for the older person. This can range from nontouching offenses, such as exhibitionism and child pornography, to fondling, penetration, incest, and child prostitution. A child does not have to be touched to be molested.

These forms of abuse can occur separately but often occur in combination. (For example, emotional abuse is almost always a part of physical abuse.)

Risk Factor #2: If You Witnessed Abuse or Violence When You Were Growing Up

Witnessing excessive fighting in the home, seeing parents lose their tempers easily, and being exposed to violence in the neighborhood while growing up are harmful to children even if they are not the direct victims. Children are more aggressive and are more likely to grow up to become involved in violence—either as an abuser or as a victim—if they witness violent acts. According to the 1994 APA's Presidential Task Force on Violence and the Family, these circumstances put children at greater risk for becoming victims of violence or participating in violence later on. In particular it was found that boys who witness their fathers abusing their mothers are at an extreme risk of using violence in their own homes as adults.

Children who are routinely exposed to violence and abuse (either by experiencing it or witnessing it) are also likely to develop patterns of coping that contribute to adult revictimization. Most survivors learn to shut down awareness of emotions to protect themselves from overwhelming emotional pain and betrayal. When a child has to constrict awareness of danger and access to emotions in order to survive he or she essentially disables self-protective mechanisms. With emotions and awareness of danger disabled in service of survival, the now-grown survivor is lacking crucial tools that are necessary in adult relationships. He or she cannot access feelings that tell how he or she is doing in relation to someone else, therefore, he or she may become involved with dangerous people.

Risk Factor #3: There Is a History of Abuse or Neglect in Your Family

Child abuse and neglect are intergenerational. This means that if one person in your family was sexually abused, for example, the likelihood is very strong that someone else in the family was, too. And the person who is being accused has more than likely sexually abused other members of the family as well as others outside of the family. The perpetrator was more than likely sexually abused, perhaps by a family member. The same holds true for neglect and emotional and physical abuse. (Recent research shows that a high percentage of battered women are incest survivors.)

Nina initially sought therapy because she had been sexually abused by her stepfather. But several months into the process, she remembered that she had also been molested by an uncle—her mother's brother. She also had another uncle, on her father's side of the family, who had been hospitalized as a sex offender for child molestation. Realizing that sexual abuse was on both sides of her family, I asked Nina to create a family tree, noting who in her family was a known sexual abuser and who was known to have been sexually abused. Nina's family tree revealed one of the most shocking cases of how child sexual abuse gets passed down from family member to family member. (See the diagram on the facing page.)

Risk Factor #4: You Had a Neurological or Psychiatric Impairment as a Child

Children with neurological and psychiatric impairments may have more difficulty controlling the rage that abuse often kindles. Hyperac-

MATERNAL

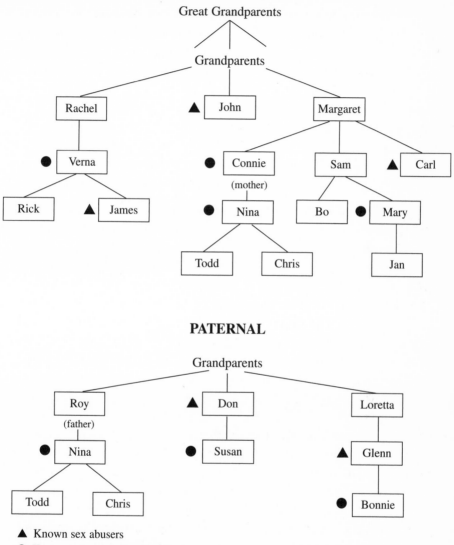

PATERNAL

▲ Known sex abusers
● Known to be sexually abused

tive or impulsive children may encourage abuse from parents who have difficulty controlling their own impulses and anger. Using psychiatric, neurological, physiological, and cognitive tests, Syndor and Sickmund, in their article entitled "Juvenile Offenders and Victims," identified the "intrinsic vulnerabilities" that predisposed juvenile males to engage in antisocial behavior. Those with a combination of an abusive family and two or more vulnerabilities were more likely to commit crimes as adults. The intrinsic vulnerabilities are: below-normal reading level, impaired memory, antisocial personality, paranoia, hallucinations, seizures, and limbic dysfunction.

Risk Factor #5: You Fit the Profile of an Abuser

Those who become abusive tend to have certain predictable traits, attitudes, and behavior patterns. Most of these traits and behaviors are actually adaptations to childhood emotional, physical, and sexual abuse. If you find that you have many or all of the items on the following list it doesn't guarantee that you will become emotionally, physically, or sexually abusive, but it means that you are at a much higher risk of doing so than the average person.

- A childhood background involving emotional, physical, or sexual abuse, or abandonment issues

- Low self-esteem, heavy shame

- A tendency to blame others for your problems

- A strong desire to remain in control, the fear of being out of control, or the need for power and control

- Difficulty empathizing with others or an inability to empathize with others

- Extreme jealousy and possessiveness

- A tendency to be emotionally needy or demanding, or a dependent personality

- Antisocial behavior (you do not believe in society's rules, you have your own set of rules that seem to accommodate your desires)

- An inability to respect interpersonal boundaries and a compulsion to violate boundaries

- An uncontrollable temper (you have a very short fuse and become immediately angry)

- Emotional volatility

- Poor impulse control

- Poor coping skills

- Poor social skills, difficulties developing adult social and sexual relationships

- Intense fear of abandonment

- Repressed anger

- A tendency to be unreasonable or to have unreasonable expectations of a partner and a relationship (i.e., to fix them or solve their problems)

- A tendency to objectify others to avoid being affected by the suffering of others

- Isolation and antisocial temperament

- Recklessness (e.g., dangerous sexual behavior, reckless driving, drug use)

- High levels of stress and high arousal levels

- Selfishness and narcissism

- A history of being abusive (physically, verbally, and sexually) as an adult or an older child

- Aggressive, demanding, or abusive behavior

Risk Factor #6: You Fit the Profile of a Victim

There are specific personality traits, attitudes, and behavior patterns that predispose one to becoming a victim of emotional, physical, or sexual abuse in adulthood. The following is a list of such traits:

- A history of childhood physical, emotional, or sexual abuse

- An intense need for love and affection

- Low self-esteem

- The belief that you don't deserve better treatment

- An inability to set and enforce interpersonal boundaries

- A strong need for a relationship to validate you

- A strong desire to avoid confrontation

- Difficulty expressing anger, a tendency to internalize it, or a tendency act it out in other ways

- A tendency to pretend things are better than they are

- A tendency to feel responsible for others

- A tendency to blame oneself for problems in a relationship

- A fear of being alone

- A tendency to doubt oneself, including one's perceptions

- A tendency to make excuses for another's behavior

- A tendency to be naive about others and to believe that love makes one a better person

Risk Factor #7: You Have Certain Beliefs That Predispose You to Becoming an Abuser

Those who become abusive tend to have certain beliefs about themselves and others that set them up to become abusive. These beliefs set the tone for the relationship and can be abusive in themselves. These include the belief that:

1. You have the right to make most of the decisions in a relationship.

2. Others should do as you say.

3. You are superior or otherwise better (e.g., smarter, more competent, more powerful) than most people, including your romantic partners, and that therefore you deserve special treatment or consideration.

4. You are usually right.

5. Those who complain about your behavior are just too sensitive or too demanding.

6. It is not important what others are feeling. Your feelings are what matters most.

Risk Factor #8: You Have Certain Beliefs That Predispose You to Becoming a Victim

Those who have developed a victim pattern also tend to have certain beliefs about themselves and about relationships. These include believing:

1. You feel inferior or less than other people.

2. You are inadequate as a partner or as a parent.

3. No one who is worth anything will want you.

4. You don't believe you deserve a loving, healthy relationship.

5. You deserve to be treated poorly.

6. Most problems in a relationship are your fault.

7. You feel you can improve a relationship no matter how unhealthy if you just try harder.

Risk Factor #9: You Are a Substance Abuser

Alcohol and drug abuse are major contributing factors to the incidence of child maltreatment. According to the National Center on Child Abuse and Neglect, recent research indicates that among confirmed cases of child maltreatment, 40 percent involve the use of alcohol or drugs.

Substance abuse has been found to be a significant risk factor for domestic violence. Studies also suggest that other factors link men's substance abuse, in particular, to violence against their partners. Among the most important of these factors are:

- Growing up in a violent and substance-abusing family

- Believing that violence against women is sometimes acceptable

- A desire for personal power (because early childhood trauma leaves one feeling helpless and insignificant)

Most notably in the United States substance abuse has been found to increase the risk that men will batter their partners, although the substance per se is not the key factor. Reported drug abuse among batterers ranges from 8 percent to 30 percent. Evidence suggests that ampheta-mines may be the only substance that serves as a possible cause of violent behavior.

Risk Factor #10: You Were Raised in a Misogynistic Environment

Those raised in a misogynistic home come to believe that females are inferior to males and that men have the right and the authority to con-trol and dominate women. Boys who are raised in this kind of envi-ronment often grow up to be emotionally or physically abusive to their wives and daughters, and girls raised in this environment often grow to believe that it is okay to be dominated and controlled and even physically abused by their mate. While not all women who find themselves in abusive relationships grew up in violent homes, what tends to be standard is that their families held strong beliefs in pre-scribed feminine sexual stereotypes.

Risk Factor #11: You Suffer from a Lack of Empathy

Research, including that conducted by the APA Presidential Task Force, consistently finds that lack of empathy is associated with a ten-dency toward family violence. Parents who are unable to empathize with their children (put themselves in their children's place) are more harsh and demanding than parents who have empathy. Men who bat-ter their wives tend to have a lack of empathy for their wives' feel-ings. In fact, having a lack of empathy is an even more powerful predictor of abusive behavior than having a problem with your anger. If you are unable to put yourself in the place of others your behavior will reflect this. You will be able to justify inappropriate, even abusive behavior more easily and you will lack the motivation necessary to change your behavior when it hurts others.

Risk Factor #12: You Have a Negative View of Your Children

Parents who have a negative perception of their children are far more likely to end up abusing them than parents who have a positive view of their children. A study conducted by researchers at Oregon State University, Corvallis, looked at 181 low-income families involved with the Oregon Healthy Start program for more than a year. Each parent's view of his or her offspring was assessed when the child was six months old and again at twelve months of age, utilizing the same measurement procedures used to assess abuse factors. The researchers found that parents who felt that their kids were difficult or deserved punishment were more likely to abuse their offspring. Other aspects of a negative view of the youngster included unrealistic expectations from parents and a perceived lack of bonding between parent and child.

Risk Factor #13: You are Highly Stressed and Have Poor Parenting Skills

Parenting can be stressful in and of itself but when parents are unusually stressed in combination with having poor parenting skills it is a recipe for abuse.

Risk Factor #14: You Have Already Begun to Exhibit Abusive Behavior

At this point you may not be clear about what constitutes abusive behavior. On the other hand, your instincts have probably told you when you have crossed the line. Being demanding and never being pleased is a form of emotional abuse. Denying the truth and trying to make your partner confused about the reality of a situation are also forms of emotional abuse. Domestic violence usually starts with degrading behavior, insults, and putdowns. One partner begins to convince the other that his or her behavior is causing trouble in the relationship and that he or she needs to change. Isolation often comes next, along with jealousy. The verbal abuse usually escalates over time and may include screaming at your partner and insulting him or her in front of others.

If you have hit, shoved, punched, slapped, or any other way physically harmed your partner, you have definitely crossed the line into physical abuse. It really is true that most people don't hit just once, especially if their partner allows it. The same is true if you have hit your child in anger.

Risk Factor #15: You Have Already Begun to Exhibit Victim Behavior

If you tend to feel helpless and taken advantage of in your relationships, you are exhibiting victim behavior. The same is true if you can't stand up for yourself in your relationships. Obviously if you are staying in a relationship that has become emotionally or physically abusive or if you have been in this kind of relationship in the past, you have already established a victim pattern. The same is true if you allow anyone to dominate, degrade, or take advantage of you.

Even when you are brutally honest with yourself, it is still sometimes difficult to determine whether you actually have some of the previously listed warning signs. We are often blind to our own behavior and patterns. The following exercise was designed to help you elicit more information from those close to you.

EXERCISE: *Getting Input from Others*

This exercise will take tremendous courage on your part, but if you are determined to break the cycle of abuse it is a necessary one.

1. One by one, explain to your partner, your children, your siblings, and your close friends that you need their help in order to break the cycle of abuse or neglect in your family.

2. Ask each person to list on a piece of paper at least *three* things that you do on a consistent basis that feels to them like either abusive or neglectful behavior or that seems to exemplify victim behavior. Specifically ask them to recall behavior on your part that has made them feel afraid, ashamed, or bad about themselves in any way. Explain that this is not an opportunity to get back at you by listing all the little things you do that irritate them but that you need their help to identify neglectful or abusive behavior that you may not be aware of. Allow each person to write his or her list in private, without any interference from you, and give them as much time as they need to write their lists. Assure each person that you will not be angry with him or her no matter what he or she writes down.

3. Once each person has completed the list, thank him or her and then go somewhere where you can be alone. Read over the list

carefully. It may be difficult to take in what you are reading, especially if the person has written down negative behaviors that you are unaware of, behaviors that are similar to those of an abusive parent you never wanted to be like, or if the list is quite long. If any of these situations is the case, take a deep breath and remind yourself that you are not a bad person and that you are committed to changing your behavior so you can break the cycle. Do not feel pressured to reconnect with the person who wrote the list right away because it may be too hard to face him or her after reading the list.

4. Write in a journal about how it feels to read the lists, or spend some time with a trusted friend or family member who can offer support. It is probably best that this person not be someone who wrote a list since that person may end up feeling bad about your reactions.

5. Once you have either written about your feelings or shared them with an objective, supportive person, you may feel like returning to the person who wrote the list and sharing your feelings together.

6. If, after reading one list and processing your feelings sufficiently, you feel strong enough to read another list, go ahead and do so. I strongly recommend that if you have a powerful reaction to one list that you do not overwhelm yourself by reading another one right away. Give yourself time to take in the awareness of your behavior before reading another.

Resiliency—Why a Fortunate Few Escape the Cycle of Violence

Not everyone exposed to family violence will become an abuser or a victim. There are a few fortunate souls who escape both of these paths. A few children demonstrate a resiliency—a psychological hardiness—almost from birth, that protects them from becoming violent or that makes them less vulnerable to the effects of violence. But psychological research suggests that resilience comes mostly from early experiences that counter the negative effects of violence and neglect. Put a check mark beside the experiences that apply to you:

- Positive role models; exposure to more positive than negative behaviors in others

- The development of high self-esteem and self-efficacy

- Support from teachers and friends

- A sense of hope about the future

- Belief in oneself

- Strong social skills

- Good peer relationships

- A close, trusting bond with a nurturing adult outside the family

- Great empathy and support from your mother or a mother figure

- The ability to find refuge and a sense of self-esteem in hobbies and creative pursuits, useful work, and assigned chores

- The sense that you are in control of your life and can cope with whatever happens

If you were fortunate enough to have many of these experiences you may have been able to resist the cycle of violence and adopt more socially appropriate behaviors that you saw in your community or at school.

Victim or Abuser?

Now that you know the risk factors you may be wondering whether you are more likely to repeat the cycle by becoming an abuser or by remaining a victim. (Of course many of you already know this due to your current and past behavior.)

Troy witnessed his father verbally and physically abusing his mother throughout his childhood. He hated his father for treating his mother this way, but he grew to hate his mother even more. "Why did she take it from him?" he'd ask himself each time he heard the familiar sounds of shouting and the inevitable thuds as his father knocked his mother around the room. "Why doesn't she take us away to someplace safe?" Terrified of his father and unable to defend his mother, Troy also began to hate himself. "What's wrong with me? Why don't I try to stop him? I'm just a wimp." he'd chastise himself.

With this kind of childhood and without intervention, Troy had only two options. Because he had only these two primary role models, he was either going to grow up to become an abuser, like his father, or a victim, like his mother. Which option do you think he chose? Troy explained his decision to me. "I was terrified of my father but I have to admit I did respect him. I didn't respect my mother. I want people to respect me. So I guess that's why I became like my father."

Think about your role models and the options available to you. Like Troy, you likely had to make the same choice in your life, although it is rarely a conscious one. What do you imagine your thinking process might have been?

Victim and Abuser

Even though you may have a tendency to be more of a victim than a victimizer, or vice versa, it is important to understand that in many respects there is significant overlap. This is true for several reasons:

1. Victimizers often see themselves as victims. If you were a victim of any form of neglect or abuse as a child you will probably consciously or subconsciously continue to react to life as a victim even if you take on the role of being a victimizer. You will continue to feel that life is unfair and that you are at the mercy of others.

2. Victims often victimize others. Victims often wreak havoc in the lives of those who love them, especially their children.

3. People usually do not remain in a victim or victimizer role throughout their lives and in all relationships. For example, you may tend to be a victim in your love relationships but be a victimizer when you are in a position of power, such as when you are promoted to manager at work or when you are with your children. Some people go from being the victim in one romantic relationship to the victimizer in the next.

Dave—Victim, Abuser, and Victim Again

When Dave was a young boy his mother emotionally abused him by constantly criticizing him. He could never do anything right as far as she was concerned. She told him he was lazy and disrespectful, and that he would never amount to anything. When he stood up to her at sixteen she put him into military school to teach him a lesson. There he learned to be as rigid and demanding as his mother was.

Dave did well in college, and soon had a good job as a manager of a major company. Although he got the kind of results the company respected, his employees often filed complaints against him because of his rigid, demanding style. Dave was just as demanding in his personal relationships. He became critical of every woman he was involved with, picking at her about the way she dressed, the way she kept her house—basically everything about her. No matter how hard each woman tried to change to meet Dave's demands, he was never pleased.

Because of Dave's rigid style and critical nature he simply couldn't keep a job or a relationship. Eventually women tired of trying to please him, or he became so critical of the woman that he ended the relationship. Employees complained so much about his abusiveness that companies simply couldn't afford to keep him on.

Then Dave met a woman who swept him off his feet. She was so beautiful and so intelligent that he fell in love with her right away. Instead of feeling like the one in charge, Dave suddenly felt like a little boy around her, eager to please her, wanting assurance from her that she cared about him. But Melissa was a strong and independent woman and she wasn't so quick to fall for Dave. This made her all the more attractive to Dave, a good-looking man who was used to women coming on to him.

Eventually, Melissa acquiesced and became romantically involved with Dave. But this was far different from any relationship Dave had had before—that is, except for his relationship with his mother. In fact, Melissa reminded Dave of his mother—in a good way. Melissa was accomplished and confident, and she kept him on his toes. He respected that. In fact, he respected Melissa more than any other woman he'd been involved with. Unfortunately, Melissa did not respect Dave. In fact, Melissa became as demanding and critical of him as he had been with other women. Caught up in trying to please Melissa, Dave did not realize he was being emotionally abused again—just as he had been with his mother. He compensated by being even more abusive with his employees at work, risking yet another job. By the time I met Dave, he was in crisis. He was afraid of losing his job and Melissa. Even though he was miserable with her, he couldn't bring himself to leave her, especially with his job on the line.

According to most experts, without intervention, violence seems to perpetuate itself throughout the life span. It can start with the abuse of a child, who might later abuse a dating partner, then a spouse, and who might even end up being abused in old age by his or her own off-spring. Dave had started out as an emotionally abused child. He turned into an emotionally abusive boss and partner in his adult romantic relationships. But Melissa changed all that. He was once again being emotionally abused, just like he had been by his mother.

CHAPTER 3

Why We Do to Others (and Ourselves)
What Was Done to Us

*A lot of people go through life beating themselves up
the same way they were beaten up.*

MARLO THOMAS

So why exactly do some people who are neglected or abused tend to
do to others what was done to them? And why do others repeat the
cycle of abuse by continuing to be a victim throughout their lives? In
this chapter, I will provide a brief overview of the most widely held
theories. This will include:

- Learned beliefs and behavior
- The family legacy
- The repetition compulsion
- Posttraumatic stress disorder
- Addiction to trauma
- We go with what is familiar
- The empathy factor
- Identifying with the aggressor
- Attempts to rid ourselves of shame
- Projection
- Learned helplessness
- Self blame
- Clinging behavior

Although these are technically theories it is important to note that they are widely accepted in the professional community, many are based on sound scientific research, and all are based on extensive clinical observation. As you read each of these theories honestly assess which ones resonate with you and which help to explain why you are the way you are. It is important to understand why we have behaved as we have because it helps alleviate the shame and guilt many survivors feel. I have included some checklists and exercises to further help you understand yourself and why you may have developed certain patterns.

Theories Concerning Abusive and Victimlike Patterns

The following theories can explain the behavior of both those who become abusive and those who develop a victim pattern.

Learned Beliefs and Behavior

Your family has passed down to you certain messages and beliefs. These include everything from the way people should treat one another to the role women play in a family. These messages and beliefs have a powerful influence on your thinking and behavior and help shape who you are today.

Joyce was raised in a home where females were considered to be second-class citizens. Her father was considered head of the household and made all the decisions. Her mother never contradicted him. At mealtime, Joyce and her sisters were expected to serve her father and brothers the best cuts of meat and to save plenty of food for them in case they wanted seconds. Joyce had to ask her father's permission before she and her mother could buy her school clothes or books, and had to get his okay before she went out with her friends, even if it was just to play in the backyard.

What Joyce learned from her parents' messages and beliefs was that as a female she was inferior to men. She learned to be passive and to not trust her own judgment. She also learned that it was okay for a man to dominate her. She ended up marrying just such a man. Today Joyce has to ask her husband's permission before she goes out with her friends from work. She has to ask his permission to spend money. Joyce learned to be a victim from both her father and her mother.

Abuse Itself Creates Certain Beliefs

Abuse and neglect tend to create certain unhealthy attitudes and beliefs that set victims up to continue the cycle of abuse. Put a check mark next to each item that applies to you.

Those who end up taking on a victim stance tend to:

- Blame themselves when something goes wrong

- Believe their needs are not as important as those of others

- Doubt themselves, including doubting their perceptions, their knowledge, and their beliefs

- Be overly trusting of others, even when someone has proven to be untrustworthy

- Be naive when it comes to the motives of others

- Believe they should attempt to meet the needs of others (especially those of their partners and children) no matter what the consequences or hardships to themselves are, and that their own needs are not as important as those of others

On the other hand, those who take on an abusive stance tend to:

- Blame others when something goes wrong

- Believe their needs are more important than those of others

- Believe they have a right to expect their needs to be met, no matter what the consequences to others are

- Believe they are always right

- Believe they cannot trust anyone and that others are constantly out to get them

- Believe that everyone is just out for himself or herself

- Underestimate the abilities of others and overestimate their own abilities

- Believe they have a right to defend themselves no matter what the consequences are

- Believe they have a right to expect others to do as they demand and that if someone refuses, he or she is now the enemy

- View his or her partner and children as property

Violence is also a learned behavior. There is overwhelming evidence that abusive behavior is learned because many children who witness abuse grow up to repeat the behavior as spouses and as parents. In one study it was found that 73 percent of batterers witnessed violence as children. When children witness abuse, or are abused, they are seeing, hearing, and learning about violence. They learn that the people you love most may hurt you, that living in fear is normal, and that violence is the way to handle conflict. As they learn, a generational cycle begins in which children grow up to be victims and abusers as adults.

The Family Legacy

In addition to your parents passing on to you certain messages, beliefs, and traits that influence whether you will become an abuser or a victim, your ancestors also passed down a family legacy of neglect and abuse. This legacy includes:

- Parental discipline styles (i.e., physical abuse)

- Physical and emotional neglect (i.e., parental unavailability, no outward signs of affection, acceptance, or approval)

- Parental abandonment, maternal rejection

- Multiple breaks in caregivers, lack of consistent caregiver in early life

- Parental discord, constant fighting

- Domestic violence

- Modeling of violent solutions to problems by key role models

- Negative sexual messages, sexual inappropriateness

- Incest, child sexual abuse

- Substance abuse (alcoholism or drug abuse)

- Personality disorders
- Mental illness or instability

Put a check mark next to each of the items that apply to your family. All of these factors make up your family legacy in regard to abuse and neglect and have influenced whether you became a victim or an abuser. The following exercise will help you get a clearer picture of your family tree and exactly what has been passed down to you.

EXERCISE: *Your Family Issues*

This exercise will help you get an overview of your family history as it pertains to the legacy of abuse and neglect. You will be investigating both sides of your family tree, paying particular attention to the issues mentioned previously.

1. On a large piece of paper write horizontally across the top of the page the names of everyone in your family, starting with yourself and going as far back as you can. For example: you, sisters, brothers, mother, father, aunts, uncles, cousins, grandmothers, grandfathers, great grandmothers, great grandfathers.
2. In the left margin, list all the important aspects of your family's history as it pertains to neglect and abuse. You may wish to use the categories I listed in the previous chapter.
3. Put a check mark in each appropriate slot as you answer the question, "Who was a perpetrator or a victim of the following?"
4. Your chart should look something like the one on the facing page.

You may also wish to make a chart for your partner's family.

This chart is a rather primitive way of completing a family tree. If you would like more detailed information on how to complete a family genogram, you may wish to read any of a number of books by Monica McGoldrick, such as *You Can Go Home Again: Reconnecting with Your Family*.

Repetition Compulsion

Originally defined by Sigmund Freud as the repetitive reenactment of earlier emotional experiences, this type of behavior is often seen in the lives of trauma survivors. It is important to remember that the rep-

	Me	Jane	Bob	Mom	Dad	Aunt Sue	Uncle Joe	Cousin Mark	Grandma Smith	Grandpa Smith
Childhood physical abuse										
Physical and emotional neglect										
Abandonment/ rejection										
Parental fighting										
Domestic violence										
Sexual inappropriateness										
Incest										
Sexual abuse										
Alcoholism										
Drug abuse										
Personality disorders										
Mental illness or instability										

etition compulsion is an *unconscious* drive. It compels us to "return to the scene of the crime," so to speak, in order to accomplish a new outcome or to gain understanding of why something occurred.

To a large extent, the repetition compulsion explains why, if one of your parents was verbally abusive to you, you will tend to be verbally abusive to your partner (and your children). If one or both of your parents were controlling and domineering, you will tend to treat your partner (and children) in a controlling and domineering way. And if one or both of your parents was physically abusive, you may end up becoming a batterer yourself. This is often how abuse gets passed down from one generation to the next.

But not everyone who was abused grows up to be abusive. The repetition compulsion can also work in the opposite way. Instead of becoming abusive yourself, you may develop a pattern of getting involved with abusive people. Instead of becoming your abusive mother or father, you may end up marrying someone very much like him or her. It is an attempt to psychologically master the previous traumatic experience. It's as if your unconscious mind is saying, "If I can only do things differently this time I'll get my mother (or father) to stop abusing me," or "If I can just be patient enough and loving enough I'll get my father (or mother) to love me." It doesn't matter that your partner isn't really your parent but only someone who acts or looks like him; it feels the same, and that's the important thing.

According to Rebecca Coffey, in *Unspeakable Truths and Happy Endings,* trauma therapists have put forth several explanations as to why survivors reenact their traumatization:

- To give a happy ending to a story whose horror still plagues them

- To prove to themselves that they now know how to handle such situations

- To relive the moment of escape or reprieve, which is the moment when the survivor felt most aware of how precious life is

- To assuage their trauma-induced biological addiction to the brain's defensive response to overwhelming fear and helplessness

The Repetition Compulsion and Repressed Memories

In order to avoid breaking down completely and becoming psychotic or comatose under the pain and fear, children who are severely abused or neglected must repress their memories of the events. But Alice Miller (author of many books on child abuse, including *For Your Own Good: Hidden Cruelty in Child-Rearing and the Roots of Violence*) and others have found that the unconscious memories and emotions of a neglected or maltreated child are stored in the body. Even before he has learned to speak, these memories drive the adult to reproduce those repressed scenes over and over again in the attempt to liberate himself from his fears. Former victims create situations in which they can assume the active role. In this way the emotion of fear can be avoided momentarily—but not in the long term, because the repressed emotions of the past don't change as long as they remain unnoticed. They can only be expressed as hatred directed toward oneself and/or scapegoats, such as one's own children. Miller sees this hatred as a possible consequence of the old rage and despair, never consciously felt, but stored in the body, in the limbic brain.

Miller has made the statement that although not every victim becomes a persecutor, she has never met a persecutor who wasn't a victim in his or her childhood. This has been my experience, as well. Parents who mistreat or neglect their children do it in ways that resemble the treatment they endured in their own childhoods, even though they may not have any conscious memory of their own victimization. Fathers who sexually abuse their children are often unaware of the fact that they had themselves been sexually abused. It isn't until they are ordered to receive therapy by the courts that some discover their own history. Then they realize they have been reenacting their own abuse in an attempt to rid themselves of their own fear. As Miller states, "The presence of a warm, enlightened witness—a therapist, social worker, lawyer, judge . . . can help the criminal unlock his repressed feelings and restore the unrestricted flow of consciousness. This can initiate the process of escape from the vicious circle of amnesia and violence."

Posttraumatic Stress Disorder

Posttraumatic Stress Disorder, or PTSD, is a psychiatric disorder that can occur following the experience or witnessing of life-threatening events such as military combat, natural disasters, terrorist incidents, serious accidents, or violent personal assaults like rape. A 1999 study by Kessler et al. in the *American Journal of Psychiatry* found that childhood abuse (particularly sexual abuse) is a strong predictor of the lifetime likelihood of PTSD. Although many people still equate PTSD with combat trauma, the trauma most likely to produce PTSD was found to be rape, with 65 percent of men and 45.9 percent of women who had been raped developing PTSD. People who have experienced assaultive violence (interpersonal victimization) at home or in the community have also been shown to be at very high PTSD risk.

People who suffer from PTSD often relive the traumatic experience through nightmares and flashbacks, have difficulty sleeping, and feel detached and estranged, and these symptoms can be severe enough and last long enough to significantly impair the person's daily life. PTSD is marked by clear biological changes as well as psychological symptoms. It is complicated by the fact that it frequently occurs in conjunction with related disorders such as depression, substance abuse, and problems of memory and cognition. The disorder is further associated with impairment of the person's ability to function in social and family life, including occupational inability, marital problems and divorces, family discord, and difficulties in parenting.

These factors play a significant role in making those with PTSD particularly vulnerable to repeating the cycle of violence for the following reasons:

1. Many people with PTSD turn to alcohol or drugs in an attempt to escape their symptoms.

2. Some characteristics of PTSD can create abusive behavior including:

   • Irritability—extreme irritation and reaction to noise or minor stimulants.

   • Explosive behavior and/or trouble modulating and controlling anger. Rage must go somewhere, either to the self or to others.

3. Some characteristics of PTSD can create victimlike behavior including:

   • Helplessness and passivity—an inability to look for and find problem-solving solutions.

   • Self-blame and a sense of being tainted or evil.

   • Attachment to trauma. Relationships that resemble the original trauma are sought. Involvement with helping figures (therapists and social workers) may end in an attempt to become one with the helper or in total rejection of the helper. A person with PTSD may vacillate between the two reactions.

Addiction to Trauma

Some traumatized people remain preoccupied with earlier trauma and continue to recreate it in some form. Victims of incest may become strippers or prostitutes and victims of childhood physical abuse seemingly provoke subsequent abuse in foster families or become self-mutilators. Still others identify with the aggressor and do to others what was done to them. Clinically, these people are observed to have a vague sense of apprehension, emptiness, boredom, and anxiety when not involved in activities reminiscent of the trauma.

We Go with What Is Familiar

Many survivors of childhood abuse or neglect equate abuse with love and affection. People often choose negative situations that are familiar over positive situations that are unfamiliar. If what is familiar in an intimate relationship is abuse, you may unwittingly get involved with someone who mistreats or abuses you. Remaining unaware of this repetitive cycle, you maintain the childhood victimization into your adulthood.

The Empathy Factor

The empathy factor involves our deep and often spiritual need to understand what was done to us. For example, by repeating the abuse we ourselves experienced we gain empathy for our abusers. We not only understand intellectually why they abused us, we can actually feel what they felt. As bizarre as this may sound, this is the way many people have chosen to find closure to what has happened to them and the way they have been able to forgive their abusers.

This was certainly the case with me. When I discovered, much to my horror, that I had become emotionally abusive in my romantic relationships in much the same way as my mother had been emotionally abusive toward me I gained a sense of empathy and understanding toward my mother that nothing else could have given me. This helped me to resolve my relationship with her by providing me with a deep understanding of why she treated me as she did and an ability to forgive her for what she did.

Abusive Patterns

The following theories help to explain why many who have been abused become abusers themselves.

Identifying with the Aggressor

When Charlie was a boy he and his brothers were severely abused verbally and physically by their father. He frequently terrorized them by waking them up in the middle of the night to inspect their closets and drawers. If he found anything out of place (which he inevitably did) he beat them all mercilessly. You would think that the boys would cling to one another for support, but instead they blamed one another when their father punished them. They also snitched on one another in order to get into their father's good graces. Charlie's oldest brother, Sam, regularly beat up the younger boys, including Charlie. Charlie's mother was afraid of his father and offered no help. Essentially, Charlie and his brothers were on their own.

As a way of adapting to the terror he lived with every day, Charlie blamed himself when his father beat him. He told himself he deserved the beating for not keeping his room cleaner or for not minding his father. He looked up to his father for being such a strict disciplinarian and vowed that he would be the same kind of father when he grew up. Charlie also became the school bully. He picked fights with most of the boys at school, and after school he singled out weaker boys and taunted them all the way home. Why did Charlie admire such an abusive father? Why in the world would he want to be like him? And why did he become like him, picking fights and bullying other boys?

Charlie had identified with his aggressor. After abuse, a victim's view of self and the world is never the same again. The experience of being violated challenges one's most basic assumptions about the self as invulnerable and intrinsically worthy and about the world being just and orderly. Assuming responsibility for the abuse allows feelings of helplessness to be replaced with an illusion of control.

The frequency with which abused children repeat aggressive interactions suggests a link between the compulsion to repeat and identification with the aggressor, which replaces fear and helplessness with a sense of omnipotence.

There are significant gender differences in the way trauma victims incorporate the abuse experience. Studies by Carmen et al., cited in the *American Journal of Psychiatry,* indicate that abused men and boys tend to identify with the aggressor and later victimize others, whereas abused women are prone to be attached to abusive men and allow themselves and their offspring to be victimized further. Boys tend to feel especially humiliated when they are victimized. Instead of risking being seen as a victim, which is typically not acceptable for males in most cultures, they prefer to deny their victimization and take on the role of the aggressor against those who are weaker than themselves.

An Attempt to Rid Themselves of Shame

Although Alice Miller and others believe that victims of childhood abuse and neglect reenact their abuse in an attempt to rid themselves of their fear, it is my belief and that of others, that they also do so in order to rid themselves of their shame. This is especially true with those who were sexually abused as children or adolescents, but it is also true of anyone who was neglected or abused in any way. The cycle of abuse continues when abusers, overwhelmed with their own shame, pass it on in a desperate attempt to rid themselves of it. The next section goes into this phenomenon still further.

Projection

Lloyd deMause, director of the Institute for Psychohistory, has concluded, after a lifetime of psychohistorical study of childhood and society, that the main psychological mechanism that operates in all child abuse involves using children as what he has termed *poison containers*—receptacles into which adults project disowned parts of their psyches. As de Mause explains it, in good parenting, the child uses the caretaker as a poison container, much as it earlier used the mother's placenta as a poison container for cleansing its polluted blood. A good mother reacts with calming actions to the cries of a baby and helps it detoxify its dangerous emotions. But when an abusive mother's baby cries, she cannot stand the screaming and strikes out at the child. Rather than the child being able to use the parent to detoxify its fears and anger, the parent instead injects his or her bad feelings into the child and uses it to cleanse himself or herself of depression and anger.

Historically, the routine use of children as poison containers to prevent adults from feeling overwhelmed by their anxieties has also been universal. Examples from the history of childhood regularly reveal children were expected to absorb the bad feelings of their caretakers. As de Mause revealed, one community in rural Greece has a saying, "You must have children around to put your bad feelings into, especially when the 'Bad Hour' comes around." An informant described the process as follows: "One of the ways for the Bad Hour to occur is when you get angry. When you're angry a demon gets inside of you. Only if a pure individual passes by, like a child for instance, will the 'bad' leave you, for it will fall on the unpolluted." This seems like very primitive thinking to most of us but it serves as a good reminder of the type of thinking that originally formed our culture and still pervades our unconscious.

Victim Patterns

The following information explains why some victims of child abuse remain victims into adulthood.

Learned Helplessness

Learned helplessness is a term developed by Martin Seligman, a pioneering researcher in animal psychology, to describe what occurs when animals or human beings learn that their behavior has no effect on the environment. This experience leaves an individual apathetic, depressed, and unwilling to try previous or new behavior. This concept is relevant to some survivors of childhood trauma who may show some degree of learned helplessness because of repeated exposure to traumatic events.

Studies have found that a true inability to control the environment is not necessary for learned helplessness to occur. In fact, even when told there is nothing a person can do, he or she is more likely to not try or to try less diligently than those who were not given this advice. Those who have been unable to escape violent situations in their homes are much more likely to refuse help and accept future violence as inescapable. This is true even when presented with real options to avoid future violence.

Self Blame

Self blame can lead to a lifetime pattern of victimization. Children blame themselves when they are abused by their parents because the child needs to hold on to an image of the parent as good in order to deal with the intensity of fear and rage that is the effect of the trauma. Victims may also blame themselves for their own victimization because it allows the locus of control to remain internal and thus prevents helplessness.

Clinging Behavior

Small children, unable to anticipate the future, experience separation anxiety as soon as they lose sight of their mothers. As we mature we develop more coping responses, but adults are still intensely dependent upon social support to prevent and overcome trauma. Upon exposure to extreme terror, even mature people will have protest and despair responses (anger and grief, intrusion and numbing) that make them turn to the nearest available source of comfort to return to a state of both psychological and physical calm. Thus, severe external threat may result in renewed clinging in adults.

When there is no access to ordinary sources of comfort, people may turn toward their tormentors. Adults as well as children may develop strong emotional ties with people who intermittently threaten, harass, or beat them. Abused children often cling to their parents and resist being removed from the home. In what has become known as the Stockholm Syndrome, hostages have been known to put up bail for their captors, express a wish to marry them, or have sexual relations with them.

Walker and Dutton and Painter have noted that the bond between batterer and victim in abusive marriages resembles the bond between captor and hostage or cult leader and follower. A woman's longing for the batterer soon prevails over memories of the terror, and she starts to make excuses for his behavior.

Making the Connection

The first step in preventing yourself from reenacting the abuse or neglect that you experienced as a child or stopping behavior you have already begun is to make a clear connection between your current behavior and the behavior of your abusers. You began to make that connection when you assessed your risk factors but now you will need to go a step further. The following exercise will help you connect the dots in order to see clearly how much your current behavior is a repetition of either your parent's or another abuser's behavior.

EXERCISE: *What Do You Have in Common
with Your Parents?*

1. On a piece of paper or on a page of your journal, write down the ways in which your mother was or still is neglectful or abusive

toward you or others. Be sure to include attitudes and verbal comments as well as behaviors.

2. On a second piece of paper write down any behavior on your father's part that was or is neglectful or abusive.

3. If you were raised by anyone other than your parents (foster parents, grandparents, aunts or uncles) make a separate list of this person's behavior.

4. On another piece of paper, write down the ways you have been neglectful or abusive toward your children, your partner, or anyone else in your life. No one else needs to read this list but you. Making this list will no doubt be difficult and painful, and you may want to put it aside or attempt to lie to yourself. If this is the case, remember your resolve to break the cycle, take a deep breath, and try again. Remember that as difficult as it is to write this list, it can make the difference between breaking the cycle or continuing it for one more generation. Imagine how much more difficult it will be to face the damage you continue to inflict on your loved ones if you aren't honest with yourself now.

5. Compare your lists. Notice the similarities between the ways you have been neglectful or abusive and the ways your parents were neglectful or abusive toward you or others. If you have established a victim pattern, do the same exercise, substituting victim behavior for abusive or neglectful behavior.

PART TWO

Facing the Truth and Facing Your Feelings

CHAPTER 4

Coming Out of Denial

*I have discovered that we are less a prey to . . . the repetition
compulsion if we are willing to acknowledge what happened to us,
if we do not claim that we were mistreated "for our own good,"
and if we have not had to ward off completely our painful reactions
to the past. The more we idealize the past, however, and refuse
to acknowledge our childhood sufferings, the more we pass them
on unconsciously to the next generation.*

ALICE MILLER, *For Your Own Good*

The second most important step in avoiding developing an abuser or
victim pattern is to face the truth about the abuse and/or neglect you
experienced either in childhood or later in life. (Although most of our
patterns develop from childhood experiences, sometimes traumatic
experiences such as rape or domestic violence in adulthood can cause
us to develop a victim or abuser pattern.) In this chapter I will help
you to face the truth. I will explain why it is so difficult to come out of
denial about childhood neglect and abuse and provide you with specific strategies that will help you to do so.

Denial is a powerful defense mechanism intended to help us cope
with intense pain and trauma. It is what allows us to block out or forget intense pain caused by severe physical or emotional trauma. Survivors of childhood abuse and neglect tend to deny what happened to
them and minimize the damage it caused them, because to do so is to
face the sometimes unbearable pain of admitting that their parents or
other family members could treat them in such horrendous ways.

One of the main reasons why adults who were abused or
neglected by one or both of their parents refuse to acknowledge the
truth about what happened to them is that children love their parents

so much that they tend to idealize them. The conviction that parents are always right and that even acts of cruelty are an expression of their love is deeply rooted in each of us. It is based on the process of internalization that takes place during the first months of life—that is, during the period of time preceding separation from the primary caregiver. Children are so dependent on their parents' love and care that it causes them to push any action on their parents' part that is unloving or cruel out of their minds. In order to preserve their faith in their parents, children must reject the first and most obvious conclusion that something is terribly wrong with them. They will go to any lengths to construct an explanation for their fate that absolves their parents of all blame and responsibility.

All of the abused child's psychological adaptations serve the fundamental purpose of preserving his or her primary attachment to his or her parents in the face of daily evidence of their malice, helplessness, or indifference. To accomplish this purpose, the child resorts to a wide variety of psychological defenses. The abuse is either walled off from conscious awareness and memory, so that it did not really happen, or minimized, rationalized, and excused, so that whatever did happen was not really abuse. Unable to escape or alter the unbearable reality in fact, the child alters it in his or her mind. The child victim prefers to believe that the abuse did not occur so he or she tries to keep it a secret from him or herself.

As an adult another reason for denial is that facing the truth about how your parents or others caretakers mistreated you can call into question a number of troublesome issues such as:

- What kind of a relationship with my parents (or other family member) will I be able to have once I face what they did to me as a child?

- Will I need to confront my parents or other abusers about their mistreatment of me in order for me to heal and for me to break the cycle?

- Are my children safe around the people who abused or neglected me?

Some survivors would rather not face the truth than to have to deal with these troublesome issues. If you have any of these concerns, don't let them get in the way of your facing the truth about what happened to you. Later on in this book we will deal extensively with each of these issues. For now, allow yourself to gradually let the truth sink in. You deserve to know the truth. It truly will set you free. It will help you to break the cycle so that you do not treat those you love in the same ways you were treated.

Unless you are able to admit that you were abused or neglected and acknowledge the damage it has caused you, you will be unable to heal. You will be blind to your own tendencies to be abusive or neglectful and you will be less able to spot abusive or neglectful behavior in others. For this reason, I begin this chapter with a questionnaire designed to help you name what happened to you as a child.

QUESTIONNAIRE: *Were You Neglected or Abused As a Child?*

Answer the following questions as honestly as you can. Put a checkmark alongside each question that applies to you. Because witnessing many forms of abuse may have also had a significant effect on you as a child, you may also wish to put a checkmark alongside these items.

Understand that even though the question says parent, if you were raised by someone other than your parents (grandparent, aunt, foster parent) it also applies to this person. The same is true if another caretaker (babysitter, teacher, nun) played a significant role in your life or if you received this treatment from another family member (sibling).

NEGLECT

Did one or both of your parents do any of the following to you or others in your family:

- Ignored you or did not respond to your needs
- Not feed you or fed you food that was inadequate or inappropriate for a child's nutritional needs (not because of financial problems)
- Forced you to feed yourself before you were able
- Not provide you adequate clothing, such as a coat in the winter
- Not wash your clothes
- Ignored your physical needs, not get you medical care when needed

- Not provide you physical nurturing, such as holding you or comforting you when you were upset

- Frequently left you alone for days or weeks in the care of others

- Frequently forgot to pick you up at the movies or after school

- Left you alone with an irresponsible caretaker

- Forced you to live in an uninhabitable place (drafty, unclean, unsafe)

- Not get out of bed to take care of you

- Not allow you to leave your room or your home for long hours, days, or weeks

- Neglected you because they were alcohol abusers or drug users

Emotional Abuse

Did one or both of your parents do any of the following to you or others in your family:

- Called you names, put you down, or embarrassed you (or others, such as your siblings)

- Belittled or made fun of you, made you the object of malicious or sadistic jokes

- Constantly found fault in you or what you did, criticized you

- Punished you unfairly

- Told you that you were stupid or ugly, or that you would never amount to anything

- Told you that you were always wrong, never allowed you to voice your opinion

- Punished you in public or in front of other family members

- Negatively compared you to others

- Made you eat something you spilled on the floor or forced you to eat something you hated and that had become cold and inedible

- Deliberately raised you as a member of the opposite sex

- Isolated you from others, refused to allow you to have friends over or to go to other children's homes

- Rejected you by openly preferring your siblings

✓ • Made you do cruel or degrading tasks

- Prevented you from going to school

✓ • Forced you to steal or do other illegal things

PHYSICAL ABUSE

Did one or both of your parents do any of the following to you or others in your family:

✓ • Shoved, or threw you across the room

✓ • Slapped, hit, or spanked, causing marks or bruises

✓ • Beat you with a belt, a tree branch or other object to the point that it left marks

- Scratched or bit you

- Burned you

- Cut you

✓ • Made you bleed or caused you to bruise

- Broke your bones

- Tied or locked you up or restrained you in other ways

- Confined you to a small space (like a closet) for long periods of time

- Locked you out of the house as punishment

✓ • Made you sit or stand for unreasonable amounts of time

- Not allowed you to urinate or defecate

- Used hunger as a consistent punishment

- Forced you to eat unhealthy or unsanitary food or food meant for animals

- Forced you into toilet training too early

- Used heat or cold (such as water) to cause pain
- Held your head under water
- Put a pillow over your head or otherwise tried to suffocate you
- Pulled your hair or used rubber bands to cause pain
- Medicated or drugged you when you were not ill
- Forced you into child labor
- Hurt or killed your pets
- Served your pets to you as food

SEXUAL ABUSE

Did one or both of your parents (or other significant adult):

- Lie around nude in a provocative way
- Flirt with you or engage in provocative behavior such as making comments about the way your body was developing
- Show you pornographic pictures or movies
- Kiss, hold, or touch you inappropriately
- Touch, bite, or fondle your sexual parts
- Make you engage in forced or mutual masturbation
- Give you enemas or douches for no medical reason
- Wash or scrub your genitals long after you were capable of doing so on your own
- Become preoccupied with the cleanliness of your genitals, tell you that your genitals were dirty, shameful, or evil
- Force you to observe or participate in adult bathing, undressing, toilet, or sexual activities
- Force you to be nude with others
- Make you share their bed when other beds were available
- Make you look at or touch adults' sexual parts
- Take photographs of you nude or engaged in sexual activities

- Allow you to be sexually molested without trying to stop it

- Tell you about their explicit sexual behavior

- In adolescence or older, ask you to tell inappropriate details about your sexual life

In order to continue to face the truth about what happened to you as a child you also need to understand just how damaging each form of abuse or neglect is to a child and how that damage is carried forward into adulthood. For this reason I have provided an overview of the damage caused to a child and types of abusive or victimlike behaviors that are common results of each type of abuse.

The Damage Caused by Child Neglect

An infant who is severely deprived of basic emotional nurturing, even though physically well cared for, can fail to thrive and can eventually die. Less severe forms of early emotional deprivation may produce babies who grow into anxious and insecure children who are slow to develop or who have low self-esteem. Early emotional deprivation has been linked to such personality disorders as borderline personality disorder and narcissistic personality disorder.

A child who is neglected either physically or emotionally will tend to be either extremely needy or extremely defensive. He or she may either exhibit clinging behavior and thus grow up to be a victim in his or her relationships or to be emotionally distant and aloof and unable to emotionally bond with others—including his or her own children.

Although many people understand that those who were abused often end up abusing others, many do not know that those who were neglected also pass on the damage inflicted on them. Direct physical and sexual abuse are not the only forms of child maltreatment that may increase the risk of aggressive, antisocial behavior in adulthood. Child neglect, which occurs considerably more frequently than abuse, seems to be an even more potent factor associated with later aggression.

The Damage Caused by Emotional Abuse

Emotional abuse is a pattern of behavior that attacks a child's emotional development and sense of self-worth. Because emotional abuse attacks a child's psyche and self-concept, the victim comes to see him- or herself as unworthy of love and affection. Those who experienced emotional abuse in childhood find it difficult to develop intimate healthy relationships as adults. Some feel smothered in their relationships, and others tend to suffer from extreme anxiety in dealing with the issues of rejection and abandonment. They may even develop antisocial behaviors that further isolate them from relating to others.

Children who are constantly shamed, humiliated, terrorized, or rejected suffer at least as much, if not more, than if they have been physically assaulted.

Marti Tamm Loring, author of *Emotional Abuse,* conducted a literature review of the effects of emotional abuse in children. She discovered that there is ample proof that children who experience emotional abuse suffer from multiple emotional and behavioral problems. She found:

> Those who internalize the abuse become depressed, suicidal, and withdrawn. They manifest self-destructiveness, depression, suicidal thoughts, passivity, withdrawal (avoidance of social contacts), shyness, and a low degree of communication with others. They are likely to have low self-esteem and may suffer from feelings of guilt and remorse, depression, loneliness, rejection, and resignation. Perceiving themselves as unworthy and the world as a hostile place in which they are bound to fail, many are unwilling to try new tasks or develop new skills.

According to Ms. Loring, those who externalize abuse may be unpredictable and violent, their behavior characterized by impulsive action rather than conformity to social norms. Some act out by mistreating animals or by emotionally or physically abusing younger siblings. They frequently become anxious, aggressive, and hostile, and they suffer from constant fear and feel ready to hit back. Emotionally abused adolescents have become truants, runaways, destructive, depressed, and suicidal.

The Damage Caused by Physical Abuse

Physical abuse breeds abusers or victims—it is just that simple. It creates intense feelings of terror, shame, and rage in a child. A child who is physically abused may act out his anger against other children by becoming a bully, against society by becoming a criminal, against women by emotionally or physically abusing them, toward his own children by being neglectful, or physically or emotionally abusive. On the other hand, he may turn his anger on himself and become deeply depressed or self-destructive (by abusing drugs or alcohol, by being reckless, or with self-mutilation). Physically abused children tend to be aggressive toward peers and adults, to have difficulty with peer relations, and to show a diminished capacity for empathy toward others. Studies have uncovered a significant incidence of neurological damage as a result of head injuries associated with physical abuse.

The Damage Caused by Child Sexual Abuse

Like all forms of abuse, child sexual abuse causes victims to suffer from low self-esteem, emotional and psychological problems, and a tendency to act out their anger in socially inappropriate ways. But child sexual abuse creates some unique problems as well. Survivors of child sexual abuse tend to have chronic relationship problems, especially regarding the ability to be intimate emotionally and sexually. More times than not, the perpetrator was someone they knew and trusted and this person betrayed that trust. Because of this, survivors often have difficulty as adults trusting others—even their intimate partners. Many also suffer from sexual problems such as lack of sexual desire, sexual dysfunctions such as vaginismus (an involuntary contraction of the vaginal muscles), promiscuity, and sexual addictions.

Most victims of child sexual abuse suffer from severe shame and self-loathing, but boys seem to suffer even more so. Boys who are sexually abused by a male often struggle with confusion about their sexual orientation. Those boys who were sexually abused by a female often suffer from sexual dysfunction, sexual addictions, or rage toward women which can manifest in date rape or physical violence against women. A girl who is sexually abused as a child is at great risk of growing up to marry a man who is a sex addict or a child molester. She may end up sexually abusing her own children or she may raise her children to feel that natural and healthy sexual feelings are bad and shameful.

EXERCISE: *Your Experiences*

1. Based on what you now understand constitutes neglect and abuse, make a list of each experience of neglect and/or abuse

you remember occurring in your childhood. Take your time and be as thorough as possible.

2. Write down all the ways you feel you have been damaged by the neglect or abuse that you experienced.

Allow Yourself to Feel

As you read the previous material you no doubt experienced strong emotions. It is quite painful to admit to yourself that you were abused or neglected in these ways and that you likely suffered from some or all of these effects. You may experience tremendous pain as you remember how it felt to be treated as you were. You may become extremely angry at those who abused or neglected you. And you may feel a deep sense of loss as your idealized picture of your childhood or your positive image of a parent, another family member, or another adored caregiver is tarnished forever.

When we finally do face the truth about what happened to us as a child we are overwhelmed with grief, sadness, and anger. Allow yourself to feel these emotions. Don't try to fight them off. You've probably been doing that for too long. Allow your emotions to flood out of you. Let the sadness wash over you. Let the tears come. Let the anger burst out. Cry for the little child who was mistreated in such terrible ways. Get angry at how the little child you once were was used or abused by adults who should have known better—adults who were supposed to protect you.

In order to heal yourself and break the cycle of abuse you must revisit the original wounding. Unfortunately, most people who were neglected or abused box off their pain and try to put it out of their minds. Although this may work to help temporarily ward off their pain, anger, and shame, the feelings are still there on a subconscious level, just under the surface, waiting to be triggered by people and events. When these feelings are triggered they lash out at those closest to them—usually their spouse or their children—and thus, the cycle of abuse is repeated. For this reason it is important to unearth those suppressed and repressed emotions and to reconnect them with the events of your childhood.

Needless to say, this will be a difficult process. But it is an extremely important one. Many people who were neglected or abused stay stuck in anger or in pain and never move through their feelings.

Instead, they project them on to those around them or turn their feelings on themselves and punish themselves with them. Others numb themselves to their feelings and are unable to access their feelings of anger and pain from the past. One of the reasons why some people reenact their own abuse by abusing others is since they cannot feel their own feelings, they must act them out. In this way they keep the unacceptable feelings at bay.

Emotions that go unexpressed often lie dormant inside us until someone or something reminds us of our past and triggers a memory—and the feeling. When this happens we tend to lash out at those closest to us when our real target is someone from the past—someone we were likely afraid to express our emotions to at the time.

It can be frightening to lift the veil of denial. The scariest part is experiencing the intense feelings that lurk just below denial's surface. You will undoubtedly need help in dealing with all these strong emotions and you'll be given help in the chapters to come. For now, allow yourself to experience whatever it is that you are feeling and remember the following:

1. Even though it may feel like it is happening in the present, it will help if you remind yourself that what you are feeling are memories of the feelings you had as a child. These things are not happening to you in the present. You have already survived your childhood and the painful things that happened to you.

2. As a child you were powerless to change your situation. As an adult you are no longer powerless. You have abilities, options and skills that can help you change.

3. It helps if you breathe into an emotion. As it is with physical pain, if you breathe into it, it tends to decrease and become less overwhelming.

4. As powerful and overwhelming as emotions can be, they are actually positive forces intended to help you process an experience.

5. As long as you don't allow yourself to become overwhelmed by them, your emotions will help you come out of and stay out of denial.

6. Allowing yourself to feel and express your hidden emotions from the past will help heal you from the past.

In chapters 6, 7, and 8 we will focus on the specific emotions of shame, anger, and fear—the emotions that are most closely tied to the reenactment of abuse and the emotions that are most important for you to get control of if you wish to break the cycle of abuse.

EXERCISE: *Your Feelings About the Abuse*

1. Earlier you made a list of all the ways you were neglected or abused as a child. Return to your list and for each item write about the following:

   - How you felt at the time
   - The effect the neglect or abuse had on you at the time
   - How you feel now as you remember the experience
   - What effect you believe the experience has had on you long-term

   As you write about each incident of neglect or abuse, allow yourself to feel whatever emotions come up for you. It is appropriate for you to feel angry, enraged, afraid, terrified, sad, grief-stricken, guilty, ashamed, or any other emotions you may feel. On the other hand, do not become alarmed if you do not feel anything. Survivors of childhood abuse and neglect often numb themselves to their feelings as a self-protective mechanism.

2. If at all possible, share your writings with at least one other person. Most victims of childhood neglect or abuse did not have what is called a compassionate witness to their pain and anguish. Telling a loved one about what happened to you and receiving your loved one's support and kindness can be a major step in the healing process. For example, experts such as Alice Miller have found that a sympathetic and understanding witness to a child's suffering is a crucial prerequisite to empathy in adulthood. Without empathy, we cannot be sensitive to the pain of others.

Now that you know the truth, the truth is yours to use for recovery. You have a better idea of what physical and emotional pain you endured and what long-term effects you are suffering from. There is healing in discovering the truth, facing it, and finally in accepting it. Your realization of the facts about your own neglect and abuse clears the way for dealing with your anger and resolving your relationships with your family. You have lived with lies, secrecy, and deception for a long time and it has been painful. Learning to live with the truth will help free you from the pain and lead you toward a fuller, richer life.

Give Yourself Time to Continue Facing the Truth

Facing the truth about the abuse or neglect you experienced will be an ongoing process. As you continue to read this book you will undoubtedly uncover more and more truths about your childhood. This can be disconcerting at times but ultimately, the more truth you face, the healthier you will become and the closer you will be to breaking the cycle.

It is incredibly painful to continue to face the truth and you will likely go in and out of denial. It takes time and courage to face the truth about the fact that the people you love most and who are supposed to love you are also capable of neglecting or abusing you. It takes time to let your mind comprehend the fact that the same people who were good to you at times could also be so neglectful or so cruel. It takes strength and time to process the pain of abuse, neglect, betrayal, abandonment, and rejection you felt as a child and still feel today. You'll need to give yourself the time that you need to become strong enough to face what you will need to face, to develop the support system you'll need to have in place so that you will not feel so alone as you emotionally separate from your abusers. And you'll need to be patient with yourself when you waffle back and forth about what is true and what isn't true.

Grieving the Loss of Your Childhood

As you remember painful or traumatic incidents in your childhood you may not only relive the feelings you once felt but may also begin to face the loss of your childhood. As you feel the loss, you will go through distinct stages similar to the stages of grieving the loss of a loved one— denial, anger, sadness, and acceptance. You won't necessarily move through each stage in a direct, linear manner since everyone's grieving process is different and there will be plateaus of acceptance and integration throughout the process. Some of you will need to grieve not only for what was lost but for what was never yours to lose.

H

CHAPTER 5

Learn to Identify and Manage
Your Emotions

*That is what learning is. You suddenly understand something you've
understood all your life, but in a new way.*

DORIS LESSING

Aside from facing the truth, one of the most important things you can
do to break the cycle is to learn to identify and manage your emotions.
While it may be the past that motivates you to act in abusive or victimlike ways, it is through your emotions today that you will be able
to break your unhealthy patterns and learn to behave in ways that are
neither abusive or victimlike. For many who were neglected or
abused as children emotions are a frightening thing. It was when their
parents' emotions got out of hand that they got yelled at, pushed
around, or hit. It was when they themselves got angry or started to cry
that they were ridiculed, punished, or abandoned by their parents,
their childhood peers, or their adult partners. For this reason, most
survivors of abuse and neglect tend to deny and repress their true
emotions. Even those who may appear to be extremely emotional,
eruptive, or volatile are usually denying their more vulnerable feelings underneath.

In addition, if you were neglected or abused in childhood you will
tend to be overwhelmed and controlled by your emotions. Many
become so overwhelmed with their emotions that their emotions
become their enemies. Dysfunctional behaviors, including abusive or
victimlike patterns, substance abuse, and suicidal behaviors, are often
attempts to cope with intolerably painful emotions. Many try to regu-
late their emotions by trying to make themselves not feel whatever it
is that they do feel. This style can be a direct result of the emotionally
invalidating environment you were raised in—one which mandated

that people should smile when they are unhappy, be nice and not rock the boat when they are angry, and confess or beg for forgiveness even when they don't feel they did anything wrong.

Because of this, you may feel sideswiped by your own emotions, or overwhelmed when your emotions build up. This, in turn, may cause you to project your feelings onto others. What is referred to as psychic numbing (stuck or frozen feelings) is another frequent result of abuse and neglect in childhood. Children shut off their feelings or dissociate in response to a traumatic situation. It is as if their mind goes somewhere else and they are disconnected from their body. Learning to reexperience frozen feelings takes time. But once these deadened feelings are liberated they can help you by providing helpful information so you can make rational decisions and take appropriate actions in your life. Reconnecting with feelings can provide you strength, courage, and joy.

In this and the following three chapters we will examine emotions up close in an attempt to take away some of the mystery and fear surrounding them. You will be encouraged to stop labeling emotions as good or bad and instead see them as important messages that can educate you about yourself, your circumstances, and your environment. You will begin to see that your emotions can empower you to take better care of yourself and in so doing, be less likely to abuse others or allow others to abuse you.

Step One: Identify and Label Your Emotions

The first step in regulating emotions is learning to identify and label your current emotions. In the course of just one day we all experience a myriad of emotions and learning to identify each and every one of them can be a daunting task. Because of this it is best to focus on only a few primary emotions, at least in the beginning.

Unfortunately those who were neglected and abused also have difficulty identifying what emotion they are experiencing at any given time. This is because they may have needed to shut off their feelings in order to survive childhood trauma or neglect, or because they may have had to pretend to feel something they didn't really feel. But it is also because many believed it was not safe for anyone to know what they were feeling and, as a result, they became adults with a jumble of feelings they now have difficulty identifying.

According to most experts, there are eight or so primary or basic emotions: anger, sorrow, joy, surprise, fear, disgust, guilt/shame, and interest (some also consider love one of the primary emotions). These are considered primary emotions because we are born with the potential, or biological readiness for them. All other emotions are considered secondary or social emotions because they are learned, and are usually some combination of the basic emotions. For our purposes we are going to focus on five of the primary emotions: fear, sorrow (or sadness), anger, guilt/shame, and joy.

Many people have become so disconnected from their emotions that they do not know when they are feeling them. Others become accustomed to covering over one emotion with another more socially acceptable one. Men typically cover over sadness with anger, especially men who tend to be abusive. This is because it is not as socially acceptable for males to cry or to be seen as weak, although it is perfectly acceptable (and often encouraged) for boys and men to be angry. Women, on the other hand, often cover over anger with sadness since it is socially acceptable for them to cry but not to get angry. You can see how this alone can contribute to the cycle of abuse.

We also become disconnected from our primary emotions by diluting them and giving them other names. For example, instead of saying they are afraid, or even realizing they are afraid, many people will say they feel anxious or worried. Instead of saying they feel sad, or even knowing they are sad, many people will say they feel tired. And instead of saying they are angry, many people will say they are disinterested or bored.

To make it more confusing, there are many other words that are commonly used to describe our primary emotions. The following is a list of words commonly used to describe the emotion of sadness. Some words describe a mild form of sadness and others describe more intense forms of sadness. For the most part, the list is in order of intensity: Unhappiness, hurt, dismay, grief, glumness, gloom, sorrow, suffering, melancholy, misery, despair, depression, agony, anguish, and hopelessness. Sometimes using one of these words instead of the word sad is beneficial because it makes it more clear exactly what level of sadness you are feeling. For example, *agony* and *hopeless* certainly describe a more intense state of sadness than the simple word *sad* does. The important thing is that you not allow the description of your state to take you away from the fact that you are basically feeling the emotion of sadness.

ASSIGNMENT: *The Words and Feelings of Sadness*

1. Study the list of words describing the emotion of sadness. Notice how often you use these descriptive words and remind yourself that no matter what words you use, you are still feeling sadness.

2. Write about the associations you have with the feeling of sadness. For example, is it okay for you to feel sadness or do you feel it is socially unacceptable? Was it acceptable to feel sadness in your home when you were growing up? Who expressed the feeling of sadness when you were growing up?

In the following three chapters we are going to focus on three of the other primary emotions: shame/guilt, anger, and fear. I'll provide a word list for these emotions in chapters 7 and 8. In this chapter we'll focus on the two emotions, sadness and joy.

How Do You Know When You Are Feeling a Particular Emotion?

Some people are so disconnected from their emotions that they simply cannot identify which feeling they are having at any given time. The best way to discover how you are feeling is to begin by asking yourself which of the eight or nine primary feelings you are experiencing (anger, sorrow, joy, surprise, fear, disgust, guilt/shame, interest, or love). It is safe to say that at any given time we are all experiencing at least one or more of the primary emotions.

Just asking yourself the question won't necessarily help if you aren't in touch with your body. Your body is your best barometer to tell you which emotion you are feeling. Emotions involve body changes, such as fluctuations in heart rate and skin temperature, the tensing or relaxing of muscles. The most important changes are in the facial muscles. Researchers now think that changes in the facial muscles play an important role in actually causing emotions. For example, we tend to feel sadness in our body in the following ways: frowning, mouth down in sad face, eyes drooping, a slumped, drooping posture, using a low, quiet, slow, or monotonous voice, heaviness in the chest, tightness in the throat or difficulty swallowing (from holding back tears), moist eyes or tears, whimpering, crying, feeling as if you can't stop crying, or feeling that if you ever start crying you will never stop, feeling tired, run-down, or low in energy, feeling lethargic, listless; wanting to stay in bed all day, feeling as if nothing is pleasurable any more, feeling a pain or hollowness in your chest or gut, feeling empty.

Conversely, joy is usually manifested in the body in the following ways: smiling, feeling excited, feeling physically energetic, active, alive, feeling like laughing or giggling, having a warm glow about you, feeling open-hearted, and loving.

You can also determine what particular emotion you are feeling by *observing your behavior.* For example, the following behaviors are all indicative of someone who is feeling sad: talking about sad things, sitting or lying around, being inactive, making slow, shuffling movements, giving up and no longer trying to improve, moping, brooding, or acting moody, withdrawing from social contact, talking little or not at all.

Someone who is feeling joyous may exhibit any of the following behaviors: smiling, grinning, being bouncy or bubbly, being affectionate toward others, jumping up and down, using an enthusiastic or excited voice, being talkative or talking a lot.

Step Two: Determine the Message

Each emotion carries with it a specific message or signal. The second step in constructively dealing with your emotions is to determine the message that any particular emotion is sending. The following is a list of the primary emotions and the message that most clearly characterizes that emotion. The next time you feel one of these emotions, ask yourself if this is the message this feeling is sending you.

- Sadness. You experienced a sense of loss or you have an expectation that did not get met.

- Anger. An important standard or rule you have in your life has been broken or violated by someone else or by yourself. Anger is also an outgrowth of hurt or an indication that a lot of hurt has built up.

- Fear. You are feeling inept or powerless to handle a situation or you need to prepare yourself to deal with something in order to avoid negative consequences.

- Guilt. You violated your own standards.

No Negative Emotions

Many people consider emotions such as anger, sadness, fear, guilt, and shame as negative emotions. But there are no negative emotions if we view all emotions as signals or messengers telling us that something important is occurring.

What makes an emotion negative is the way we deal with it and the interpretation we give to it. For example, most people deal with these emotions in one of four negative ways:

1. They try to avoid feeling the emotion entirely (suppression).

2. They try to deny the feeling by pretending that it is not that bad (minimizing).

3. They blame someone else for making them feel as they do.

4. They deny their feeling by projecting it onto someone else.

All four of these methods prevent you from heeding the signal that the emotion is sending, from learning from the emotion and utilizing the emotion to your best advantage. When we try to avoid feeling an emotion we prevent ourselves from growing. Denied or repressed emotions tend to fester inside us and then burst out of us unexpectedly, often causing us to become emotionally, verbally, or physically abusive. And no matter how much you try to blame others, no one else makes you feel anything. It is what you allow yourself to feel. The truth is, your emotions are your responsibility and no one else's.

You'll learn a lot more about the messages that your primary emotions send you in later chapters. For now, the following exercise will help you begin to notice and appreciate the messages they send.

EXERCISE: *The Messages of Emotions*

1. Note which of the primary emotions you have the most difficulty with.

2. For each of these emotions, list at least two messages. For example, "I'm feeling sad. I need to allow myself to grieve the loss of my dog."

Step Three: Feel Your Emotions without Becoming Overwhelmed by Them

The third step to managing your emotions is to experience them without inhibiting, judging, or distracting yourself from them. This is called being mindful. Being mindful of our emotions, instead of fighting them or walling them off, actually helps us let go of them. The following steps will help you to experience your emotions in a mindful way:

- Begin by simply observing your emotion. Notice how it makes you feel. Notice what happens in your body as you feel the emotion.

- Do not judge the emotion as good or bad. Just breathe into it.

- Fully experience your emotion. Allow it to rise up in your stomach, burn in your throat, spread through your body.

- Allow yourself to feel the emotion as a wave, peaking and then subsiding. Try not to suppress the feelings or push the emotion away. On the other hand, don't hold onto the emotion or amplify it. Just let it pass through you like a wave.

- If the feeling doesn't fade, try stepping back from your emotion. This experience of simply witnessing an emotion will put you in a better position to detach from it and to let go of the intense energy you may have invested in it. Once you are more detached from the emotion you can begin to let it go—it has served its purpose.

Why It Is Important Not to Judge Our Emotions

Whenever we judge our emotions as bad the natural consequence is to feel guilt, shame, anxiety, and/or anger. The addition of these secondary feelings simply make the distress more intense and intolerable. Often you will find that you can tolerate a distressing situation or painful affect a lot better if you refrain from feeling guilty or anxious about feeling the painful emotion in the first place. Think of some occasions when you have had a secondary emotional reaction to a primary emotion (i.e., getting angry or feeling ashamed for getting angry, getting depressed about being depressed). Which causes you more pain or trouble—the primary or the secondary emotion?

How to Observe an Emotion Nonjudgmentally

1. Simply observe the emotion—where you feel it in your body, what sensations it elicits—without any kind of judgment or evaluation whatsoever. Restrain from labeling it good or bad, painful or pleasant.

2. Notice the thoughts that go through your mind as you feel this emotion, the associations you have with the emotion. Acknowledge the helpful, the healthy, but do not judge it. Acknowledge the harmful, or unhealthy, but do not judge it.

3. Notice the opinions you have about this feeling and about the fact that you are feeling it. Let go of your opinions and simply feel.

4. When you find yourself judging, don't judge your judging. Just stop and move on.

Further Tips to Help You Not Become Overwhelmed by Your Emotions

- Remember that you are not your emotions.

- You do not necessarily need to act on your emotions.

- Remember times when you have felt different.

- Remember times when you have overcome the emotions.

By learning to observe your emotions, you learn to be separate from them and also at one with them. In order to be in control of your emotions you must be separate from them so that you can think and use coping strategies. But you also need to be one with your emotions, in the sense that you identify them as part of you and not something outside you.

Step Four: Determine Whether It Is Appropriate to Be Feeling This Emotion at This Time

Our emotional reaction—how we respond to a given situation—often has to do with the meaning we have given to the experience. In other words, it is the way we *interpret* our experience that determines how we will feel about it. For example, let's say that you are out running errands when you spot a friend across the street. You feel happy to see her and wave and call to her enthusiastically. Your friend looks your way but she doesn't wave back. How do you interpret this? Some people will interpret this experience as rejection and feel immediately shamed. Others will interpret the very same experience by telling themselves that their friend simply did not see them and they will move on feeling perhaps a little disappointed but not give it a second thought. And so we can see that a friend not waving back doesn't actually *cause* you to feel a prescribed emotion, even though many people in your situation might interpret the experience as you did.

How the Past Affects Our Interpretation of the Present

We often base our interpretation of an event on our previous experiences. Let's say that you are one of those who interpreted the experience of your friend not waving back as rejection. Most people in your situation would feel a momentary pang of shame in reaction to feeling rejected and exposed in public but the feeling would subside within minutes. But let's say that you have a childhood history of being severely rejected and ignored by your parents or by other children. In either case your immediate and automatic response would be a far more intense shame reaction than the average person's. In fact, the incident may trigger a full-blown shame attack so intense that you may be unable to complete your errands. You may feel so bad about yourself that you need to return home and to bed. When your husband comes home he finds you in bed. When he discovers that you didn't run the few errands he asked you to do for him he becomes angry with you and accuses you of being lazy and selfish. Too shamed to defend yourself, you just take in his criticisms as the truth, causing you to feel even more shamed and even worse about yourself.

If you are the kind of person who immediately turns shame to rage, you may become irate at the person who didn't wave back at you. You may storm off, cursing at the person under your breath. You rerun the incident over and over in your head feeding your shame and your rage. By the time you get home you are really worked up. You tell your husband about the fact that your friend snubbed you and what a bitch she is. Your husband tries to console you by suggesting that perhaps your friend didn't see you. You dismiss your husband's suggestion with an air of contempt—after all, he's always in la la land as far as you're concerned. When he suggests you call your friend on the phone to check it out you become enraged with him and tell him to mind his own business. You continue to snap at him throughout the evening and don't even want him near you.

What happened in both of these scenarios was that the person was *triggered*—meaning that a situation that occurred in the present reminded her of something in the past to such an extent that in her mind and in her senses she felt as if the past event was actually reoccurring. She once more experienced all the emotions and sensations she felt in the past and was unable to distinguish the past from the present.

Those who have a history of abuse or neglect in childhood are often triggered by past memories and therefore often react inappropriately. Discovering when you are acting inappropriately because you are not in the present can be a daunting task.

LEARNING TO HANDLE TRIGGERING SITUATIONS

So how do you handle triggering situations so they don't snowball out of control? What do you do so you don't become so depressed that you take on the criticism and or even the abuse of others? What do you do to take responsibility for your reaction so you don't become abusive to others?

The first step is to become aware of your particular triggers or automatic reactions. Triggers can include anything that touches off the stored up anger, fear, or shame that you have concerning your childhood abuse or neglect experiences. They can also include stored up resentments, regrets, and insecurities. By identifying specific actions, words, or events that seem to trigger these automatic emotional reactions, these reactions may become easier to anticipate and to handle.

EXERCISE: *Be on the Lookout for Triggers*

- Start by jotting down all the triggers you can think of based on your most recent reactions.

- Continue making notes about your moods and behavior for the next several weeks, noticing in particular the things that seem to trigger you the most. In addition to the words and actions of others, pay attention to such factors as the immediate environment, time of day, and the presence or absence of alcohol.

- Keep in mind that your intent is not to make judgments about how many times you are triggered but to gain information.

Exercise: *Your Triggers*

Those who were abused or neglected as children tend to have certain predictable triggers. Put a checkmark next to the ones that apply to you:

- Feeling rejected

- Feeling abandoned

- Feeling ignored

- Feeling smothered

- Feeling controlled

- Feeling criticized

- Feeling that others are unpredictable

- Feeling that others are inconsistent

- Feeling invalidated

- Feeling envious

- Feeling labeled or stigmatized

- Being told to snap out of it

Distinguishing between Triggering a Reaction and Causing a Reaction

Just because someone triggered a reaction in you doesn't mean they caused your reaction. This is a very important distinction. Let's go back to our example of the friend not waving back. Let's say that you saw your friend later and discovered she hadn't seen you wave to her.

Now that you know that she didn't even see you, you certainly can't blame her for your reaction, right? Believe it or not, some people in this situation would still blame their friend. They would still harbor anger at her for *causing* them to feel so shamed. The next time they saw her on the street they might not wave, either out of anger or out of fear of being rejected again. And when they were in her presence they might either act aloof or angry.

Making the distinction between when someone triggers your reactions and when they cause it is even more important in intimate relationships. But what if your friend did see you and chose not to wave to you? Did she cause your reaction in that case? This is a little more difficult to discern. While her snubbing behavior was certainly hurtful and was responsible for *triggering* your reaction, it still did not *cause* you to feel as intensely as you did. The real cause was your history of being rejected in childhood and the fact that you did not have a better way to handle your feelings once they were triggered.

COPING STRATEGIES FOR DEALING WITH TRIGGERS

- Defuse the trigger. This is the optimum way to cope with triggers. By catching yourself in the moment and realizing that you are being triggered, you can minimize the damage. This will be difficult at first and in some cases and for some people, may remain difficult since the very act of being triggered often prevents you from being in the present and having all your wits about you. One of the best ways to defuse a trigger is to talk to someone you trust about your situation.

- Minimize exposure to situations that trigger you. It is, of course, impossible to do this completely. There will always be someone or something that can trigger you. But knowing your particular triggers will help you to eliminate some potential trouble spots.

Step Five: Take Action to Remedy the Situation

Our emotions often tell us that something needs to be addressed or changed. Our typical reaction when we feel an emotion is to blame someone else for *making* us feel a certain way and our normal focus is to expect the other person to change how they behave so we won't have to feel as we do. But the message our emotions are sending us provides other possibilities for change. These are:

1. Do I need to change my perception of the situation? ("Am I over-reacting? Are my expectations too high? Have I been triggered? Is this an appropriate emotion to be feeling with this person at this time?")

2. Do I need to communicate my needs and feelings?

3. Do I need to behave differently in order to achieve different results?

Let's say that you feel hurt when you come home and your spouse doesn't stop what she's doing to greet you. This hurts you because it makes you feel like you aren't important to her. After all, you always make sure you drop everything you're doing to make sure she feels welcomed home.

You've now identified the emotion and the message. What action do you need to take? Let's go through the steps I've outlined above. Let's say that you answered no to question #1 (Do I need to change my perception?), because you've decided that it is an appropriate emotion to be feeling with your spouse. So the next step is to ask yourself, "Do I need to communicate my needs and feelings?" Have you ever told your partner that it hurts you that she doesn't stop what she is doing to greet you? If you haven't, do you think it is really fair of you to expect her to do so? Remember, we become hurt when one of our expectations has not been met but we often need to communicate what our expectations are in order to have them fulfilled. Telling your partner how much it would mean to you to have her greet you when you come home will let her know how important it is to you.

On the other hand, maybe your answer to question #2 (Do I need to communicate my needs and feelings?) is also no. You have already let your partner know how you feel about the fact that she doesn't stop what she's doing when you come home, but she still hasn't changed. Okay, so let's move on to question #3 (Do I need to behave differently?). Let's say that you have communicated to your partner that you'd like her to greet you when you come home. But did you do it in a very negative, accusatory way? For example, if you said something like, "Oh, honey, I'm so glad you're home. I missed you so much," in a sarcastic way, or if you complain, "Can't you stop what you're doing long enough to say hello to me? Am I that unimportant to you?" chances are your partner will not be very receptive to changing. In this case the answer to question 3 is yes, you need to change the way you behave. You need to communicate your needs and feelings in a more straightforward, direct way, with no accusations, no sarcasm, and no self pity.

For example, if you were to go to your partner and explain why it is important to you to be greeted she would likely be far more open to really hearing you and may even be more open to changing. One client of mine explained to her husband that she had been a latch key kid growing up and had always come home to an empty house after school. It used to make her feel lonely and sad. Now when she comes home and no one greets her she tends to be reminded of those feelings. When she explained this to her husband he gained a great deal of empathy toward that little child that she once was and he understood, for the first time, why it was important to stop what he was doing to greet her. From that time on he made a point of doing just that.

To review, the steps to coping with your emotions in a healthy, empowering way are:

1. Identify the emotion.

2. Determine the message.

3. Feel your emotions without judging them or becoming overwhelmed by them.

4. Determine whether it is appropriate to be feeling this emotion at this time.

5. Take action to remedy the situation, (i.e., change the way you: look at things, communicate your desires, treat other people).

In this chapter I've shared a lot of important information and provided you with a program for identifying and managing your emotions. Reviewing this information from time to time will help you understand it on a deeper level and facilitate you in learning skills that can help you to break the cycle of abuse, whether you tend to be abusive or a victim.

CHAPTER 6

Learn How to Identify
and Manage Your Shame

*Experience is not what happens to you; it is what you do
with what happens to you.*

ALDOUS HUXLEY

We all know that those who end up abusing their partner or their children have a problem with anger and we will focus on this in the next chapter. But in order to prevent yourself from becoming abusive it is as important to manage your shame. Shame is at the core of every form of neglect and abuse and is a key factor in the behavior of both abusers and victims. Shame plays a significant role in the cycle of abuse in the following ways:

- Those who abuse others are often trying to rid themselves of their own shame.

- Shame can cause emotional outbursts. It is often shame that triggers the kinds of rage that cause abusiveness.

- It is often shame that prevents victims from believing they deserve to be treated with love, kindness, and respect.

- It is shame that causes a person to humiliate and degrade his or her partner or children.

- It is shame that causes an adult to believe he or she deserves to be treated with disrespect and disdain.

- Shame can cause a person to sabotage any happiness or success they experience in life, including pushing away those who care about them by being abusive.

Shame is a feeling deep within us of being exposed and unworthy. When we feel shamed we want to hide. We hang our heads, stoop our shoulders, and curve inward as if trying to make ourselves invisible. Shame is also the emotion that we most often experience when those parts of ourselves that we defend against the most—our weaknesses, deficits, and mistakes—are exposed. The more we hide our weaknesses, the bigger our shame. The bigger our shame, the more defenses we need to build up. Those who become abusive tend to have the most defenses. In actuality, they are defending against their own victimization and shame.

How Children Are Shamed

When you recall the neglect and/or abuse you experienced as a child you may feel the emotion of shame. Those who are victimized feel humiliated and degraded by the violation. When a child is traumatized, as in the case of parental violence or sexual abuse, the child also feels helpless and powerless. In response to this sense of helplessness the child feels shame. If the child was physically forced to do things he or she did not want to do, he or she will also feel the shame of the violation of bodily integrity and the indignity suffered in the eyes of another person.

In addition, most victims of abuse and neglect blame themselves for the way others treated them, feeling that somehow they deserved to be treated in such a way. This is an attempt to regain some sense of power and control. To blame oneself and assume one could have done better or could have prevented an incident is more tolerable than to face the reality of utter helplessness.

Abandonment and Rejection

According to the author Gershen Kaufman in his important book *Shame: The Power of Caring*, breaking the interpersonal bridge is the critical event which induces shame in children. The interpersonal bridge is broken when a child's expectations are exposed as wrong or when someone he or she values (such as a parent) unexpectedly betrays his or her trust. This is because a young child, especially a preverbal child, often experiences shame as abandonment. If a parent becomes emotionally unavailable (i.e., silent withdrawal), overtly contemptuous, or in some other way withdraws love and support, whatever feelings of abandonment the child may be harboring can rapidly intensify to the point of sheer terror.

Other Parental Shaming Experiences

Sometimes parents deliberately shame their children into minding without realizing the disruptive impact shame can have on the child's sense of self. Statements such as "You should be ashamed of yourself" or "Shame on you" are obvious examples, and yet because they are overtly shaming they are actually easier for the child to defend against. More damaging are the kinds of public shaming many parents engage in. For example, often behavior that was once acceptable at home is suddenly seen by parents as bad when they are in public. Or the parent seems to be ashamed because his child is not adhering to certain social norms that the child was completely unaware of. Such comments as, "Stop that, you're embarrassing me in front of everyone," not only causes a child to feel exposed, judged, and ashamed, but burdens him with his parent's shame as well.

Another way that parents induce shame in their children is by communicating to them that they are a disappointment to them. Such messages as "I can't believe you could do such a thing" or "I am deeply disappointed in you" accompanied by a disapproving tone of voice and facial expression can crush a child's spirit.

Belittling

Another form of shaming frequently done by parents is belittling. Comments such as "You're too old to want to be held," or "You're just a cry-baby," are horribly humiliating to a child. When a parent makes a negative comparison between his child and another such as, "Why can't you act like Tommy? Tommy isn't a cry-baby," it is not only humiliating but teaches a child to always compare himself with peers and find himself deficient in the comparison.

Blaming

When a child makes a mistake, such as accidentally hitting a ball through a neighbor's window, he needs to take responsibility. But many parents go way beyond teaching the child a lesson by blaming and berating their children: "You stupid idiot! You should have known better than to play so close to the house! Now I'm going to have to pay for that window. Do you think money grows on trees? I don't have enough money to constantly be cleaning up your messes!" According to Gershen Kaufman, all this accomplishes is to shame the child to such an extent that he cannot find a way to walk away from the situation with his head held high. Blaming the child like this is like rubbing his nose in the mess he made, and it produces such intolerable shame that he may be forced to deny responsibility or find ways of excusing it.

Contempt

Expressions of disgust or contempt communicate absolute rejection. The look of contempt (often a sneer or a raised upper lip), especially from someone who is significant to a child, can be a devastating inducer of shame because the child is made to feel disgusting or offensive. Having an overly critical parent, one who always finds something wrong with the child, guarantees that the child will be constantly subjected to shame.

When I was a child my mother had an extremely negative attitude toward me. Much of the time she either looked at me with the kind of expectant look that said, "What are you up to now?" or with a look of disapproval or disgust over what I had already done. These looks were extremely shaming to me.

In addition to her shaming looks, my mother would accuse me of intentionally doing bad things. One incident stands out in particular. I think I was about six years old. She had sent me to the store with a quarter to buy a can of tuna (yes, it was a long time ago). I picked up the can of tuna from the shelf but in the process I dropped the quarter. I bent down to look for it but it had dropped under the shelving where I couldn't reach it. I went home and told my mother what happened, but she didn't believe me. She assumed I was lying and that I'd spent the money on candy. She dragged me back to the store to check with the store clerk. I felt so humiliated. I begged her to believe me and not to embarrass me by making a scene, but she wouldn't listen. The store clerk backed me up telling my mother that he had seen me looking for the money, but by that time I was so thoroughly humiliated and enraged that it made no difference to me.

My mother's accusatory looks and continual assumption that I was a liar caused me to constantly feel that there was something terribly wrong with me, that I was a bad person. Because I felt like a bad person with her this feeling carried over into my relationships with other people. Even though I was a gregarious person by nature, I began to assume that people wouldn't like me when they met me and was quite surprised when someone actually showed me some kindness. This set me up to be a target for child molesters, exhibitionists, and later on in my teens and early twenties, men who would take advantage of me sexually and emotionally.

But the way she treated me also set me up to be a delinquent. Because my mother treated me like I was a bad person I figured I might as well become a bad person. By the time I was twelve and had already been sexually molested, I started acting out. I started shoplifting, drinking, smoking, and sneaking out of the house at night.

Humilation

In addition to shaming me with her contemptuous looks, my mother also punished me physically if I had done something that really made her angry. As a young child she hit me with the switch of an apricot tree. Usually this was done outside, in front of all the neighbors. As Gershen Kaufman stated in his book, "There is no more humiliating experience than to have another person who is clearly the stronger and more powerful take advantage of that power and give us a beating." I can personally attest to this. The humiliation I felt was like a deep wound to my soul.

Disabling Expectations

Appropriate parental expectations serve as necessary guides to behavior and are not disabling. Disabling expectations, on the other hand, have to do with pressuring a child to excel or perform a task, skill, or activity. Parents who have an inordinate need to have their child excel at a particular activity or skill are likely to behave in ways that pressure the child to do more and more. According to Kaufman, when a child becomes aware of the real possibility of failing to meet parental expectations he or she often experiences a binding self-consciousness. This self-consciousness—the painful watching of oneself—is very disabling. When something is expected of us in this way, attaining the goal is made harder, if not impossible.

EXERCISE: *Your Shaming Experiences*

You no doubt recognize some or all of the examples of parental shaming listed above. This exercise will help you further identify and process what you personally experienced as a child.

- Make a list of experiences in childhood and adolescence that shamed you the most.

- Write about how each of these experiences made you feel.

- How do you think these shaming experiences have affected your life? Write your insights down.

How We React to Being Shamed

Whenever someone experiences rejection, especially by a significant other, he or she will likely become upset or angry. This is a typical and normal response. But there is a very different scenario, described by Herbert E. Thomas, M.D., in his book *The Shame Response to Rejection*, in which rejection causes a person to experience a primitive physiological response in one's body. Thomas calls this the shame response. Others have written about this as well, referring to it as a shame attack.

When the shame response is sufficiently intense, it can be extremely painful and causes an equally intense psychic trauma. This trauma, according to Thomas, can be a precursor to violence when the energy associated with the trauma is directed outward. At other times, it can be directed inward, against the self.

According to Thomas, the more intense the shame response is, the more painful it is. The physical pain experienced can range from a slight pain in one's chest, often in the region of one's heart, to a pain so intense that one feels one's chest will explode. Shame responses can occur elsewhere in the body as well. (Thomas states that there is evidence to suggest that the pain associated with the shame response is located in a particular region of the brain known as the cingulated gyrus or nearby.)

Thomas believes that to reject someone is to objectify that person. Several factors determine the intensity of a rejection. These include:

- The significance of the person who is doing the rejecting to the one who is being rejected.

- The significance of the person rejected to those who witness the rejection.

- The rejected person's vulnerability to experiencing rejection.

- Whether what is rejected is an aspect of one's self or one's whole self.

- The degree of surprise associated with the rejection.

- The correlation of the rejection's intensity to the intensity of the shame response.

The intensity of the shame response determines what follows. One may become angry and direct that anger outward. In such cases, the anger may be manifested as violence against others. When anger is directed inward it may lead to a vicious cycle of self-hatred in which the person becomes isolated and withdrawn in order to avoid the possibility of further rejection. The trauma associated with the pain of an intense shame response can lead to all the phenomena we associate with a post-traumatic stress disorder.

Because the wounds that result from the pain of rejection are especially difficult to heal, those who have experienced intense rejection are often dominated by a desire to avoid further acts of rejection. They do this by building defensive walls around themselves, walls that keep out rejection but at the same time keep out intimacy and love.

Choosing Guilt over Shame

Since shame is so debilitating it makes sense that we would do almost anything possible to try to avoid it. Human beings strive to remain in control. We are raised to believe that we are responsible for what happens to us and that we can control our own lives. When something goes wrong we tend to feel ashamed about the fact that we have lost control of our lives. This is especially true of trauma victims who, instead of simply believing that something bad just happened, tend to believe that they somehow caused or contributed to the events and are therefore responsible. Being victimized causes us to feel helpless and it is this helplessness that leads us to feel humiliated and ashamed. As a protection against feeling this helplessness and shame we take personal responsibility for our own victimization, in other words, we trade guilt for shame.

Shame is often confused with guilt but it is not the same emotion. When we feel guilt we feel badly about *something we did or neglected to do*. When we feel shame we feel badly about *who we are*. When we feel guilty we need to learn that it is okay to make mistakes. When we feel shame we need to learn that it is okay to be who we are. Another distinction between guilt and shame is that shame comes from public exposure to one's own vulnerability whereas guilt is private. It comes from a sense of failing to measure up to our own internal standards. When others discover or know that we were once helpless, we tend to feel ashamed. We also feel exposed. If, on the other hand, we feel we caused our own problems, we cease to feel as vulnerable, or as exposed.

Shame to Anger

Turning shame to anger can actually be a positive way of reacting to shame. Instead of taking the negative energy in, against oneself, the energy is directed outward, against the person who is doing the shaming or causing the shame. Most children are unable to do this because of their tendency toward self-blame.

Rage occurs spontaneously and naturally following shame. It serves a vital self-protective function by insulating the self against further exposure and by actively keeping others away to avoid further occurrences of shame. Extroverted children are more likely to express rage at being shamed while introverted children often tend to keep their rage inside, more hidden from the view of others (we'll discuss this distinction further in the following chapter on anger).

Humiliation can be a fertile breeding ground for hatred and for revenge-seeking. By hating one's oppressor and nursing revenge fantasies, the shamed and wounded person can salvage something of his or her dignity. To do otherwise, to give in to the power of others, may feel to some like a relinquishing of one's integrity and in doing so, a loss of respect for oneself.

Identifying with the Aggressor

A related way that victims suppress their feelings of helplessness is identifying with the aggressor. We discussed this phenomenon earlier in this book. We find the phenomena of identifying with the aggressor to be particularly common with boy victims. In most societies it is not acceptable for males to be perceived as victims. A boy who is sexually molested, for example, will likely blame himself rather than face the shame of having been a victim. He will also be less likely to tell anyone about it, for fear of being further shamed. Because he has told no one and because he begins to blame himself and even to convince himself that he may have wanted it, he may also begin to identify with the aggressor—that is, become like his abuser. The only way left for him to discharge his shame and aggression is to do to others what was done to him.

Your Shame Inventory

The following inventory will help you understand how shame has affected you in the past and in the present.

1. How did you react to the shaming experiences of your childhood? Did you blame yourself? Did you become angry?

2. Notice what triggers shame in you today. Is it criticism from others, being called on your stuff (or as one client described it, "Having my covers pulled,") or is it being rejected?

3. When are you most likely to feel shamed? Is it when you are feeling the most insecure? Is it when you are trying to impress someone?

4. Who is most likely to trigger shame in you? Is it the people you care about the most? Or is it those you are trying to impress? How about the people you feel inadequate around or those who have rejected you in the past?

How Shame Can Cause You to Develop Abusive or Victimlike Patterns

The inner experience of shame is to feel seen in a painfully diminished way. The self feels exposed and it is this sudden, unexpected feeling of exposure and accompanying self-consciousness that characterizes the essential nature of shame. Within this experience of shame is the piercing, overwhelming awareness of ourselves as fundamentally deficient in some vital way as a human being.

In addition to feeling deficient when we feel shame we also tend to feel impotent because it feels as though there is no way to relieve the situation. It is easy to see, therefore, that those who were heavily shamed in childhood can easily come to believe that they are power-less to change things. This leads to a victim mentality. To live with shame is to feel alienated and defeated. It is to believe you are never quite good enough. This can set the stage for getting involved with emotionally or even physically abusive partners who are demanding and hard to please. If you already feel like a failure you will be more likely to put up with unreasonable demands and put-downs, and be less likely to leave a relationship, no matter how abusive.

Rage

Whether held inside or expressed more openly, rage serves the purpose of defending against shame. It may also, secondarily, transfer the shame to another. This can create an abusive style of relating to others.

As Gershen Kaufman explains in *Shame: The Power of Caring:* "If rage emerges as a strategy of defense, what we will see is an individual who holds onto rage as a characterological style. This manifests itself either in hostility toward others or bitterness. Although this hostility or bitterness arises as a defense to protect the self against further experiences of shame, it becomes disconnected from its originating source and becomes a generalized reaction directed toward almost anyone who may approach."

Becoming Shamebound

Sometimes a child has been so severely shamed or experienced so many shame inducing experiences that he or she becomes what is referred to as shamebound or shame based, meaning that shame has become a dominant factor in the formation of the person's personality. Shame based people suffer from extremely low self-esteem, feelings of worthlessness, and self-hatred. They feel inferior, bad, unacceptable, and different from others. They were often taught that they were worthless or bad by hearing adults say such things to them as: "You are in my way," "I wish you were never born," or "You'll never amount to anything."

Shame based people are commonly survivors of severe physical discipline, emotional abuse, neglect, and abandonment—which all send the message that the child is worthless, unacceptable, and bad. These acts also convey the message that the adult will treat you any way he or she wants to because you are a worthless commodity. Many were also humiliated for their behavior (i.e., being chastised or beaten in front of others, being told, "What's wrong with you?" or "What would your precious teacher think of you if she knew who you *really* are?"). Last but not least, shame based people often had to endure shame inducing traumas like child sexual abuse.

Shame based people tend to defend against any feeling of shame with anger. Although most people react with anger whenever they are made to feel humiliated, devalued, or demeaned, shame based or shamebound people tend to be extremely sensitive and defensive and they go into rages when they feel criticized or attacked—which is often. Because they are so critical of themselves they believe everyone else is critical of them. And because they despise themselves they assume everyone else dislikes them. If you are shamebound, one teasing comment or one well-intentioned criticism can send you into a rage that lasts for hours. Because you feel shamed by the other person's comment you may spend hours making the person feel horrible about themselves, in essence, dumping shame back on the other person.

Shame based people feel very vulnerable underneath all their defensiveness. Another way a shame based person uses anger as a defense is by attacking others before they have a chance to attack him. It's as if they are saying, "I'll show you. I'll make you feel like shit because that's what you think of me."

If you are shamebound you may also use anger to keep people away from your vulnerability by raging at them. In essence you are saying, "Don't get any closer to me. I don't want you to know who I really am." Their raging works—it drives people away or keeps them at a safe distance. Of course this also makes you feel even worse when you realize that others are avoiding you.

Contempt

When children experience contempt directly at the hands of a parent they perceive themselves as offensive to the parent and feel utterly rejected and disgusting to the parent. When children observe a parent treat someone else contemptuously (i.e., the other parent, a sibling) they become vulnerable to taking on this way of treating others themselves. By looking down upon others and perceiving them as lesser or inferior beings, a once-wounded child can insulate himself against further shame. We then see the beginnings of a judgmental, fault finding, or condescending attitude, which in itself is emotionally abusive.

Striving for Power

As Gershen Kaufman stated in his book: "While rage keeps others away and contempt both distances the self from others and elevates the self above others, striving for power is a direct attempt to compensate for the sense of defectiveness which underlies internalized shame. To the degree that one is successful in gaining power, particularly over others, one becomes increasingly less vulnerable to further shame."

A person who reaches a position of real power over others not only becomes less vulnerable to having his own shame activated but is in a good position to transfer blame to others. In the same way, a parent can both wield power over her children and blame her children for any mistakes she makes with them. Power seeking individuals also prefer to remain in control in any interpersonal situation and to gain control in their intimate relationships. They will even seek out those who are weaker or less secure to gain influence or power over.

For these individuals, power not only becomes a way to insulate themselves from further shame but a way to compensate for shame internalized earlier in life. By gaining power over others they in essence reverse roles with those who controlled or abused them early in life.

Striving for Perfection

Instead of striving for power, some people fight against shame by striving for perfection. Like power seeking, this is a way to compensate for an underlying sense of defectiveness. The reasoning goes like this: If I can become perfect, I am no longer vulnerable to being shamed. Unfortunately, the quest for perfection is doomed to fail and the realization of this failure reawakens the sense of shame the person was trying to run from in the first place. Since he or she already feels that he or she is inherently not good enough as a person, nothing he or she does is ever seen as good enough.

If you expect perfection from others you will end up being demanding and critical. If you do this with your children you will be emotionally abusing them. If you expect perfection from yourself you will constantly be disappointed in yourself and constantly be damaging your self-esteem.

The Transfer of Blame

When a child is often blamed for things that go wrong or observes a parent or significant other repeatedly fixing blame on others, he or she may take on blaming as a defensive strategy against shame. For example, in a blame oriented family environment, attention is focused not upon how to repair the mistake but on whose fault it was and on who is to blame. The child learns to blame in order to counter blame received from others. If responsibility can be transferred to someone else the child has preserved her own belief that she has done nothing wrong.

Such a child grows up unable to accept inevitable mistakes on his part. He takes on the same blaming strategy as his parents and often becomes emotionally abusive to his own children or to his own spouse by chastising and shaming them when they make a mistake.

Gershen believes that when blaming becomes directed outside oneself—externalized—we often see a person who perceives the source of all that goes wrong to lie outside of himself, and, paradoxically, beyond internal control. And though this person resents the resulting feeling of powerlessness, he never recognizes that he has colluded in the very process of creating that powerlessness. As Gershen stated, "By perpetually seeing fault to lie externally to himself, he is inadvertently teaching himself to experience the control over events as wholly external to himself as well." This is a typical pattern for male batterers.

Although full control is not attainable, we do have control over how we perceive and handle what comes our way, and how we internally experience ourselves. While blaming others may help us avoid taking responsibility for wrongdoing or mistakes and thus avoid shame, we render ourselves powerless by doing so. When the source of what goes wrong in life becomes external to the self, we have also relinquished the power to affect or alter what happens to us.

Self-Blame

Sometimes children growing up in a blaming family will learn to blame themselves—to internalize rather than externalize blame—as a way of avoiding blame from significant others. Such a person learns that if he or she is quick enough to blame himself or herself, a parent's blaming will subside or be altogether avoided. It is as though the child makes an implicit contract with the parent: I will do the blaming so you will not have to. In this way, the intolerable blaming, which induces shame in the child, is placed under the child's own, internal control. It becomes internalized in such a way that the child's inner life is forever subject to spontaneous self-blame.

THE CONNECTION BETWEEN SHAME, SELF-BLAME, AND A VICTIM MENTALITY

Self-blame and shame are closely related. For example, there has been considerable research on the relationship between self-blame and abusive experiences in adulthood. Self-blame is congruent with the way children tend to think—making themselves the reference point for all events. It is also consistent with the thought processes of traumatized people of all ages, who search for faults in their own behavior in an effort to make sense out of what happened to them. When a child is being chronically abused, there is neither time nor experience to help modify this tendency toward self-blame, instead, it is continually reinforced. The abused child's sense of inner badness may also be directly confirmed by parental scape-goating. Survivors frequently describe being blamed, not only for their parents' violence or sexual misconduct, but also for other family misfortunes.

In the case of sexual abuse, a child's participation in forbidden sexual activities also confirms his or her sense of badness. Any gratification that the child is able to experience from the exploitative situation becomes proof in her mind that she instigated and bears full responsibility for the abuse. If she ever experienced sexual pleasure, enjoyed the abuser's special attention, bargained for favors, or used the sexual relationship to her advantage, she will view these things as further evidence of her innate wickedness.

Survivors of child sexual abuse often describe themselves as being damaged goods, as evil, or beyond contempt. I've had clients who do not think they are even human and many use the imagery of excrement or filth to describe themselves. By developing a contaminated, shame-laden identity, a victim takes the evil of the abuser into herself and thereby preserves her primary attachment to her parents (or other abuser). Because the inner sense of badness preserves a relationship, it is not readily given up even after the abuse has stopped but becomes a part of the child's personality structure.

Exercise: *How Shame Has Affected You*

1. Think about how you have coped with the shame you endured in childhood. How did you defend against the shame? How has shame contributed to your abuser or victim style of relating to others?

2. If you internalized the shame, think about the ways shame has contributed to your victim mentality.

3. If you have externalized shame think about the ways you have projected your shame onto others.

4. Some people defend against shame by projecting it out on others and by raging at others. If you tend to do this, particularly if you tend to lash out at people or have sudden, unexpected fits of rage, pay attention to the ways in which you convert shame into anger. Do you put other people down because you feel rejected by them? Do you go on a verbal rampage in an attempt to shame anyone who dares to criticize you? Do you yell at anyone who makes you feel inadequate? Do you become difficult or insulting when you feel like a failure?

In order to break the shame/rage cycle you will need to ask yourself, "What am I ashamed of?" each and every time you get angry. Think of your anger as a red flag signaling the fact that you are feeling shame. This is especially true whenever you experience sudden bursts of anger or when you become enraged. It may be difficult to find your shame at first and you may not be feeling shame each and every time you feel angry but with some practice you will be able to recognize those times when you are feeling ashamed and discover what has triggered it in you. Once you've identified the shame/rage connection you will need to break it. This means you will have to stop yourself from becoming angry as a way of defending against your shame.

How to Cope with Shame

Until you can learn to manage your sometimes debilitating shame you will not be successful in your attempts to break the cycle of anger, pain, and abuse that have likely defined you and your family. Shame can trigger abusive reactions. It can cause us to compensate by needing to have power over others, and it is often responsible for encouraging people to stay in abusive situations.

You can learn to cope with shame by following the process outlined in the previous chapter: (1) Identify the emotion; (2) determine the message the emotion is conveying to you; (3) feel the emotion without becoming overwhelmed by it—breathe into it and accept it; (4) ask yourself if it is appropriate to be feeling this emotion at this time; and (5) take action to remedy the situation (e.g., communicate your feelings to someone, change the way you look at things).

Identify the Feeling

Identifying the emotion of shame is not as easy as it is with some of our other emotions.

"I just want to dig a hole and hide myself in it."

"I wish I could just disappear. I'm so ashamed I can't look anyone in the eye."

"I can't tell anyone about it. It's just too humiliating."

These are the kinds of comments that clients have made through the years concerning how they feel about incidents in their lives when they felt humiliated or shamed. When we feel strongly shamed it is common for us to want to hide. In fact the word *shame* is thought to derive from an Indo-European word meaning *hide*. There seems to be a consensus among theorists, researchers, and lay people that the experience of shame involves an impulse to hide from others, to avoid having one's personal failure observed by anyone and to escape from judgment.

But the problem with shame is that there is also a tendency to want to hide from ourselves when we are feeling shame. Many people are simply unaware of the fact that they are feeling it. H. Lewis in *Shame and Guilt in Neurosis* coined the phrase *unacknowledged shame* to refer to the fact that shame can be concealed from our conscious awareness. As she put it, "Difficulties in identifying one's own experience as shame have so often been observed that they suggest some intrinsic connection between shame and the mechanism of denial."

According to Lewis, denial operates in two ways, the first being that shame affect is overt or available to consciousness but the person experiencing it either will not or cannot identify it. Another person may identify that the person is having a shame reaction, or the person may identify it as it recedes, but while shame is occurring the person is unable to communicate. He or she often says only that he or she feels blank or tense or awful. This kind of shame is referred to as *overt, unidentified shame.*

The second kind of denial-tempered shame is referred to as *bypassed shame.* This type of shame can involve a great deal of worry and obsessing about what other people think of you. There seems to be little feeling connected to this type of shame except for a momentary wince, or jolt that consists of a peripheral, nonspecific disturbance in awareness.

"I felt exposed and speechless." This highlights the fact that many people feel such utter self-consciousness when they are shamed that speech can become silenced. In addition to finding it difficult to talk about their experiences with shame many people simply do not have the ability to articulate their feelings. Often, instead of identifying our feelings as shame we mistakenly use words such as *hurt* or *awkward.*

To make matters even more complicated, instead of expressing or showing shame we often manifest secondary reactions such as fear, hurt, or rage instead. For example, feeling exposed is often followed by fear of further exposure and further occurrences of shame. The feeling of distress more commonly referred to as hurt also frequently accompanies shame. And the instant flash of rage, whether expressed or held inside, often protects the self against further exposure. When rage predominates in reaction to shame, all that anyone sees in the shame experiencing person is that very self-protective rage. It is as if the shame experiencing person were vehemently saying, "Keep away!"

So, as you can see, it is difficult to identify shame or to communicate about feelings of shame. Instead of saying we feel shame we often use the following words to label or describe the feeling: embarrassment, humiliation, guilt, remorse, regret, mortification, contrition, culpability, insult, or invalidation.

Once again, checking in with your body can help you discover your shame. We tend to feel shame in our body as a *sense of dread,* an overwhelming desire to hide or cover our face, a pain in the pit of our stomach. Some people blush (a hot or red face) or others experience feelings of jitteriness, nervousness, or a choking or suffocating sensation. Some people experience what is commonly referred to as a shame attack in which they feel completely overwhelmed with shame. Feelings commonly reported by those having a shame attack are: feeling dizzy or spacey, disoriented, and nauseated.

Behavior associated with shame includes: withdrawing, hiding or covering the face, bowing the head, eyes down, darting eyes, avoiding the person you harmed or the people you have wronged, saying you are sorry or apologizing, asking for forgiveness, making amends, giving gifts, trying to repair the harm, fix the damage, or make restitution.

Exercise: *Your Experience of Shame*

1. How do you know when you are feeling shame? Do you react emotionally in a particular way? Does your body react in a consistent way? If so, identify where you feel shame in your body and how you experience it.

2. Do you deny shame, mislabel it, or cover it over with another emotion? If so, list the ways you do so.

Determine the Message Shame Is Conveying to You

We are told that shame is the painful feeling of being a flawed human being and that therefore it is an unhealthy emotion. But this isn't necessarily true. First of all, all emotions are natural and healthy reactions. Second, shame can be a message that we are failing to be who we were meant to be. Shame can expose us to parts of ourselves we have been reluctant to acknowledge. In this way, it can help us to know ourselves on a very deep level.

There are two kinds of shame, healthy shame and unhealthy shame. The purpose of healthy shame is to remind us that we are less than we ought to be and less than we want to be. If you can still feel shame, it is because you are healthy enough to feel uncomfortable about this fact. Many people have been so shamed in their lives that they are completely defended against it. This is why some people are able to commit horrendous crimes without feeling any remorse for their actions. If you still feel shame for your less-than-noble actions you should feel grateful that you still have the power to feel it.

Healthy shame keeps us in touch with our better or true self. When it comes down to it, it is not the threat of punishment or the wrath of God that keeps us true to ourselves. Most of us do the right thing because we would be ashamed of ourselves if we did the wrong thing. If you have done something that you know is wrong, feeling shame can be your first hope for healing.

Unhealthy shame, on the other hand, has no basis in reality. It is false because, unlike true shame, it is not a signal that something is wrong with us. It is unhealthy because it kills our joy and saps our energy and creative powers. As Lewis B. Smedes explained in his book *Shame and Grace: Healing the Shame We Don't Deserve,* "It is a shame we do not deserve because we are not as bad as our feelings tell us we are."

So how do we know if we are feeling healthy shame or unhealthy shame? It can be difficult at times since most of us feel both forms of shame from time to time and can even feel both at once. But there are some significant differences.

Unhealthy or false shame:

- Is put on us by others. False shame comes from outside of us: from being abused, neglected, or controlled by nonaccepting parents, from unforgiving, noncompassionate churches or church people; and from a culture that shames us if we are not attractive, rich, or smart enough.

- Causes us to be unable to distinguish between minor mistakes and major offenses. Every trivial failing feels to us like a crime or a sin.

- Causes us to be shamebound. Nearly anything can bring on a shame attack—a mild criticism, a memory of a past mistake, the suspicion that we are being ignored, or mocked by others.

- Is indiscriminate and all pervasive. Unlike healthy shame that zeros in on the problem area, unhealthy shame has no focus. It leaves us feeling like total failures.

The next time you become aware that you are feeling shame, ask yourself whether it is healthy shame or unhealthy shame. If it is healthy shame, ask yourself what the message is that your shame is sending you. By probing your healthy shame you may discover a great deal about yourself. You may discover things about yourself that disappoint you, but healthy shame can also give you the gift of self-understanding. It can also cause you to be grateful for and give yourself credit for your good qualities. As Lewis B. Smedes in *Shame and*

Grace explained, "Whatever there is to discover about ourselves, shame may be the push we need to make us look and see."

If it is unhealthy shame, work at discovering where the shame originated. Did someone say something to you that was shaming? Were you criticized, belittled, or made fun of? Did someone reject you or do something that felt rejecting? Did something trigger memories of the past? Were you reminded of a past shaming experience?

EXERCISE: *Healthy Shame or Unhealthy Shame?*

1. What type of situations cause you to feel healthy shame?

2. When do you tend to feel unhealthy shame?

3. What ways have you found to tell the difference between healthy and unhealthy shame? If you haven't developed any ways to help you make the distinction, think of some now.

Feel the Emotion without Becoming Overwhelmed by It

The next time you become aware that you are feeling shame you need to first determine whether it is healthy or unhealthy shame. If it is healthy shame simply breathe into it as you have learned to do with your other emotions. Allow it to be. Don't be alarmed by it and don't allow it to overwhelm you. Accept it as the normal and healthy emotion that it is. Refer back to chapter 5 for instructions on how to feel and accept an emotion.

If it is unhealthy shame do as I suggested earlier, try to discover the source of the shame—what triggered your shame response. Certain things can trigger memories of earlier experiences when you felt shamed and this can cause you to have a shame attack. These shame attacks can be extremely debilitating. A shame attack is usually experienced as a sinking feeling or feeling wounded. Some people actually become dizzy or disoriented and others become nauseated.

How to Deal with an Attack of Shame

If you are having a full-blown shame attack you may need to talk to a *trusted* friend or someone else close to you (your therapist, your sponsor, a member of your support group, someone at a hotline). Explain that you are having a shame attack and that you are feeling horrible about yourself. Don't blame the person who triggered your shame for making you feel bad, take responsibility for your own shame. Try to make a connection between this current incident and what it is reminding you of (from your childhood, from a more recent traumatic shaming). Ask your friend to remind you that you are not a horrible person by telling you of at least one good attribute you have.

If you can't find someone you trust to talk to, write your feelings down on paper or in a journal. Describe what you are feeling in detail, including your physical reactions. Trace these reactions back to other times and incidents when you felt similar feelings.

If you find a connecting incident, write about it in detail. Then spend some time reminding yourself of your good qualities and accomplishments.

Ask Yourself if It Is Appropriate to Be Feeling Shame at This Time

We've already covered this question in the previous material. Just be aware that we often feel shame when we really have nothing to be ashamed of. This is particularly true for adults who were neglected or abused as children who are overwhelmed with unhealthy shame. The following exercise will help you discover what your shame triggers are.

EXERCISE: *Discover Your Triggers*

1. Take some time to create a list of the most embarrassing experiences in your childhood or adolescence. Include the times when you felt humiliated or shamed by someone else.

2. Once you have completed your list, read through it slowly. Pay attention to how you feel emotionally and how your body feels as you read each item.

3. Put a check mark beside each of the items on your list that you still feel an emotional charge about.

4. Think about the possibility that these items might be your triggers. For example, if you remembered an experience where you were chastised or punished in front of a group when you were a child and thinking about the event (or events) still makes you feel humiliated and/or angry, it is possible that when you experience any kind of public embarrassment it may trigger the memory of this event. This may then cause you to

have a shame attack and to overreact to the situation in the present.

At this point it is also very likely that you may feel a great deal of shame when you realize just how much you have already perpetuated a legacy of abuse or neglect. While it is important to face the truth about your victimizer or victim mentality, it will serve no purpose for you to become overwhelmed with shame. Remember it was the abuse or neglect that you experienced that has caused you to react as you have and not some inherent badness or evil inside of you.

While it is important to take responsibility for your actions, constantly putting yourself down for your past actions will only increase your shame. Research shows that painful and debilitating feelings of shame do not motivate constructive changes in behavior. In fact, unhealthy shame serves to escalate the very destructive behavior we aim to curb. This is true whether someone else is shaming you or you are shaming yourself.

Take Action to Remedy the Situation

If your shame is justified you will need to take action to remedy the situation. Here are some suggestions:

1. Repair the transgression. Say you're sorry. Apologize. (For information on how to make a meaningful apology, refer to my book *The Power of Apology*.) Make things better. Do something nice for the person you offended (or for someone else if that is not possible).

2. Commit to avoiding that mistake in the future.

3. Accept the consequences gracefully.

4. Then let it go.

Healing Your Shame from the Past

You no doubt feel shame when you recall and acknowledge your own abuse and neglect. In addition to being shamed by the abuse itself, it is likely that you also took on the shame of the abuser. When a parent abuses a child it is often because he or she is in the middle of a shame attack and is, in essence, projecting his or her shame onto the child.

When a child molester is abusing a child he or she is usually reenacting his or her own abuse and therefore is also feeling a great deal of shame. While any form of abuse is taking place the child feels the shame of the abuser and is overwhelmed by it—causing the child to actually take on the shame of the abuser.

In order to avoid passing on the abuse and the shame to another child or to a partner, you need to work on ridding yourself of your shame. This will include the following:

1. First you need to fully accept the fact that you did not deserve the abuse—that no matter what you did or did not do you did not deserve to be abused.

2. You need to tell significant others about the abuse or neglect you experienced.

3. You need to separate your own shame from the shame of the abuser and give back the abuser's shame.

4. You need to work on gaining self-acceptance and compassion for yourself. Stop rejecting in yourself that which was rejected by your parents or other significant people in your childhood.

5. Expect others to accept you as you are. Surround yourself with people who like and accept you just as you are, as opposed to people who are critical, judgmental, or otherwise shaming.

Let's examine each of these items more closely.

Accept the Fact That You Did Not Deserve the Abuse or Neglect

Absolutely nothing you did as a child warranted any kind of emotional, physical, or sexual abuse that you experienced. You did not make your father so angry that he had to hit you, you did not make your mother feel so humiliated that she had to lock you in the closet, you did not turn your father on by sitting on his lap. Your parents' (or other abusers') abusive reactions were their responsibility and theirs alone. It is vitally important that you understand this.

Many times my clients have told me that while they believe other children did not deserve to be abused, their situation was different.

They tell me how they instigated the sexual abuse or how they were so rebellious that they forced a parent to beat them. Sadly, most have lost touch with how very vulnerable and innocent they really were when they were a child. For these clients, I recommend the following:

1. If you have a child who is around the age you were when you were abused, or if you know a child this age, spend time really observing this child closely. If you don't know a child, observe children you come in contact with. Notice that no matter how mature a child is or how much she sometimes tries to act like an adult, she is really just a vulnerable, innocent child who needs to be protected.

2. If you were physically abused, ask yourself, "Is there anything this child could do that would justify an adult beating him?" If you were sexually abused, ask yourself, "Does this child want to have sex with an adult? Is there anything a child could do that would warrant an adult becoming sexually involved with this child?"

Tell Others about Your Experiences

As the saying goes, "We are only as sick as our secrets." This particularly applies to the shaming that continues by keeping the secret of your abuse from those you love. In order to heal your shame from the past you will need to share your experiences with someone you love and trust (your partner, a close friend, a therapist, members of a support group).

Give Back the Abuser's Shame

Several years ago during one of my group sessions for survivors of child sexual abuse, several of the women were talking about how they always felt as if they were damaged goods. They discussed how they felt ashamed of themselves and their bodies. This is a common experience for survivors, often causing them to spend the rest of their lives trying to make up for the bad things they have done by being very good people. Although these women *intellectually* understood that the abuse had not been their fault, they didn't seem to get it *emotionally*. They still blamed themselves.

You may have been told many times by your therapist, by your friends and loved ones, that the abuse you endured was not your fault, but you may still blame yourself. Releasing your anger toward your abuser will help you stop blaming yourself since he or she is the appropriate target for your anger. Getting angry at your abuser will affirm your innocence. And the vital force of anger will be moving in the right direction: outward instead of inward.

EXERCISE: *Give the Shame Back to Your Abuser*

1. Sit comfortably and breathe deeply.

2. Imagine you are looking inside your body. Find any shame or "bad" feelings you might have there.

3. Imagine you are reaching down inside your body and pulling out all that dark, ugly stuff.

4. Now imagine you are throwing all that dark ugliness at the abuser, where it belongs.

5. Open your eyes and make a throwing motion with your arms. Say out loud as you do it, "Take back your shame. It's not mine. It's yours." Do this until you can feel the truth of what you are saying.

Ridding Your Body of Shame

Victims of child abuse, especially those who were sexually abused, tend to hold shame in their bodies. It is important to discover where you hold your shame. This will be an important first step in beginning to manage it and eventually in alleviating it.

EXERCISE: *Self-Healing Ritual*

The following self-healing ritual will help you to exorcise the shame from your body. This self-healing ritual can bring a sense of being reborn and cleansed.

1. Soak yourself in a hot bath or Jacuzzi. As you do so, imagine that all the residues of the abuse are being soaked out of you through your skin. Visualize the impurities flowing *out* of your genitals, breasts, lips, mouth, or anus—any place that was contaminated by the abuser.

2. Take a large sponge and use it to wipe your body free of all the shame you have held in your body. As you do so, say out loud to yourself, "It was not my fault."

3. Imagine loving energy pouring *into* your body. Visualize yourself being reborn into a pure body that will keep its integrity throughout your lifetime. Emerge cleansed, inside and out.

Trade Self-Criticism for Compassion and Self-Acceptance

Compassion is the antidote to shame. In order to heal your shame it is vitally important that you trade your tendency to be impatient or self-critical with compassion. My client Judy came into her session feeling very down. "I don't know what is wrong with me. I just can't get in touch with my feelings the way you are encouraging me to. I seem so stuck, so defended. I really want to change but I'm just not able to move forward."

It was clear to me that Judy was being impatient and critical with herself in the same way that her mother had been with her. I explained to Judy that not only was she treating herself in the same destructive way as her mother had but that this treatment was actually going to stifle her progress. She needed to have compassion for herself, not self-criticism.

I encouraged her to remember the way her mother had treated her as a child and how it made her feel. To help her gain compassion for the child that she was and the pain she endured. I asked her to look at pictures of herself as a child. I suggest you do the same.

Judy's impatience and self-criticism was, in computer-speak, a dowload of her mother's critical, negative voice. She needed to replace her mother's voice with a more nurturing, compassionate inner voice. If you tend to be critical or demanding of yourself, you too may have downloaded the voice of an abusive parent or other caretaker into your head. There are several ways to create a nurturing inner voice that can eventually crowd out or replace the negative inner voice so many survivors have:

1. Close your eyes, take some deep breaths and connect with the inherent strength, goodness and wisdom within you.

2. If you notice that you tend to have a lot of negative or critical inner chatter, begin to speak to yourself in the same voice you use to speak to a small child or a beloved pet. If you make a mistake, comfort yourself the way you would a child who has accidentally spilled some milk.

3. Adopt the voice of someone who is nurturing and strong (your therapist, a sponsor, a loving friend). Give yourself credit for the progress you have made and for the good things you have done.

Having compassion for yourself will give you the strength and motivation to change, whereas self-criticism will only tear you down and take away your motivation and strength. If you don't have compassion for yourself you won't be able to have it for anyone else and this can help create an abusive mindset. Those who are unable to have empathy or compassion for others tend to act selfishly and callously toward others because they are unable to understand how their behavior affects others.

Stop Comparing Yourself to Others

Another aspect of accepting yourself as you are is to stop comparing yourself to others. People who carry a great deal of shame react to the awareness of differences between themselves and others by automatically translating it into a comparison of good versus bad, better versus worse. Rather than valuing the difference, they feel threatened by it. Those who have adapted perfectionism as a defense against shame inevitably feel less than the other person when they compare themselves to someone. Those who have adapted contempt as a defending strategy against shame feel enhanced at the expense of devaluing the other person. Each strategy, perfectionism and contempt, may be employed by the same person at different times or situations.

But there is a third outcome possible. Neither you nor the other person needs to emerge as the lesser if your awareness of your differences can remain just that—a difference to be owned and valued. Unfortunately, for those whose differences were not valued by significant others, this third option is difficult to fathom.

Expect Others to Accept You As You Are

In order to heal your shame from the past you also need to consciously work on believing that it is okay to be who you are. The following suggestions will help you do this:

1. Stop relying on anyone who treats you as if you are not okay the way you are.

2. When someone treats you poorly tell him or her to stop it! I realize this is easier said than done but start out with someone who is not threatening and work your way to the harder cases. Tell them you do not deserve to be treated poorly even if you don't believe it yet. The more often you say it the more you will believe it. If the person continues to treat you poorly don't keep telling them over and over. This is like begging and it makes you look weak in their eyes and makes you feel weak and to lose respect for yourself. Instead determine that you will try to stay away from this person as much as possible.

3. When someone treats you poorly or insults you make sure you don't absorb it. Those who really care about you will not insult you if they don't like something about you, they will kindly take you aside and have a talk with you. Even then you are not obligated to take in everything everyone says because often people have a hidden agenda in pointing out your faults. The important thing is that you do not allow someone else to make you feel bad about yourself or make you feel like you are not a valuable human being. Even more important, don't allow yourself to replay negative messages over and over in your mind.

4. Spend more and more time with people who know you and accept you for who you are. Choose your relationships based on how you are treated as opposed to whether the person makes you feel comfortable. We are often most comfortable with the kind of people we are used to being around—including those who treat us poorly and remind us of those from our childhood who treated us poorly.

5. Open up more with those people who already accept you as you are. The fewer secrets you have the less shame you will experience.

6. Treat others the way you want to be treated. If you treat others with respect and consideration they are far more likely to treat you the same. And the better you treat others the less shame you will experience.

7. When someone treats you well make sure you absorb it. When someone does something nice for you take a few minutes to

take it in and feel the good feelings. Don't doubt the person's sincerity or tell yourself they are being nice because they want something. Trust that they are being nice because they simply want to and because they like you. If someone gives you a compliment, take a deep breath and really take it in. Don't negate the compliment or talk yourself out of believing it. Most people don't give compliments unless they really mean them.

8. Let the person know you appreciate their kindness. This will encourage him or her to continue being kind.

9. When you are treated well make sure you give yourself time to enjoy it. When you are alone remember the positive or kind things the person said or did. Replay the positive experience in your mind so you can really take it in.

CHAPTER 7

Managing Your Anger

Hostility cannot simply be passed off as something we inherit and hence we can do nothing about. On the other hand, excessive hostility is regularly found to be a disease of personality, transmittable from person to person and from group to group, and basically by contact from parents to children, from generation to generation.

LEON J. SAUL, M.D., *The Causes of Hostility*

Anger is an especially important emotion for those with a history of neglect or abuse for several reasons.

1. Neglect and abuse are violations against the human spirit and we tend to become angry when we are violated. Unfortunately, most children are unable to express their anger at the time, for fear of further abuse or rejection.

2. This repressed or suppressed anger is often reignited when they themselves become intimately involved with a partner or when they have children and reexperience some of the same feelings and experiences they did as children.

3. Those who take in the rage of the parent tend to become depressed, fearful, and hopeless. They turn their anger inward and take their anger out on themselves in the form of self-destructive behavior or a tendency to allow others to be abusive toward them.

4. Those who externalize their rage become bullies and juvenile delinquents as children. As adults they emotionally or physically

abuse their partners or their children and sometimes, become criminals.

5. Parents who abuse their children are doing so partly because they are taking their anger out on their children.

6. Anger is a major avenue for repeating the cycle of abuse. We tend to repeat the way our parents disciplined us, the way they expressed their anger, and the way they misused or abused their anger against other people.

How Trauma Affects a Child

Humans and animals respond in similar ways when they are threatened. Both either ready themselves for battle or they flee—fight or flight. Adrenaline circulates, the heart pumps hard and fast, and the muscles tense, enriched by oxygen and nutrients that arrive within a few seconds. But humans also know how to think and how to talk their way out of a predicament. One special human quality is the ability to control the environment—to use impulse control and long-range planning to master circumstances. Children learn this ability a little at a time, beginning in late infancy when they can nod their heads no to the time when they can waddle on two feet and achieve bladder and bowel control.

What happens when a child who has already learned this skill and achieved some autonomy is suddenly robbed of it, such as in the cases of child abuse? According to Lenore Terr, M.D., author of *Too Scared to Cry*:

> The same autonomic releases for fight or flight come about—adrenaline is released, nutrients flow quickly to the muscles, and oxygen supply is augmented. But motoric discharge is blocked. The child's body—all ready for taking risks—cannot move. There is no hope for success. The child's mind, thinking overtime and totally on the alert, cannot create a plan because the shock of the ambush feels too overwhelming, the attack, too devastating, and the attackers, too powerful. A child in such circumstances, is totally helpless, and he knows that he is. He has temporarily lost a very human attribute and an early accomplishment, the ability to exert autonomy.

Anger and powerlessness are strongly connected. We become angry when we feel hurt or frustrated and are unable to do anything about it. If someone is responsible for our pain, they rightly become the object of our anger. When a child is abused, either emotionally, physically, or sexually he becomes terrified. But he may also become enraged. Since there has been no outlet for the stored up adrenaline, fear and aggression tend to build up. This stored up fear and aggression can lead to a pattern of abusiveness or victimlike behavior.

Those abusers who are known to the child and those who repeatedly abuse the child, tend to stir up the most anger in a child. In fact, frequently repeated and long-standing traumatic experiences of neglect and abuse create in its victims an extreme rage and its mirror image, extreme passivity. Parental abuse in particular creates intensely angry reactions in a child. The physically abused child may be quite open with his rage and may fight back with everything in him. On the other hand, he may be so afraid of further retaliation that he must submerge his anger. This can result in a pattern of becoming numb to feelings, self-destructiveness, self-injury, or even suicide attempts. Those who were abused also tend to repress their anger at their abusers for fear of abandonment or rejection. This anger is stored in the unconscious and is only expressed when something in their current life triggers the memories. At these times the person is likely to strike out without warning at those nearest to them—most especially their children and their partner or to become self-destructive.

In general a repeatedly abused or sexually exploited child may express his anger in one of three pathological ways. The child may:

1. Identify with the aggressor. At its extreme this may lead to the child developing a cruel, bullyish, abusive, or even criminal personality.

2. Retreat into passivity and reenact the old victimization out of habit or reenactment. Such a child may retain the victim stance for life.

3. Continue to act in an acceptable way but break out into wild rages or self-destructive behavior whenever frustration occurs or whenever he is reminded of the traumatic incidents (triggered).

As a way of protecting himself from the horrible shame he felt because of his overly critical and demanding father, Max identified with his aggressor. As an adult he is emotionally abusive to everyone close to him: his employees, his wife, and especially his children. He belittles and berates people when they make the smallest mistake and expects far too much of others.

As a child, Marnie retreated into passivity whenever her father began to go off on one of his tirades. She tried to stay out of his way as much as she could in order to avoid being on the receiving end of her father's wrath. Today Marnie continues to be passive and to deny her anger, espeically her anger toward her father.

Debbie frequently blows up at her children and husband for no apparent reason. In actuality, Debbie is often triggered by past memories of the abuse she sustained at the hands of her tyrannical mother.

Whichever configuration the abused child's personality eventually takes, angry children grow up to be angry adults who often use and abuse alcohol, illegal drugs, and prescribed medications in order to dampen their rage and numb their feelings. (Unfortunately, alcohol and drugs first anesthetize the parts of the brain that control judgment and self-restraint, which can lead to abusive behavior.) Others use food to stuff down feelings of anger. Some project their rage onto others, assuming that everyone is against them. Still others become involved with abusive partners who act out their anger for them or become involved in risky or self-destructive activities as a way of reenacting their abuse.

The Role Anger Plays in the Cycle of Abuse

As you can see, the role that anger plays in the cycle of abuse is profound. It is so profound, in fact, that if you are truly serious about breaking the cycle of abuse or neglect you must take a close look at the way you express anger for this may signal current or future abusive or victimlike behavior more than anything else.

Whether a person has an aggressive, passive or eruptive anger style, make no mistake about it, all victims of childhood abuse are enraged. That rage bursts out of them whenever they are shamed, under stress, or under the influence of alcohol or drugs, or when they are reminded of the abuse.

If you tend to act out your anger in aggressive, abusive ways like Max, you need to learn to manage your anger in more productive ways, such as taking a time-out when your anger builds up. You also need to direct your righteous anger toward your original abusers instead of taking it out on innocent people.

If, like Marnie, you reacted by denying and disowning your anger toward your abusers you will also need to begin to own and express your anger toward your original abusers. Instead of turning your anger against yourself and becoming self-destructive or further damaging your self-esteem you need to give yourself permission to express your anger. If you tend to passively stand by and allow others to abuse you or your children you need to give yourself permission to stand up to your abusers. You will need to confront your fear of anger—both your fear of others' anger and the fear of your own, otherwise you will attract and be attracted to angry people who will act out your anger for you. This disowning and denying of anger can also set you up to be what is called a silent partner (someone who will stand by while their child is being abused).

If you break out in wild rages like Debbie you need to learn constructive ways of calming down when you are triggered by memories of the past, when you are stressed, or when you are shamed and to manage your anger in more productive ways. You also need to become aware of your triggers, to be able to trace them back to your original abuse and to begin to express your anger toward your original abusers.

Discover Your Anger Legacy

One of the first steps to changing an unhealthy way of coping with anger is to discover its origin. For example, the suppression of anger is a pattern that gets passed down from generation to generation. Marnie, the woman who retreated into passivity from the previous example, shared with me that every woman in her family on her mother's side was very passive. "I never saw my mother express anger, nor did I ever see my grandmother or my aunts. They all put up with horrible treatment from their husbands, and even their grown children, but they never showed even the slightest bit of anger toward them. In many ways, I'm just like them."

We often "inherit" the way we cope with anger and our beliefs about anger from our parents' example, from their beliefs, and from the way they treated us. Unfortunately, those who have a history of abuse or neglect seldom had positive role models when it came to practicing healthy ways of dealing with their anger. They tend to repeat the ways their parents interacted with one another or the ways they were treated. Others fear taking on one of their parents' anger styles to such an extent that it causes them to take on the opposite anger style. Some become so afraid that they will repeat one or both of their parents' ways of expressing his or her anger that they avoid certain situations—like getting married or having a child.

The following exercise will help you identify any patterns you may have established based on parental messages and your parents' behavior.

WRITING EXERCISE: *Your Anger Legacy*

1. List the ways your mother and father dealt with their anger. Which of your parents do you feel handles anger the best?

2. List the messages you received from your family about expressing anger. For example, was it acceptable or unacceptable to confront someone when you were angry? Were you ever punished for expressing your anger? Were you ever rewarded for not expressing your anger?

3. Which of your parents are you most like when it comes to expressing your own anger? List the ways you are like this parent in terms of anger expression.

4. Which of your parents are you most like when it comes to dealing with other people's anger? List the ways you are unlike this parent in terms of coping with the anger of others.

This exercise may have unearthed some painful truths for you. As much as we often try hard not to be like our parents, especially a parent who was explosive, abusive, or who put up with the abuse of others, we often become more like them than we care to admit. If you have found this to be true, don't get discouraged. Now that you are aware of the similarities, you can do something about it.

Strategies for Those with an Aggressive Anger Style

Although you may feel better immediately after releasing your anger in an aggressive way, the good feeling usually doesn't last very long. This is because aggression creates its own problems. Responding aggressively (yelling, throwing things, hitting walls, controlling, blaming) can damage someone's self-esteem, frighten them, or harm them physically. By responding in an aggressive way you set yourself up to feel guilty when you recognize the effect your words or actions had on the person (your child looks at you with fear in his eyes, your wife cries herself to sleep and is unable to be physically close to you for days afterward). Last but not least, sometimes when those with an aggressive anger style vent their anger the desire to keep it going actually increases. In actuality, although the impulse is to get a release from the built-up tension by forcing the angry energy out—in a sense you may just be priming the pump. The more you ventilate your anger, the more anger you feel you need to ventilate. This is partly due to the fact that aggressive anger increases rather than decreases aggression.

Even though there are serious consequences to releasing your anger in aggressive ways, because there is such a feeling of temporary relief, aggression can be difficult to give up. So what do you do when you are angry and your adrenaline starts to pump? You'll need other outlets that will feel just as good and offer the same kind of release.

The following are some effective activities for releasing anger energy:

- Taking a brisk walk or run.

- Writing your angry feelings down is also a good way to find relief. Write down all the negative, hateful things that are going through your head. Don't censor yourself, just let it all out.

- As a further way of releasing tension you can tear up what you have written.

- Playing a sport such as basketball, racket ball, or swimming

- If you are extremely angry and competitive it is best to play an individual sport in order to avoid physical skirmishes with others. I suggest you shoot hoops, play one-person racket ball, go to a batting cage and hit some balls, or practice your tennis game. (Activities such as boxing, wrestling or hockey are usually not recommended for those with an aggressive anger style because they are aggressive sports that may actually reinforce aggressive behavior instead of releasing energy. Instead find physical activities that make you feel calm and relaxed.)

Take Time-Outs

Another way of calming down is to take time-outs. It takes about thirty seconds from the time you begin to notice your anger signals before you finally explode. This gives you just enough time to get away so you can cool off. There's no time for a discussion, no time to work off your anger in a physically appropriate way. A time-out will give you a chance to let your anger subside and ultimately to regain control of yourself.

Go to a place where you can relax such as your car, your room, or a park. If you're inside, distract yourself by watching TV, listening to music, or reading. If you're outdoors, take a walk, ride a bicycle, or go for a run. Even though you may feel like doing something like hitting a punching bag, throwing something, or chopping wood these activities may actually fuel your anger or even be dangerous. And don't call up a friend or go to your local hangout where you can talk to your friends and get more angry. The point is to calm down.

Once you've accomplished your goal it is time to go back to the scene of your upset. Don't go back too soon or you will get angry all over again. Take all the time you need. It is far more important for you to avoid a blow-up with someone than it is to avoid keeping someone waiting.

If you were having a discussion with someone close to you when you started to get angry go back and continue the conversation. Hopefully you will be able to stay calm this time. If not, table the conversation until you can remain calm. The goal is to be able to discuss things more calmly, even issues that are controversial or hot-buttons for one or both of you.

The following guidelines will help you to take time-outs when you need them:

- Explain to those close to you that you are going to take time-outs when you start to get angry. Do this in advance because you don't want people to come after you when you leave suddenly (a natural thing to do) or to think you're just running away from an argument or trying to punish them by not talking. Most people will want to support you with this endeavor since your anger has likely been a problem for them as well as for you.

- Don't just leave. Say something like, "Excuse me, I need time to cool off." Assure the person that you will be back and then keep your word. Time-outs are not an excuse to avoid dealing with conflicts.

Strategies for Those with a Passive Anger Style

Those of you who have submerged your anger out of fear or denial and are unable to defend yourself against the anger of others need to assert your anger in safe ways and to stand up for yourself and your children. Many of my clients have natural rage that they have suppressed for decades. As Marnie shared with me, "As a child I learned to not make any noise in order to avoid upsetting my father. I believed if I just remained quiet and stayed out of his way I could avoid being abused. Even when my father physically abused me I didn't make a sound. I thought that doing so would make him even more angry. When I grew up and got married I carried those same beliefs into my marriage. I believed that if I didn't make waves with my husband he wouldn't get angry with me and become abusive. Unfortunately, the reverse happened. Because I didn't speak up for myself it gave him permission to be controlling. The first time he hit me I just took it. I didn't fight back; in fact, I didn't even make a sound. That just gave him permission to hit me again." It wasn't until Marnie was given permission to express all the anger that she had kept in check for so long that she was finally able to let out the screams that she had suppressed for so long.

Work Past Your Fear of Anger

Many who have a passive anger style or a victim pattern are afraid to feel and express their anger. Some of the most common fears are: the fear of retaliation, the fear of becoming like those who abused you, the fear of losing control, the fear of hurting someone, the fear of rejection, and the fear of becoming irrational, or looking like a fool. If you have any of these fears, it often helps to visualize your anger being released in a safe way. The following exercise will help you to do this.

EXERCISE: *Gradual Release*

1. Get into a relaxed, comfortable position, either lying down or sitting up. Close your eyes and begin to breathe deeply and evenly. Allow yourself to relax with each breath you take.

2. Visualize your anger as steam that has built up in some pipes. Imagine that the steam (anger) has filled the pipes almost to the bursting point (losing control).

3. Slowly let some of the steam out of the pipes by carefully and gradually opening a valve. Allow only a small amount of steam out at a time. Eventually all the steam will be released and no pipes will burst. Your anger is the steam building up inside you. If you release your anger a little at a time, you will not lose control.

EXERCISE: *Getting Past Your Resistance*

If you are reluctant to express your anger openly, the following exercise may help uncover still more reasons why you are afraid of your anger.

1. On a piece of paper, write and complete this sentence: "I don't want to express my anger because . . ." Don't think about your answers beforehand, just write.

2. Continue completing this sentence for as long as you have responses.

Practice Becoming More Assertive

If you have a passive anger style, you probably don't stand up for yourself. The following suggestions will help you become more assertive:

- Resist the temptation to take the easy way out by responding passively and avoiding conflicts at all costs.

- Practice saying the word no. Say it out loud when you are by yourself. Say it silently to yourself whenever you would like to say it to someone out loud but are afraid to do so. If you continue practicing and telling yourself you have the right to say no, eventually you'll gain the confidence to speak your mind out loud.

- Remind yourself that being assertive is different from being aggressive. You are not being mean, demanding, or abusive when you say no to unreasonable demands or when you express your own ideas, feelings, and opinions.

- Practice being assertive in low risk situations in order to build up your courage. For example, would you be more comfortable being assertive toward someone you know or toward a stranger?

Would it be easier to be assertive over the telephone or in writing instead of in a face-to-face encounter?

- Understand that by being the silent partner, that is, allowing your mate to be emotionally, physically, or sexually abusive to your children you have a part in the damage caused to your children.

For more help on the issue of the fear of anger refer to chapter 14.

Strategies for Those with an Eruptive Anger Style

Although your current anger may feel new, it is often old anger that has come back to haunt you. Past pain from traumatic events often lingers to resurface again and again together with renewed anger. Instead of reacting to a present day situation we are really reacting to another incident. Someone may remind you of a parent or other caretaker or a particular situation may bring back unpleasant memories. In order to prevent this from happening on an ongoing basis, disrupting your life and causing problems in your relationships, you need to identify your anger triggers and work on your unfinished business from the past. The best way to do this is to examine why you got angry in any particular situation and then try to make connections with your past. Refer back to chapter 5 for information on how to discover your triggers.

For All Anger Styles—Find Constructive Ways of Releasing Your Anger toward Your Abusers

It is normal and healthy for you to feel and express your anger toward your parents or other abusers. One aspect of completing your unfinished business will be for you to name, own, and release this anger.

Exercise: *Express Your Angry Feelings*

1. Make a list of all the people who hurt, betrayed, or abandoned you as a child.

2. Find a creative outlet for the unexpressed feelings you have toward each of these people. For example, write about the pain you experienced, paint the rage you feel when you think of the treatment you received, use clay to express how the abuse made you feel about yourself. These forms of creative expression are wonderful cathartic outlets, especially if you

give yourself permission to express yourself freely without censor.

3. If you need something more physical, express your anger through dance or physical exercise, scream into a pillow or scream in the shower (if you can do so without anyone hearing you).

4. Write an anger letter in which you confront your parent or caretaker with your anger. Don't censor yourself; say everything you need to say. You can choose to keep the letter, tear it up, or burn it.

5. Role play your anger. Have an imaginary conversation with the person you are angry with. Tell that person exactly what you feel: don't hold anything back. It may help to look at a picture of the person or to imagine that the person is sitting in a chair across from you. If you are still afraid of this person, imagine he or she is tied up and gagged and cannot get to you or say anything to you.

How to Cope with Anger on a Daily Basis

You can learn to cope with your anger by following the same process we have been following throughout this book: identifying the emotion; discovering its message; feeling the emotion without becoming overwhelmed by it; determining whether it is appropriate to be feeling it at this time and taking action to remedy the situation. But underneath your anger, or your refusal to get angry, are other core feelings that you will also need to unearth if you are going to find healthy ways of managing your anger. And in addition to learning how to handle your anger in a healthier, more balanced way, you also need to learn to communicate your angry feelings in ways that will be heard and to resolve conflicts in ways that take into account the other person's needs.

Identify Your Anger

For many of you, identifying when you are angry will not be difficult. Some people experience anger as an overwhelming feeling of tightness and heat. They feel that they will literally burst with emotion. Others don't feel much of anything. They are what is commonly referred to as blinded by rage—they don't seem to feel their anger building up. Instead they immediately go into action by screaming, yelling, pushing, or hitting the person who angered them. Still others experience anger as an imaginary wall that comes up to protect them from someone who has hurt them.

But for some of you, identifying your anger will be extremely difficult. There are people who just don't know when they are angry. They have not yet been able to identify the body signals that alert them to their anger. If you don't know you are getting angry you don't have the opportunity to short-circuit your anger before it builds up to the point where you are out of control. If you don't know your body's anger signals you may deny you are angry even when others are keenly aware of it. What about you, do you know your body's anger signals? When we become angry we all experience an increase in our heart rate, our blood pressure, and our skin temperature, although the intensity and volatility differs from one person to the next.

The following exercise will help you begin to get in touch with the anger signals your body sends out.

EXERCISE: *How Your Body Experiences Anger*

- How do you know you are angry? Think about what happens in your body when you become angry. Does your jaw become tight? Do you tend to make a fist with your hands or to tighten up your shoulders? Do you get a splitting headache or does your stomach feel queasy?

- Make a list of all the signals your body gives you alerting you to your anger.

Determine the Message

We tend to become angry when we feel threatened, hurt, frustrated, or betrayed—as when we feel victimized by an injustice or disloyalty. We especially become angry when our freedom, autonomy, boundary, and personal space are violated or when our body and/or psychological integrity are being threatened or attacked. We also become angry when we feel disrespected, discarded, or ignored; in which case there is a sense of insult and humiliation along with injury.

Although it may not actually be a life or death struggle, we often feel threatened by the behavior or remarks of others, in other words, we experience a threat to our emotional well-being. When someone hurts or insults us by saying something inappropriate, disrespectful, or vicious we become righteously angry.

Our angermay also signal to us that we are not addressing an important emotional issue in our lives or in a relationship. It may be a message that our wants or needs are not being met or it may warn us that we are giving too much or compromising too much of our values or beliefs in a relationship.

Oftentimes we become angry because there is a conflict of some kind (internal or external). For example, perhaps you want something from someone but your needs are not being met. This impasse causes frustration, which in turn causes anger.

The next time you become angry at your spouse or your child, ask yourself: What is the message this anger is sending me?

Feel Your Anger without Becoming Overwhelmed by It

Since anger is a natural defense mechanism designed to protect us from pain and abuse, it is not a good idea to deny feeling angry. In fact it is extremely beneficial to feel and acknowledge angry feelings when they occur. Otherwise we lose out on the benefits of anger— empowerment, protection, energy, and motivation. Anger energizes us and can serve as a catalyst for resolving interpersonal conflict. It can promote self-esteem and can foster a sense of personal control during times of peak stress. This is especially important for those with a passive anger style to understand.

Don't fool yourself into thinking that just because you don't express your anger it will miraculously go away. Each emotion has a purpose and that emotion will remain with you, buried inside your body, locked up in your psyche, until that purpose is recognized and understood. Anger arises within us to tell us that what is occurring is undesirable or unhealthy. Suppressing your emotions—that is, consciously trying to bury them—does not eliminate them. In addition to causing you to become numb to your feelings, including your positive feelings, your suppressed emotions will often cause physical symptoms such as muscle tension, back problems, stomach distress, constipation, diarrhea, headaches, obesity, or maybe even hypertension.

Your suppressed anger may also cause you to overreact to people and situations or to act inappropriately. Unexpressed anger can cause you to become irritable, irrational, and prone to emotional outbursts and episodes of depression. If you carry around a lot of suppressed or repressed anger (anger you have unconsciously buried), you may lash out at people, blaming them or punishing them for something someone else did long ago. Because you were unwilling or unable to express how you felt at the time, you may overreact in the present, damaging your present relationships.

IF YOU TEND TO BE ABUSIVE WITH YOUR ANGER

Although it is generally important to feel and express our anger, this is not necessarily the case if you have explosive episodes with your anger or have a history of being abusive with your anger (e.g., erupting in a rage and yelling at people, losing your temper and starting physical fights or pushing, slapping, or beating your partner or kids). Instead of trying to rid yourself of your anxiety or discomfort by making someone else bad, work on *containing* your anger. When you stay with your discomfort you create a rich environment from which to better learn about yourself, the feelings underneath your anger and your true self.

Those who become abusive with their anger are not just dealing with anger, but with aggression. Aggression has been defined as any behavior directed toward another person (or a person's property) with the intent to do harm, even if the aggressor was unsuccessful. Everyone has aggressive impulses when they feel threatened but you must learn to either find appropriate ways to release them or to *contain* them. For example, when your child says something insulting you may become enraged. Your first instinct is to slap him in the face. He has shamed you and after all children are supposed to respect their elders. *Your* father certainly would not have allowed you to talk to him like that. But wait a minute. Slapping your child in the face will only shame, humiliate, and enrage him, just like it did when your father slapped you. Research tells us that slapping, spanking, or beating children does not teach them lessons as much as it teaches them to be afraid of their parents and teaches them defiance, shame, and violence.

In this case and in most others, it is best to control your impulse to become aggressive. Unfortunately, you may be one of those who are unable to do so. As soon as you feel threatened and your adrenaline starts to pump you put all reason aside. All you can focus on at the moment is getting back at the person who threatened you, no matter who it is and what the personal cost is to your loved ones. So how can you stop yourself? Take a time-out or find alternative ways to release your anger energy.

Ask Yourself if It Is Appropriate to Be Feeling Anger at This Time

A person with a healthy relationship with anger is able to make a distinction between which situations warrant an angry response and which do not. We are all bombarded daily with situations that could cause us to become angry. If we became angry at all these situations we would end up being angry all the time. It is the healthy person who recognizes that in the interest of their mental and physical well-being they have to ignore some of the less important infractions. They must make a distinction between what is merely annoying and what is important to address—in other words, they must choose their battles. Getting angry every time you get a slow cashier at the grocery store is a waste of time and energy so you need to take a deep breath and let it go. The same holds true of every time someone cuts you off on the freeway or takes the parking space you were waiting for. On the other hand, telling a friend who keeps you waiting for forty-five minutes that you are angry may be a necessary move in order to maintain the relationship or to avoid having to wait for her in the future.

It is also important to ask yourself if you are using anger to cover up another emotion. It is especially important for those of you with an aggressive anger style to pay attention to what lies underneath your anger. This is because for you, anger is more than likely an all-consuming feeling that prevents you from experiencing other feelings. Anger has probably become a way of life and a way you are used to feeling, rather than a message that something is wrong. But without the message there is no chance for positive change.

There is almost always another emotion under your anger, another emotion that will lead you to the real cause of your feelings of being upset. Some people even believe that anger is not a primary emotion at all, but a reaction to other emotions. Anger wells up when we feel any of the following feelings: fear, sadness, shame, or guilt.

Fear. Some believe that fear and anger are, in many ways, variations of the same emotion. This is based on the fight or flight response we discussed earlier. Other people believe that there is always fear underneath anger. Some people are so used to responding with anger to threatening situations that they become oblivious to any feelings of fear.

Often the angriest person is actually the most frightened person. This person is often covering up deep fears of inadequacy and fear of failure. We often intuitively sense this whenever we experience bullies. We sense that those who have to prove to us that they are tough are actually compensating for deep feelings of inadequacy.

Hurt, sadness, loss. It is often hurt and pain that causes us to become angry in the first place. Unless someone has hurt us we usually do not become angry with him or her, especially in an intimate relationship. And all too often we hang on to our anger in order to avoid facing the underlying pain. Those who become abusive often have a great deal of pain underneath their need to control, criticize, or blame.

Like so many boys, my client Brad was not allowed to cry or to talk about his hurt feelings when he was a child. Instead of receiving any sympathy from his parents when he was bullied by some boys at school, his father insisted that he toughen up and become a man. And that's exactly what Brad did. He not only doesn't cry but he doesn't allow himself to feel sadness or pain. Instead he covers it up with anger. If someone hurts his feelings he puts them down.

Shame. For many people, shame is the emotion that often motivates their anger. Shame can create a need to hide or disappear to such an extent that we distance ourselves from others because of it. We usually do this by blaming or attacking others or by projecting on to others.

As discussed earlier, shame can be one of the most devastating of emotions, causing a shrinking sense of worthlessness, of feeling small and powerless. In reaction to this debilitating feeling, and in an attempt to provide temporary relief from it, many people experience what is referred to as a humiliated fury.

Guilt. We often defend against feelings of guilt with anger. For example, parents can't help feeling guilty when harm comes to their child in some way. It's a natural reaction even when a parent is not responsible for the incident. But instead of facing their guilt over not being able to protect their child better, many parents cover it up with anger. Some take their anger out on their child, blaming her for causing her own accident, for not minding them, and so on. While anger is sometimes warranted, in many cases it is just a way to defend against guilt feelings, especially when there actually was something one could have done to prevent harm to someone.

Why should we allow ourselves to feel the guilt under our anger? Feeling our guilt over an act or a failure on our part helps us to feel empathy for others. It motivates us to take responsibility for our actions by confessing, apologizing, making amends, or repairing the harm we caused. By defending against our guilt with anger we enable ourselves to continue harming others (and ourselves) by repeating unacceptable behavior. We don't learn from our mistakes but instead blame others for them.

By discovering the emotions underneath your anger you will be better able to define the problem clearly and this affords you a better chance of solving the real problem. The following assignment will help you in this endeavor.

ASSIGNMENT: *Identifying Your Underlying Emotions*

For one week make a note in your journal of each and every time you become even slightly angry. For each incident, describe what happened and try to identify your underlying emotions (i.e., fear, shame, guilt, frustration, disappointment). Then write about this underlying emotion. For example: "I'm afraid Mark's going to leave me now that he knows who I really am. I guess that's why I started the argument. I wanted to push him away before he could reject me."

Take Action to Remedy the Situation

When you have a healthy relationship with anger you view your anger as the warning sign that it is and you take the time to look for the reason for your anger. Sometimes the reason may be obvious and other times it may take a little more investigating before you discover the cause. When you do discover what is wrong either in your environment, a relationship with someone else or with your relationship with yourself, you take action. This change may involve modifying something in your environment, communicating your feelings or difficulties with the other person, or addressing the feelings that triggered your anger in the first place.

Reclaiming our power is the key to taming anger. If you are to gain real control of your anger you must also discover the root of your powerlessness. Each time you become angry you need to ask yourself, Am I feeling hurt or threatened? If so, why? Am I feeling helpless? If so, why?

The purpose of anger is to solve problems, not just to ventilate your feelings and certainly not to hurt other people. You need to take responsibility for what you say and do, even in the heat of anger and not use your anger as an excuse to become inappropriate or abusive. Instead of losing control and yelling, screaming, or belittling the other person, you need to express your anger appropriately and in moderation. The person with a healthy relationship with anger has learned how to transform anger from a weapon that wounds others and oneself to a tool that promotes understanding and healthy change in relationships. Communicating your angry feelings in a direct and constructive way is one of the most important steps to transforming your anger into a positive force. Research shows that the direct expression of anger at the time that it occurs and toward the immediate cause is the healthiest and most satisfying way of releasing tension.

How do you know whether it will be constructive to express your angry feelings directly to the person that you are upset with? There are at least four constructive expressions of anger. Before you choose to confront someone with your anger, ask yourself if you are motivated by a desire for at least one of the following:

- To communicate feelings of hurt.
- To change the hurtful situation.
- To prevent a recurrence of the same hurt.
- To improve the relationship and increase communication.

If you are motivated by one of the above, the appropriate action is for you to communicate with the other person in a very direct way what it is that you feel, as well as what you want or need. The most effective way of communicating your anger is to translate your anger into clear, nonblaming statements that establish boundaries. This is commonly referred to as being assertive. Many people associate being angry with yelling and being out of control but expressing anger can become a positive thing when done with a firm, controlled tone of voice, good eye contact, and a confident posture that's neither aggressive nor robotic. With assertive confrontation, you need to take responsibility for your emotions and clarify your expectations and limits. Unlike aggression, assertive behavior does not push others around, deny their rights, or run over people. Instead, assertiveness reflects genuine concern for everyone's rights since it is grounded in the belief that every human being is of equal value.

Assertive Statements

What you say and the way you say it makes all the difference between being heard and being ignored or dismissed. No matter what your anger style, learning assertiveness will help you to communicate your feelings and needs more effectively. Those with an aggressive anger style often become frustrated because they lack good communication skills and feel like others can talk circles around them. Those with a passive anger style are usually afraid to communicate their feelings directly and firmly and so others tend to speak over them or outshout them.

For those with an aggressive anger style, becoming more assertive means learning how to get your needs met more satisfactorily, without aggression. It means being able to say what you want (or don't want) without having to get angry first. And it means taking care of yourself without abusing other people. It is not necessary to put the other person down (aggressive) to express your feelings (assertive). It is important to express yourself and take responsibility for your feelings, not to blame the other person for how you feel. Many with an aggressive anger style believe that anger has to be forceful, emotional, loud, or explosive to be effective. But the truth is that when you learn how to be effectively assertive you will find that you are far better able to express the intensity of your true emotions to others and that others will be better able to listen to you and take in what you are saying.

For those who have a passive anger style, assertiveness is especially important. Assertiveness is an alternative to personal powerlessness and manipulation and a tool for making your relationships equal, for avoiding the one-down feeling that often comes when you fail to express what you really want. Being assertive also may increase your self-esteem, reduce anxiety, gain a greater respect for yourself and others, and improve your ability to communicate more effectively with others.

An assertive statement to communicate anger needs to contain two thoughts:

1. The fact that you are angry and the reason why you are angry.

2. What you want the other person to do about it.

A simple form for such a statement is: "I feel angry because _____. I want you to _____." Every situation is different of course and so the words may differ. Be sure to follow these simple rules:

- Avoid using "you" messages which not only put the person receiving the message on the defensive but can reinforce feelings of helplessness in the person sending the message.

- Always use "I" statements in order to take responsibility for your reactions. I statements give information about you as opposed to making judgments of others.

- Avoid name calling, insults, or sarcasm.

- Avoid using the words *never* and *always,* which tend to shame the other person and make them feel hopeless and misunderstood.

- Always express why you are angry and what you want done about it.

Reduce Your Anger through Stress Reduction

Sometimes taking action means finding a way to reduce the stress that created your anger. This is especially true for those with an aggressive anger style. For you, much of your battle against uncontrollable anger can be won if you learn how to relax the physical tension in your body that accompanies anger. If you can relax your body and keep it relaxed it is almost impossible to become angry. Learning stress reduction techniques can help you calm down, think more clearly and handle almost any provocative situation in a more effective manner.

Researchers have discovered that higher stress is associated with higher anger levels. It has also been found that stress-related anger is more likely to find expression in venting or abusive behavior such as blaming statements or put-downs rather than being suppressed or discussed in constructive ways. Many people end up turning this stress into anger and taking their anger out on those around them—most especially their loved ones. They blow up at their partner or their kids after an especially stressful day. They overreact when someone says something that hurts their feelings. Over time stress can create depression, anxiety, pessimism, and dissatisfaction. It can make you difficult to live with because people under stress are often irritable, irrational, and hostile.

Here are some stress reduction strategies to get you started. I've also included more information on stress reduction and stress reduction exercises in chapter 8 and recommended some books on stress reduction at the end of the book.

1. *Keep a stress diary.* Begin to keep track of situations that cause you stress. Describe situations and people that you have conflicts with, or those that make you anxious. Ask yourself why a particular situation or person caused you to feel upset. How might you think or act differently in the future to help you cope more effectively?

2. *Be active.* Exercise helps eliminate stress hormones from the bloodstream and stimulates the release of endorphins that provide a feeling of well-being. Aim for at least thirty minutes of moderate activity a day.

3. *Avoid stimulants.* Stimulants such as caffeine, nicotine, and alcohol stress out the body and can make you more irritable and impatient. Try herbal teas and drink lots of water.

4. *Breathe.* Once every hour stop and take ten to twenty slow deep breaths. Breathe in through your nose, hold it a second, and then breathe out through your mouth.

5. *Get a pet.* If you have a pet spend quality time with it, stroking it, brushing it, taking it for a walk. Research shows that people who have pets generally have less stress.

6. *Laugh more.* Use humor to get yourself out of a bad mood. Numerous laboratory experiments lead to the conclusion that amusing a subject sharply reduces the likelihood that he or she will subsequently engage in overt acts of aggression. When you begin to get annoyed at someone, try seeing the humor in

the situation. It is especially important that those with an aggressive anger style learn how to laugh at themselves. If you find yourself in a compromising situation, instead of becoming defensive and blaming or attacking someone else, try making fun of your own self-importance, impatience, need to be right, or tendency to control.

7. *Have a good cry.* Stress chemicals are released through emotional tears.

8. *Find a spiritual outlet.* Medical research has repeatedly shown that individuals who regularly attend a religious service have less stress-related illness, such as heart attacks and high blood pressure.

Let It Go

Another measure of having a healthy relationship with anger is the ability to let go of anger once it has served its purpose. Once you've recognized the problem and communicated your feelings and needs, it is time to let it go. Unfortunately, many of us have a difficult time letting go of our anger once it is activated. It's almost as if we want to punish the other person for causing us to become angry in the first place instead of recognizing our choice in becoming angry. This is especially true of those who view anger as a negative emotion and those who don't like losing control. But once the problem has been addressed and solved it is time to move on, not to continue to wallow in your anger.

Whether your anger style is aggressive, passive, or eruptive, by following the steps listed previously you can develop a healthy way of coping and expressing your anger that will help prevent you from either becoming abusive or allowing others to abuse you.

CHAPTER 8

Coping with Fear

Be not afraid of growing slowly; be afraid only of standing still.

CHINESE PROVERB

Fear plays a significant role in both creating the cycle of abuse and in perpetuating it. The emotion of fear is a pivotal motivator for both abusers and victims. Those who need to control others do so because they feel so out of control. They do it because they are afraid. Those who need to have power over others do so out of fear of someone having power over them. And those who put up with abusive behavior do so out of fear of more extreme violence, the fear of abandonment, the fear of being alone, or sometimes, the fear of their own anger.

How Trauma Creates Fear

According to the *Comprehensive Textbook of Psychiatry*, the common denominator of psychological trauma is a feeling of "intense fear, helplessness, loss of control, and threat of annihilation." Survivors of childhood abuse consistently report an overwhelming sense of helplessness. In an abusive family environment, children are rendered helpless by tyrannical parental power and rules that are erratic, inconsistent, or patently unfair. Survivors frequently report that what frightened them the most was the unpredictable nature of the violence. Unable to find any way to avert the abuse, they learn to adopt a position of complete surrender.

Chronic childhood abuse creates a climate of pervasive terror for the child. Many survivors describe a characteristic pattern of totalitarian control, enforced by means of violence or even death threats, inconsistent enforcement of petty rules, intermittent rewards, and

138

elimination of all outside or competing relationships through isolation, secrecy, and betrayal.

The constant fear of death is reported by many survivors. Sometimes the child is silenced by violence or by a direct threat of murder. The man who molested me at nine threatened to kill me if I told anyone and I believed him since I knew he had already been in a mental hospital. More often survivors report threats that resistance or disclosure will result in the death of someone else in the family. Violence or murder threats may also be directed against pets; many survivors report being forced to witness the sadistic abuse of animals.

How We React to Being Terrorized

Children in an abusive environment become what is commonly referred to by professionals in the field as hypervigilant, meaning that they develop extraordinary abilities to notice any warning signs of an impending attack. They learn to recognize subtle changes in the facial expression, voice and body language as signals of anger, sexual arousal, intoxication, or dissociation.

When abused children note signs of danger, they attempt to protect themselves either by avoiding or by placating the abuser. Even though they are in a constant state of hyperarousal, they must also be quiet and immobile. The result is the peculiar, seething state of frozen watchfulness noted in abused children.

When avoidance fails, children attempt to appease their abusers through obedience. The arbitrary enforcement of rules, combined with the constant fear of serious harm or death, produces a paradoxical result. On the one hand, it convinces children of their utter helplessness and the futility of resistance. Many develop the belief that their abusers have absolute or even supernatural powers, can read their thoughts, can control their lives entirely. On the other hand, it motivates children to prove their loyalty and compliance. They double and redouble their efforts to gain control of the situation in the only way that seems possible—by trying to be good. It is easy to see how this learned helplessness and need to please can translate into a victim pattern in adulthood. We see the very same behaviors in battered women.

Another commonality between child abuse and domestic violence is the issue of isolation. Isolation is often enforced by abusive parents in order to preserve secrecy and control over other family members.

Children are often forbidden to participate in ordinary peer activities, and abusive parents often intrude into the child's activities at will. Survivors often describe a pattern of jealous surveillance of all social contacts. Once again, we see this exact pattern with an emotionally and physically abusive man who insists on knowing his partner's every move and who refuses to allow his partner to continue to see her friends and family.

Like a Deer Caught in the Headlights

When I first met Jenny I knew she had been terrorized in some way. She had the look of a deer who had been caught in the headlights. She stared straight ahead and didn't blink her eyes and her eyes also had the familiar glazed-over look that I have seen so often in abuse victims.

But Jenny did not come to see me because of an abusive child-hood. She came because she was having trouble getting along with people. Her friends, and especially her husband, frequently complained that she snapped at them, was sometimes explosive for no apparent reason, and was too intense. She also complained about a lack of energy, losing track of time, and of frequently being late for important appointments.

While taking her history it came out that Jenny's mother had been an extremely abusive woman who would fly off the handle at little or no provocation. "You never knew when she was going to go off," Jenny explained. When Jenny's mother went off she tore into Jenny with horrendous accusations and insults. She'd scream and yell obscenities and attack Jenny where she was most vulnerable. After such an attack, Jenny said she felt like "a Mack truck had run over me—I just felt like crawling off somewhere to die."

As a result of these surprise attacks, Jenny was always on the alert for any sign that her mother was getting ready to blow up. This caused her body to be in a constant state of tension and stress. As a result, even when Jenny grew up and moved away from her mother, she maintained her hypervigilant frame of mind. She was always leery of other people, even her husband, constantly expecting them to attack her as her mother had. She was unable to relax her body and suffered from severe neck, shoulder, and back pain most of her life.

Jenny also walked around in a constant state of dissociation. She was seldom, if ever, really present. As a child she protected herself from her mother's attacks by going away in her mind (dissociation).

She got into such a habit of doing this that she did it habitually, even when there was no real threat.

Jenny's intensity and her attacks on others were a direct result of the trauma she experienced as a child. She was not only repeating her mother's behavior (she suspected that her mother had been traumatized in a similar way by her abusive grandfather) but was doing so because she was frequently being triggered by other people's behavior. Constantly on the lookout for abuse, when someone disagreed with her, it triggered the memory of her mother's outbursts and she attacked the other person before they had a chance to attack her.

Posttraumatic Stress Disorder

Threat initially arouses the sympathetic nervous system, causing the person in danger to feel an adrenaline rush and go into a state of alert. It also concentrates a person's attention on the immediate situation and alters ordinary perceptions—for example, people in danger are often able to disregard pain. These changes in arousal, attention, perception, and emotion are normal adaptive reactions. They mobilize the threatened person for strenuous action, either in battle or in flight.

Dr. Judith Herman, an associate clinical professor of psychiatry at the Harvard Medical School, is an expert on trauma. In her classic book *Trauma and Recovery* she explains that when neither resistance nor escape are possible, the human system of self-defense becomes overwhelmed and disorganized. Each aspect of the ordinary response to danger, having lost its function, tends to persist in an altered and exaggerated state long after the actual danger is over. Traumatic events produce profound and lasting changes in physiological arousal, emotion, cognition, and memory. For example, the traumatized person may experience intense emotion but without clear memory of the event, or may remember everything in detail without any emotion. Like Jenny, she may find herself in a constant state of vigilance and irritability without knowing why. Traumatic symptoms tend to become disconnected from their source and to take on a life of their own. The perceptions become inaccurate and pervaded with terror, the aggressive impulse becomes disorganized and unrelated to the situation at hand. These reactions characterize what is commonly referred to as PTSD.

We discussed the many symptoms of PTSD in chapter 3. These symptoms fall into three main categories: hyperarousal, intrusion, and constriction. Hyperarousal reflects the persistant expectation of danger; intrusion reflects the indelible imprint of the traumatic moment; constriction reflects the numbing response of surrender.

Fight, Flight, or Freeze

Many children who grow up with abuse make fight-or-flight their standard response to fear. Earlier I explained that children actually learn that there are other options when faced with danger, but children who are abused lose the ability to call upon these options. They become stuck. Violence toward others and self often becomes a distorted fear response.

Actually, the response many survivors stay stuck in could more accurately be called "fight, flight, or freeze." They learn to fight off their enemy, run away, or play dead. While some survivors vacillate between these three defense strategies depending on the circumstances, many get stuck using only the strategy that seems to work best for them based on past experiences. Unfortunately, this severely limits their ability to deal with physical and emotional threats and often keeps them from developing other important aspects of their personalities.

For example, those who tend to *fight* when confronted with danger are often highly defended individuals who are as successful at hiding their vulnerability from themselves as they are from others. When they feel threatened they immediately puff themselves up and take on a defensive stance (we talked about these types of people in chapter 7 on anger). This often convinces the other person to back off, certain they would lose any battle they might start. But fighters tend to be almost paranoid when it comes to being attacked. They are always on the lookout for anyone who dares to attack them, insult them, criticize them, or question them in any way. They are so hypervigilant that they often imagine someone has attacked them when they really haven't.

They also tend to build up a wall of nonchalance and bravado in order to avoid the pain they feel inside and to prevent themselves from being further abused by those outside the home. These are often the people who become schoolyard bullies and juvenile delinquents as children, and partner and child abusers as adults.

Fighters often imagine others are criticizing them and are against them. Any comment that comes even close to sounding like criticism is pounced on immediately and used to prove that the other is the enemy. This is even the case in love relationships where a partner is seen more as an enemy than an ally.

Those who choose the option of *fleeing* when faced with possible danger are convinced that they could never win at any confrontation. Therefore they must get away as soon as possible in order to save themselves. Or they may have simply decided that it is best to avoid conflict at all costs. This person has lost touch with the fighter inside—that part of ourselves who feels compelled to stand up for ourselves, who refuses to allow another human being to subjugate, abuse, or bully us into submission. Their only hope for survival seems to be to flee the situation—either literally or figuratively. If at all possible they will physically escape but they are also experts at disappearing even when they have to stay physically present. They may do this by ignoring their attacker—acting as if the other person is not even present and that his or her words are not getting to them at all. Or they may smile sweetly and agree with their attacker or try to distract him or her by changing the subject. Whatever tactic they use the point is to avoid confrontation at all costs and try to get back to the status quo as soon as possible.

Much like the person who flees, the one who *freezes* is probably convinced that she would be annihilated if she chose to fight. Like the possum who plays dead or the dog who turns over on his back to expose his vulnerable underbelly to his attacker, the freezer believes that by waving a white flag she will save herself from harm. And just as it often happens in the animal world, this tactic often succeeds at disarming an attacker by taking the fun out of the kill. The problem is that the freezer, like the weaker dog, has lost all sense of pride. Constantly humiliated by her show of weakness, she comes to despise herself.

How Fear Contributes to the Cycle of Abuse

And so you can see, fear can motivate people to become abusive or to remain helpless victims in abusive situations. Here are some specific ways that fear contributes to the cycle of abuse:

1. Those who were abused in childhood often grow up to be hypervigilant adults who are constantly on the lookout for further abuse. This can cause them to misunderstand the actions

or motivations of others, to be hypersensitive to criticism or feedback and to behave as if they have a chip on their shoulder.

2. Living in a constant state of terror can also contribute to learned helplessness. The child grows up believing that there is no action they can take that will be effective in stopping the abuse. This transfers into their adult relationships. A woman who was trained to believe she does not have any choices is more likely to put up with abuse.

3. Children who grow up constantly afraid become immobilized by their fear. Their fear becomes so all-encompassing that it often crowds out other reactions, such as anger, that would be natural under the circumstances.

4. Children who grow up in a climate of domination and abuse often develop pathological attachments to those who abuse and neglect them, attachments they will strive to maintain even at the sacrifice of their own welfare, their own reality, or their very lives. A childhood history of placating an abusive parent or other caretaker naturally leads to placating a partner, especially an abusive one. The idea of being able to say no to the emotional demands of a partner, parent, or authority figure may be inconceivable to them.

5. Although an adult woman or man does not actively seek an abusive relationship, when abuse does occur it is often experienced as the inevitable price of having a relationship.

6. Those who are afraid of being reabused often take on a defended, hardened stance that prevents others from getting close. This kind of person often keeps others away by being overly critical or overly demanding.

7. Those who are afraid they will become like an abusive parent often submerge their anger and take on a passive stance allowing others to treat them unfairly or even to abuse them.

8. Those who were neglected or abandoned as a child are often consumed with a fear of being alone. This can cause them to be overly possessive or to put up with unacceptable or abusive behavior from others.

9. Many neglected and abused children grow up to be adults who are afraid to take risks, including the risk of striking out on their own. Many people who were terrorized as children will remain dependent on their abusive parents and be unable to separate from them. Others leave their abusive parents only to attach themselves to a partner who is controlling.

10. Those raised by domineering and authoritarian parents grow up fearing their parents and were taught to equate respect with fear. Many abusive adults, especially men who batter women, believe the only way they can gain the respect of others, particularly their spouse, is to make them afraid of them.

11. Children who were raised in an environment of unpredictability, emotional chaos, and terror tend to grow up with the inability to trust. This may be because they did not have a secure attachment to a parent, because their parent betrayed them by crossing important personal boundaries (as in sexual abuse), or because their parents could not be relied on because of their inconsistency or neglect. In adult relationships this lack of trust is expressed by extreme insecurity, possessiveness, and jealousy, which can translate into emotional and even physical abusiveness.

12. Closely related to the lack of trust is the fear of abandonment. For example, abusive men have a terrible fear of abandonment and become desperate when they feel they could lose their partner. They tend to believe that the only way they can gain security against abandonment is through control.

13. Those who were abused (and therefore terrorized) or neglected (and therefore abandoned) will either become overly fearful parents or overly angry parents. Either scenario can set someone up to become an abusive parent (for further elaboration, refer to the control issues section in this chapter).

EXERCISE: *How Fear Turns to Abuse*

This writing exercise will help you become more clear about how fear has contributed to your tendency to be abusive or victimlike.

- What fears do you think may have motivated the aggressive or violent actions of those who were abusive to you?

• How has the fear you felt as a child affected you as an adult, especially in your relationships with your partner and your children? For example, do you use aggression when you are afraid? Do you attack others before they have a chance to attack you? Or do you tend to placate those you are afraid of?

The Connection between Anxiety and Fear

Anxiety and fear are related emotions, even though they are often experienced differently by the body and mind. Anxiety is frequently a response to fear. Children who have been abused or neglected often develop anxiety to such a degree that it becomes a part of their body's physiological pattern, as it did with Jenny. If as a child you lived in fear, never knowing what was going to happen next, and if you were not helped to feel safe and secure, your response to the sudden, surprising or unexpected could well be anxiety or panic. You may be unable to enjoy life because you are always waiting for the other shoe to drop and may suffer from constant worry and anxiety which causes insomnia, anxiety disorders, and obsessive thinking.

This in turn can cause you to behave in victimlike or abusive ways. It causes victimlike behavior by causing you to be overly dependent on others, afraid of being alone, and afraid of asserting yourself in your relationships. It can cause abusive behavior because constant anxiety and stress reduces a person's ability to cope with day-to-day or life challenges, makes you irritable and short-tempered, and affords you little ability for tolerance.

Symptoms of anxiety include muscle tension, aches or soreness, restlessness and fatigue, trembling, twitching, or feeling shaky, shortness of breath or sensations of smothering, palpitations or accelerated heart rate, sweating or cold, clammy hands, exaggerated startle reaction, irritability, dizziness or light-headedness, need to urinate frequently, trouble swallowing or feeling a lump in throat, feeling keyed up or on edge, nausea, diarrhea, or other abdominal distress, hot flashes or chills, difficulty concentrating or mind going blank, trouble falling asleep or staying asleep.

Panic and panic reactions are the most extreme form of anxiety. Panic is an overwhelming terror and feeling of fright. Phobias are a form of anxiety—they are fears specific to a thing or a group of things (such as fear of heights, crowds, snakes).

Fear and Stress Reduction

Some people think that stress is just another word for fear. Others believe that stress feels so much like fear in our bodies that we react to the two states in the same way. In either case, relaxation is the primary antidote. According to Herbert Benson, a Harvard physician and noted stress researcher, each of us possesses an innate protective-mechanism against overstress—the relaxation response. By developing this relaxation response we can counteract the increased sympathetic-nervous-system activity that accompanies the arousal of the fight-or-flight response and restore our body to its normal balance. Relaxation can be intentionally induced by activities that decrease sympathetic-nervous-system activity by programming the hypothalamus to trigger lower blood pressure and a reduced heart rate. A relaxation response decreases oxygen consumption and carbon-dioxide elimination. The heart and breathing rates simultaneously slow and blood flow to the muscles is stabilized. The state is one of a quiet, restful relaxation.

There are numerous techniques that you can use to develop your relaxation response, such as meditation, yoga, progressive relaxation, self-hypnosis, autogenic training, and bio-feedback. I'll describe some techniques later on in this chapter. For now it is important that you understand that there are four components necessary no matter which method you use. These include:

- *A quiet environment.* Choose a quiet, calm environment without distractions.

- *A mental device.* Having a mental device—a sound, word, image, statement, fixed gaze—helps you shift your mind from being externally oriented to being internally oriented. This is important because it enables you to feel what is going on in your body and because it helps you to overcome your tendency to let your mind wander. Use the same image, word, sound each time you practice your relaxation response.

- *A passive attitude.* This is probably the most important component. Adapt a let it happen attitude instead of trying to force yourself to relax. When distracting thoughts occur, just return to your mental device.

- *A comfortable position.* Remain in a comfortable position so that there is no undue muscular tension. When a position gets uncomfortable it is a sign that tension is increasing. Switch to a position that makes you feel more comfortable.

The Connection between Control and Fear

Most people who were neglected or abused as a child have control issues and these issues are a key factor in determining whether they will repeat the cycle of abuse. Some try to make up for the fact that they were overly controlled and dominated by their parents or other caretakers or authority figures by controlling and dominating others when they become adults. Others, in their determination to never become like their domineering or abusive parents, will go to the other extreme and submerge all assertiveness and aggression to the point that they allow others to dominate them even as adults.

The most typical arena where we act out our control issues is with those we love—namely our partners and our children—but we do so with our bosses, coworkers, and employees as well. If, for example, your parents were overly controlling you may either follow in their footsteps with your children or, fearful of becoming like them, raise your children without limits or restrictions. Unfortunately, you can't escape your past quite so easily. By doing the opposite of your parents you may once again find yourself living under authoritarian rule—only this time the person in who is ruling you is your own demanding, tyrannical child.

We resort to trying to gain control over others when we feel we have lost control of our own lives. Real control comes neither from controlling others nor from allowing others to control us. While nearly everyone who was abused will have issues with control, some forms of childhood abuse cause a person to have more of a need to maintain control than others. These include:

- If one or both of your parents (or primary caretakers) were overly protective. Parents who do not allow their children to explore their worlds out of fear that they will get hurt, who hover too close and too anxiously send the message that their children cannot make it on their own, that they must depend on others to care for them and protect them. They teach their children that acts of independence can be fatal, that safety resides in other people's control.

- If one or both of your parents (or primary caretakers) were overly controlling. Parents who insist on controlling all aspects of their children's lives, who are unable to relinquish their power over their children, even after they are old enough to assert some independence teach their children that there is always someone in control in a relationship and that equality in relationships does not exist. It can also teach that control is really caring or it can cause children to grow up believing that if they ever get close to someone, he or she is going to control them.

- If one or both of your parents were emotionally or physically abusive. When our early experiences with power are not just intrusive or controlling but humiliating and hurtful, we may grow up to do unto others what was done to us or to be overly compliant in order to protect ourselves from further harm. Or, we may undermine anyone, including a therapist, who offers to help us or who reminds us of our dependency. This resistance to emotional dependency may compel us to attack those on whom we depend, causing us to become overly critical and to try to reduce or destroy their power. The most compassionate expressions of caring and concern may remind us of our powerlessness. To value and accept help is equated with surrendering to a malevolent control.

A Case of Fear Turning to Control

Barbara insists on having things her own way. When one of her children goes against her wishes she becomes furious with them. She storms around the house accusing them of not respecting her and she punishes them by taking something away from them. She believes she can make people do what she wants by punishing, accusing, shaming, yelling, shoving, throwing things, or hitting. She wants her children to be afraid of her because then she knows she's in control.

How did Barbara get this way? Barbara had absolutely no control when she was growing up. She lived in a state of constant fear. Her father was an extremely controlling, abusive man who ruled his wife and children by intimidation. Everyone in the household was afraid of him. If something didn't get done or if one of the children made a mistake, even something like spilling their milk, they would be punished severely, usually by being beaten with their father's belt. At times he became even more abusive and would torment them throughout the night.

Most abusive people have a great deal of anger. And most abusive people are also highly defended. Underneath all that anger and all those defenses is tremendous fear. In fact, the purpose of the anger and the defenses is to cover up their fear. Fear is a very debilitating emotion. It causes us to feel powerless, hopeless, and small. Anger, on the other hand, causes us to feel powerful, hopeful, and big. When you think of this, why wouldn't someone who is overwhelmed with fear not choose to trade it for anger? Why wouldn't someone choose to defend themselves against their fear by covering it up? Why in the world would someone who is terrified of their own fear choose to face it when controlling, dominating, and abusing others works so well to mask their fear?

How to Cope with Fear

We will follow the same formula for coping with fear as we have for shame and anger.

Identify the Emotion

Understanding how your body reacts to fear can help you recognize when you are afraid. Unfortunately, we often deny or dismiss the fact that we are afraid. Think about how your body responds when you are frightened. Our body normally experiences the emotion of fear in all the following ways: sweating or perspiring, feeling nervous, jittery or jumpy, shaking, quivering or trembling, breathing fast or breathlessness, muscles tensing, cramping, eyes darting or quickly looking around, lump in throat, choking sensation, diarrhea, vomiting, feeling of heaviness in stomach, getting cold, hair standing on end.

Determine the Message That Fear Is Sending

The message of fear is that something requires your attention. It means that you need to be prepared for something. Most often, fear signals danger. Unfortunately, those who were abused as children often live their life in a state of fear, even when there is no imminent danger. If you are aware that you are feeling afraid or anxious, ask yourself if there is something currently going on in your life that you need to be afraid of or concerned about. If you cannot find anything in the present, assume it is your anxiety and fear from the past.

Feel the Emotion but Don't Become Overwhelmed by It

You may have heard the phrase, "What you resist, persists." This can sometimes be true of fear. By simply acknowledging your fear, allowing yourself to feel it, and then breathing into it, you may be amazed at how your fear diminishes. The same is true of anxiety. Simply trying to accept it, letting yourself feel it, may be the best way to handle it. Battling with it is likely to create a greater internal struggle. Refer to chapter 4 for a reminder of how to feel and accept an emotion.

Ask Yourself If It Is Appropriate to Be Feeling This Emotion at This Time

Your fear or anxiety today may be the same as you experienced in childhood abuse situations, albeit in a different form. By connecting your current fear to past experiences you will put distance and perspective on the situation. Doing so will enable you to reduce the fear and help you work through it.

EXERCISE: Connecting Your Current Fear to the Past

- Make a list of your specific fears (i.e., fear of closed-in spaces, fear of being alone, fear of snakes).

- Which of your fears do you relate to abuse, incest, or neglect experiences? For example, your fear of closed-in spaces may very well come from having been locked in a closet when you were a child, your fear of being alone may come from the fact that you were left all alone at night while your parents went out to bars. Your fear of snakes may not be as direct, but many survivors of child sexual abuse have such a fear.

Stress Reduction Exercises

If your fear is based on irrational thoughts or childhood fears, you may need to actively work on calming yourself down and relieving your stress. The following exercises will help you to do so.

Deep Breathing Exercises

Slow breathing from the diaphragm is one of the most effective ways of managing stress and can help release tension in a difficult situation.

1. Slowly inhale as you count to two, hold your breath for two counts, exhale your breath for two counts.

2. Repeat this pattern twenty times. Notice how much more relaxed you are.

3. Once you have become proficient in this technique, slow down your breathing even more by inhaling as you count to four, holding your breath for four counts, and exhaling to four counts.

Relaxation Exercises

By following these instructions for only fifteen minutes a day you can substantially lower your stress level and your tendency to erupt in frustration or anger:

1. Lie on your back on your bed or a mat.

2. Allow your feet to flop outward and your hands to rest by your sides (make sure your hands are not in a fist or otherwise tightened).

3. Close your eyes and sigh several times to release tension.

4. Begin to breathe slowly, pausing after each exhalation.

5. Relax your toes, feet, and legs. Allow all tension to drain out.

6. Do the same with your fingertips, arms, and neck.

7. Ease the tension in your shoulders by lowering them.

8. Mentally smooth the muscles in your face.

9. Be aware of the relaxation in your muscles. When you are ready, slowly open your eyes and stretch. Bend your knees and roll on your side before getting up slowly.

Mind/Body Techniques

The following techniques are powerful methods of stress control that have worked for many people.

- Meditation—induces deep physical relaxation and mental awareness.

  1. Sit comfortably and upright, close your eyes and relax.

  2. Focus your mind on an object, breathing out and in to the count of four, or look at an object such as a candle flame or flower.

  3. Repeat a word such as peace or Om either out loud or silently. Continue for at least fifteen minutes.

- Visualization—assists in calming you before or after a high pressure event, situation or conflict.

  1. Either sit comfortably or lie down.

  2. Relax your body and clear your mind by either doing the breathing or the relaxation exercise described above.

  3. Imagine yourself in a peaceful, beautiful place, perhaps a serene garden, a quiet beach, or on top of a hill with a beautiful vista. Smell the scents and hear the sounds.

  4. As you take in a deep breath, imagine yourself being there and feeling comfortable, safe, and relaxed.

  5. Continue taking slow, deep breaths, allowing yourself to enjoy the relaxation.

  6. Repeat affirmation phrases such as "I feel peaceful," or "I am completely relaxed."

  7. Remind yourself that this place is available to you whenever you feel stressed out. It is just a few slow, deep breaths away.

- Mindfulness or active meditation—helps you stay in the moment instead of worrying or obsessing.

  1. Focus all your attention on whatever you are doing. Observe shapes, colors, textures. Focus on the movement of your body.

  2. Stay in the present moment without worrying about the past or the future.

Take Action to Remedy the Situation

So what do you do when you are afraid? What you don't want to do is to cover up your fear with a false bravado that turns into an aggressive or abusive stance. You don't want to bully your way through life as a way of covering up your own fears. Instead of trying to control others as a way of dealing with the fact that you feel so out of control, do things to give yourself a sense of mastery and control (practice a sport until you are good at it, learn a skill that you can excel at). Neither do you want to allow your fear to keep you in a one-down position with others. Here are some other suggestions for handling fear on a daily basis:

- Discuss your fears with others. Ask your friends how they would handle the situation.

- Change what you normally do when you are fearful. Do something different.

- Visualize the situation with yourself as a strong person, unafraid and able to handle the situation.

- Develop a set of fear mantras. For example: "I will get through this." "I'm strong enough to handle this situation."

- Do what you are afraid of doing, over and over again.

- When overwhelmed, make a list of small steps or tasks you can do. Start with the first thing on the list.

PART THREE

ABUSE PREVENTION STRATEGIES

CHAPTER 9

How to Prevent Partner Abuse

The only person you can control is yourself.

MARIAN WRIGHT EDELMAN

When Vanessa was a child she endured horrible beatings by her father whenever she did something that upset him—and this was often. Her father would take off his belt and beat her viciously on the back until she was in such pain she could hardly walk.

Vanessa got married right out of high school and soon had a little girl. Shortly after the birth of her daughter, her husband began to slap Vanessa in the face whenever he got upset with her. Over the years her husband's slaps escalated into full-blown beatings. Vanessa endured the beatings for fifteen long years, partly out of the fear that she wouldn't be able to support her daughter, partly out of the fear of being alone, but mostly because she didn't know any other way of living. She was merely doing what her parents had raised her to do: be obedient and blame herself for the inappropriate and abusive behavior of others.

By the time I met Vanessa she had already fled her abusive husband. She had hidden out in a shelter for battered women for several months before feeling safe enough to start a new life in a new town. Vanessa and I worked together for several years helping her to recover first from the abuse of her husband and then the abuse of her father. During this time, Vanessa, a very attractive woman, was approached by many men. For a long time she became angry at their advances and made it clear to them that she simply wasn't interested. But as Vanessa began to heal she also began to think about the possibility of having a healthy, loving relationship with a man. This was not without a great deal of trepidation, however. "How will I avoid getting myself into the same kind of mess I was in before?" she'd ask. "How can I tell if a man is an abuser?"

While you may not have the kind of history that Vanessa had, the chances are extremely high that if you were neglected or abused as a child, without some healing and intervention on your part you will end up getting involved with someone who is similar to one of your parents or abusers. It is what we talked about earlier in the book: the repetition compulsion. This means that if you tend to be a victim you will attract and become involved with someone who tends to be abusive. It you tend to be abusive yourself, you will be attracted to and become involved with someone who tends to be passive and will allow you to be domineering, controlling, or otherwise abusive.

So how do you avoid reenacting your childhood abuse or neglect experience in your romantic, intimate relationships? How do you avoid getting involved with someone who is a replica of a parent or other abuser? And how do you prevent yourself from treating your partner in the same abusive ways as you were treated as a child? That is what this chapter is about.

All the information and strategies that you have learned so far will help you to avoid repeating the cycle, as will the work you will continue to do in the section on long-term strategies. But there is also some specific information that you will need to know now in order to avoid repeating the cycle of abuse in your romantic relationships.

Your choice of partner is one of the best indicators of how much you have recovered from the abuse or neglect you sustained as a child and whether or not you are at risk of continuing the cycle of abuse. In this chapter you will learn some specific strategies to help you break your pattern of continually choosing partners who will victimize you or allow you to victimize them. For those of you who are new to relationships, you will learn suggestions and strategies that will keep you from developing a negative pattern in the first place. You will also learn what a healthy relationship looks like so that you can begin to replace your unhealthy patterns with healthy ones.

Reevaluate Your Relationships

Because we tend to surround ourselves with people who are similar to those in our family of origin or to our abusers, to take on the same roles we had in our family and to treat our partners in the same ways we saw our parents treating one another, it is often necessary to reevaluate your relationships in order to break the cycle.

The first thing you will need to do is to identify your pattern. When you look back on your previous relationships, do you recognize the fact that many of your partners were very similar in terms of temperament, personality characteristics, and possibly even physical characteristics? Have you found that you tend to pick the same kind of partner over and over—someone who is excessively critical like your mother, someone who is passive like your father? If you are having difficulty seeing the parallels, the following exercise will help.

EXERCISE: *Discover Your Pattern*

1. Draw a line down the middle of a piece of paper. On one half of the page, list the positive personality traits of your most current lover; on the other half, list his most predominant negative personality traits.

2. On two separate sheets, do the same for each of your parents or primary caretakers.

3. Notice if there are similarities between the traits of your most current lover and those of your parents. Pay special attention to whether he or she shares *negative* traits with one or both of your parents.

4. Now, once again on separate sheets, list the personality traits of your previous three lovers (if you have had that many).

5. Notice if they share any personality traits, particularly negative ones.

6. Compare these traits with those of your parents.

7. Circle the negative traits that your partners (both present and past) and your parents have in common.

Most people with a history of neglect or abuse notice a close correlation between the traits of their partners and their parents. With only a few exceptions, the traits that matched up most closely tend to be the negative traits.

While it may seem logical to look for partners who compensate for, rather than duplicate our parents' inadequacies, the fact is, we tend to do the opposite—we attempt to recreate the conditions of our upbringing in order to correct them. We attempt to return to the scene of our original wounding in an effort to resolve our unfinished business. If one or both of your parents were overprotective or engulfing, instead of looking for someone who allows you plenty of space and freedom so you can overcome your fear of engulfment, you find yourself repeatedly attracted to partners who smother you. If one or both of your parents neglected or abandoned you, instead of looking for someone attentive and reliable so you can overcome your fear of abandonment, you find yourself attracted to partners who are unreliable and neglectful.

The repetition compulsion is so powerful that even after you have become aware of the fact that you have developed a pattern of choosing a particular type of person you can still fall into the trap. This is why you need to make a list of your new partner's characteristics and compare them with the list of your parent's (or other abusers') characteristics each time you enter a new relationship.

Any or all of the following warning signs may also help alert you to a pattern:

- You fell in love at first sight.

- You developed extremely intense feelings toward him or her in a very short time.

- He or she is your type.

- Whenever you are around him or her it is so intense it feels like there is electricity in the air.

- Something about him or her feels very familiar.

- You feel so comfortable with him or her, it is as if you've known each other all your lives (in fact, you have).

- You can't really explain why you like him or her, you just do.

- Ever since you met him or her you've been obsessive—you just can't get him or her out of your mind.

Once recognized, these patterns can be broken by completing your unfinished business from the past. We'll discuss this in part four. For now, begin by saying no to an intense attraction to a person who is your usual type and opt instead to explore relationships with those who may not give you that initial feeling of intensity and power that someone who represents your past will give you. This may seem boring at first, but give it a chance. As you continue to get healthier you'll be surprised how attractive partners who are more healthy will become to you.

Other Strategies for Preventing Abuse in Your Relationships

In addition to working on changing your patterns, preventing abuse in intimate, romantic relationships involves the following:

- Choosing to have equal relationships

- Taking your time and choosing your partner wisely

- Not losing yourself in your relationships

- Setting and enforcing appropriate boundaries and limits

- Having reasonable expectations of your partner and of what a relationship can provide you

- Not making assumptions

- Not confusing the present with the past

- Taking responsibility for your own feelings, reactions, and projections

- Working on developing your empathy skills

- Agreeing to disagree and taking time-outs

- Learning conflict resolution and fair fighting techniques

- Recognizing abuse in its early stages and getting help

Choose to Have Equal Relationships

One of the most significant mistakes people who tend to be victims or victimizers make when entering an intimate relationship is in choosing a partner who is not their emotional equal. Some choose partners

who they know they can control and dominate. Others choose partners that have what they perceive as superior qualities to theirs. Both
of these choices are open invitations for abuse to take place.

When you get involved with someone *you* perceive as being more
powerful or better than you are in some way, either because he seems
more intelligent, more successful or more attractive, you will tend to
give in to him far more than if you felt you were his equal. You will
tend to keep quiet when you should speak up, to tolerate unacceptable
behavior, and to generally allow him to control the relationship. You
may bend over backward to please your partner, including putting up
with abusive behavior. This is particularly true for women. Since most
women have a strong motivation to maintain harmony in their relationships, they tend to make the changes their partner requests, even
when the requests are unreasonable.

When you become involved with a partner who has more power
or perceives himself as being more powerful, or better than you are,
he will tend to expect and demand more from you, tend to take advantage by pushing limits, taking you for granted, or trying to dominate
you. If you are the one who holds the most power you will undoubtedly behave the same way. It is human nature.

In the previous chapter on shame you learned that those who seek
power over others do so as a way of compensating for the sense of
defectiveness which underlies shame. For this reason many survivors
choose partners who are weaker or less secure than they are in an
attempt to remain in control and to insulate themselves from further
shame. By gaining power over their partner they are also reversing
roles with their abuser. Should their shame be activated in the relationship these people are usually in a position to be able to blame their
partner for their own mistakes or shortcomings.

On the other hand, many survivors choose partners who they perceive as their superior as a way of compensating for their inner sense
of defectiveness. Other survivors are driven by the hunger for the protection and care they did not receive as a child. In a quest for rescue,
they may seek out powerful authority figures who seem to offer the
promise of a special caretaking relationship. Also haunted by the fear
of abandonment and exploitation, they may choose someone who
appears to offer security and undying love.

Because of these unhealthy dynamics, it is vital that you aim for
equal relationships—ones in which both you and your partner view

each other as equals. This doesn't mean that you are equal in all respects, but that overall, your qualities balance each other out. More important, it means that you each have equal power in the relationship.

Take Your Time and Choose Your Partner Wisely

In order to establish a healthy relationship, one based on mutual respect, sharing, and intimacy, you need time—time to get to know the other person, time for her to get to know you, and time to determine whether you are compatible. We all try hard to impress a potential partner at the beginning of a relationship and it takes time before we are willing to let down that false persona and risk our real selves.

The problem with instant romance is that by the time you finally get to know your partner you are already emotionally and sexually involved and can no longer be objective. This makes it nearly impossible for you to perceive the person for who he or she really is.

Although many abusive partners are initially quite charming, most exhibit similar behaviors and attitudes, and have very similar personality traits. By being able to spot these behaviors, attitudes, and traits you can avoid becoming involved with an abusive partner. Refer back to the list of behaviors and attitudes common to abusive partners that I provided in chapter 2. The following questionnaire will also help.

QUESTIONNAIRE: *How to Identify a Potential Abuser*

1. Was this person abused as a child or raised in a violent household?

2. Does he or she drink alcohol excessively or abuse drugs?

3. Is he jealous of your other relationships—not just with other men but with your friends and family members as well?

4. Does she keep tabs on you? Does she want to know where you are at all times?

5. Does he expect you to spend all your free time with him? Does he act unusually possessive of you and your time?

6. Does she lose her temper frequently and more easily than seems necessary? Does she over-react to small problems?

7. Does he become enraged when you don't listen to his advice?

8. Does she become angry if you do not fulfill her wishes or if you cannot anticipate what she wants?

9. Does he appear to have a dual personality, experiencing extreme highs and lows in a short period of time?

10. If there a sense of overkill in her cruelty or kindness?

11. Does he believe in a gender-specific supremacy, or hold a strong stereotype of gender roles in the family?

12. When she becomes angry, do you become afraid of what she will do?

13. Has *not* making her angry become an important part of your behavior?

14. Does he punch walls or throw things when upset?

15. Does he use violence to solve problems? Does he get into fights with others?

16. Does he have a history of violent offenses?

17. Does he keep guns or other weapons? Does he threaten to use them when upset with someone?

Scoring: If you answered yes to any of questions 1 through 12 you may have reason to be concerned, especially if you answered yes to more than one question. If you answered yes to even one of questions 14 through 17 you definitely have reason to be concerned. This person has an abusive personality and is very likely to become physically abusive toward you.

Don't Lose Yourself in Your Relationship

Whenever we care deeply about another person we care about what that person thinks of us. When this occurs we have essentially given over to this person some degree of power to affect how we feel about ourselves. Whenever we openly admire someone we are more open to their guidance or influence and in essence, have surrendered power to them. And whenever we permit ourselves the vulnerability of needing someone emotionally we inevitably give that special person a measure of power which can be either respected or abused.

This makes entering into an intimate relationship a risky endeavor for those who were neglected or abused as a child. The adult survivor is at great risk of losing themselves in their relationships and thus repeated victimization in adult life. The following tips will help you avoid this.

1. Be honest about who you are and what you want in a relationship.

2. Maintain time for yourself and time to take care of yourself.

3. Maintain your own friends and social life.

4. Do not allow yourself to become isolated.

5. Remain financially independent.

6. Maintain your own separate space—this means not moving in together too soon and even when you do move in together, having a separate space for time alone.

7. Don't change who you are just to please your partner.

8. Speak up when you disagree or when you don't like how you are being treated.

9. Don't allow your partner to make decisions for you.

Women tend to lose themselves in their relationships more than men. For more information on how to maintain a separate life and sustain your sense of self in relationships, refer to my book *Loving Him without Losing You.*

Set and Enforce Appropriate Boundaries and Limits

Many of you are probably familiar with the concept of boundaries; for those of you who are not, here is a brief overview of exactly what boundaries are and how to set them. A boundary is a limit, a demarcation. Personal boundaries define the territory of your personal space. There are physical and emotional boundaries. They are what separate us from other people. Your skin is an example of a physical boundary since your skin creates a physical barrier that separates you from all other living and nonliving organisms. We also have an invisible boundary around our body that is often referred to as our comfort zone. Our comfort zone varies depending upon the situation. For example, you are no doubt much more comfortable allowing a friend to stand close to you than you would a stranger.

An emotional boundary usually takes the form of a limit. We all have limits as to what feels appropriate and safe when it comes to how others treat us emotionally. What may feel fine to you may feel uncomfortable to your partner. But unless you tell your partner you are uncomfortable, he will never know, and he will continue treating you in a manner that is uncomfortable to you. This doesn't help either one of you. If you allow someone to emotionally abuse you, for example, you are not honoring and protecting your boundaries and you are participating in the erosion of your relationship.

A boundary violation occurs when someone crosses the physical or emotional limits set by another person. All relationships, even our most intimate ones, have limits as to what is appropriate. When someone crosses the line between what is appropriate and inappropriate, whether they do it knowingly or unknowingly, that person has violated our boundary.

Most of us begin a relationship thinking we have certain limits as to what we will or will not tolerate from a partner. But as the relationship progresses, we tend to move our boundaries back, tolerating more and more intrusion or going along with things we are really opposed to. Although this can occur even in healthy relationships, in abusive ones partners begin tolerating unacceptable or even abusive behavior and then convince themselves that these boundaries are normal and acceptable, and they believe their partner when he or she tells them they deserve such treatment.

EXERCISE: *Establishing Your Boundaries*

1. Only you can decide what you will and will not accept in your relationships. In order to set your boundaries, you need to know what they are. Spend some time thinking about the kinds of behavior that bother you the most, behaviors that push your buttons, or behaviors that are morally unacceptable to you. Make a list of these behaviors. Your list might include such things as: reading your mail, going through your private papers, making fun of you in front of others.

2. Make another list about what your personal limits are regarding your partner's behavior. For example, you may think it is

okay for your partner to have two drinks, but no more since you have noticed that his personality changes after two drinks and you come from an alcoholic family and have no intention of being involved with a drunk.

Communicate Your Limits and Boundaries

Your partner needs to know you have limits and boundaries. In order to establish your boundaries you will need to state them clearly. At an appropriate time sit down together and share your lists with your partner. Explain why you have the limits and boundaries you have and ask your partner if she will honor them. You may also take this opportunity to ask your partner to share her boundaries and limits with you.

Don't expect your partner to be perfect. Boundary violations can be healed in the moment if you gently tell your partner about it at the time and she apologizes for it and assures you that it will not happen again. Unfortunately, this doesn't always happen. Your partner may get defensive or deny that she violated your boundary. Don't let this discourage you from bringing up offenses, however. While she may deny the violation at the time, after thinking it over she may realize what she has done and try harder to honor your boundaries. Plus, you need to stand up for yourself and assert your limits.

Have Reasonable Expectations

A good romantic partner is supposed to bring pleasure, security, and joy into your life. He or she is not supposed to be able to make up for all the neglect, deprivation, or abuse that you sustained in your childhood. All too often survivors of abuse and neglect expect their partners to provide the nurturing, unconditional love, and support that they missed as a child. Unfortunately, this is impossible for an adult partner to give. Adult partners have needs of their own and a healthy person has limits and boundaries in terms of what they are willing to put up with.

It is a common pattern for those who were neglected or abused to really be looking more for a mother or father than for an equal romantic partner. This kind of unreasonable expectation is a setup for abuse. For example, the typical female survivor enters an intimate relationship with a hunger to be protected and cared for and a fear of abandonment or exploitation. In a quest to be rescued, she seeks out a powerful authority figure who seems to offer the promise of a special caretaking relationship. Inevitably, her chosen partner fails to live up to her expectations. In reaction to being disappointed she becomes furious and denigrates the same person she had put on a pedestal.

Don't Make Assumptions

One of the most damaging aspects of coming from an abusive or neglectful background is that we make certain assumptions about people and their motives that are unrealistic and can even be destructive to a healthy relationship. For example, those who were abused often have a difficult time trusting other people and may, in fact, grow up to believe that no one can be trusted. This, in turn, can cause their perceptions to be distorted. By assuming that another person cannot be trusted they will tend to read into her behavior, seeing deceit and dishonesty in everything she does. When someone they love makes an honest mistake, they will assume she deliberately intended to hurt or deceive them. This assumption is the cause of many marital problems, causing partners to view one another as enemies instead of allies.

The way you feel at any given time has to do with the meaning you attach to the experience. We all attach different meanings to things. What I experience as someone being inconsiderate or selfish you might interpret as normal behavior. For this reason we need to stop making assumptions about the meaning of our partner's actions or inaction. The next time you become upset with your partner for something he or she said or did (or didn't say or do) ask yourself this question: "What else could this mean?" For example, instead of assuming that the reason your partner did not call you one night when he was out of town on business was because he doesn't love you or because he was with someone else, see if you can come up with some other, less negative possibilities. Maybe his business meetings were delayed, or perhaps he went out to eat with some colleagues. Or maybe he had intended to call you later but fell asleep.

Rosemary's Assumptions

Here's another example of how assumptions can affect a relationship. My client Rosemary's father cheated on her mother and was sexually inappropriate with Rosemary. "My father was obsessed with sex. It's all he ever talked about. He constantly made sexual innuendoes and told dirty jokes and he was always flirting with women. My mother just seemed to tolerate it, she even put up with him having numerous affairs. But it made me mad. Then, when I was a teenager he started making comments about the way I was developing, how I had nice tits. It made me sick to my stomach. When he was drinking he'd always want me to come sit on his lap like I was still a little girl, but I knew I was too big for that. I knew he just wanted to cop a feel as he always put it. It didn't matter to him that I was his own daughter."

What do you imagine Rosemary's beliefs were about men based on her experience with her father? I asked her to write them down and here is what she wrote:

- All men ever think about is sex.

- No man is capable of being faithful to his wife.

- Men are ruled by their penis—they put all other reason aside.

- You can't trust a man to have boundaries when it comes to sex.

Rosemary made sure she married a man who was very different from her father. He hadn't pushed her for sex all the time they were dating; in fact, he respected the fact that she was a virgin. He didn't flirt with other girls and he never told off-color jokes. But even so, Rosemary often became upset whenever Frank talked with other women at a party or gathering and if he made any comment at all about how a woman was dressed, she became furious. The truth was, Rosemary still believed that all men were like her father. She was unable to make the distinction between her father and her husband, even though they were drastically different people. Whenever Frank did anything at all that remotely reminded her of her father, Rosemary was triggered. She was no longer in the present but was instead reliving the pain she experienced with her father.

Exercise: *Your Negative Assumptions and Beliefs*

Like Rosemary, if you were neglected or abused as a child you have certain negative assumptions about people and beliefs about relationships that have affected your expectations and perceptions of others.

1. Make a list of the negative beliefs you have about other people, the opposite sex, and relationships based on your experiences growing up.

2. Circle those assumptions and beliefs that you believe have caused you or will cause you the most difficulty in relationships.

Don't Confuse the Present with the Past

Everyone enters romantic, intimate relationships with a great deal of baggage—memories of the past, unrealistic expectations, and fantasies of how a relationship should be, and unhealthy beliefs about how a relationship should work. Those with a history of abuse or neglect carry even more baggage than the average person and this baggage prevents them from seeing their partners clearly. It is as if they place a mask of the face of their parents or other significant caretakers or abusers onto the face of their partner.

In the mind of a survivor, even minor slights can evoke past experiences of callous neglect, and minor slights can evoke past experiences of deliberate cruelty. Like Rosemary, confusing the past with the present is a common problem for survivors. Just because your present partner broke a date does not mean that he is going to constantly disappoint you like your father did. While you may feel similar feelings of disappointment and rejection and it may bring back terrible memories, you must remind yourself that he is not your father and you need to give him a chance to prove to you that he will not make it a habit.

To prevent the past from contaminating your present relationship I suggest you try the following:

- Take responsibility for your reactions. Instead of blaming your partner for your reaction or immediately assuming that he is just like someone from your past, first allow yourself to process the feelings that have been stirred up. Does this remind you of something from the past? Then, once you are more clear, see if you can make a distinction between the past and the present.

- Learn from the past but don't dwell on it. Take responsibility for releasing your pain and anger from the past, either in therapy or through a self-help program. Work on learning to trust again and then try to enter each new relationship with the lessons of the past but not the burdens.

- Become familiar with your triggers or hot buttons. Each of us have triggers that set us off emotionally. It may be a situation that reminds us of the past, or something someone says that reminds us of what someone from the past said to hurt us. Getting your buttons pushed can send you into a tizzy without warning, causing you to become enraged, deeply hurt, fearful, or depressed.

- Make a list of your triggers. The next time your partner does something to trigger you, such as using a particular phrase, tell him you do not want him to use it again, that it hurts you deeply and reminds you of the past. If he seems to be sympathetic, you may wish to share your entire list of triggers, explaining why each item upsets you so much. While you're at it, ask him to make his own trigger list and share it with you.

Don't Place the Face of an Abuser on Your Partner

It is unfair of you to place the face of an abuser on your partner or to hold your current partner responsible for what others have done to you in the past and it is unhealthy for you to live in the past in this way. By working on differentiating the past from the present you can begin to feel less insecure or intimidated by your present partner and be more able to respond to him or her as an adult, as opposed to as a child. The following suggestions will help you make this distinction:

1. Determine who your partner reminds you of (your mother, your father, a sibling, an abuser).

2. Make a list of the ways in which your partner is different from this person.

3. Whenever you are reminded of a person from the past, bring yourself back to the present by looking at your current partner in the face. See your partner clearly and remind yourself of who you are with now.

This last step is especially important for those who were sexually abused as a child. This is because certain things that partners say and do, particularly when they are making love, can remind survivors of the abuser and cause them to confuse their partner with their original abuser.

Take Responsibility for Your Own Feelings, Reactions, and Projections

The truth is, just because something upset you doesn't mean that the other person did something wrong. This is a very difficult concept for most people to understand, especially those with an abusive or neglectful background. It only stands to reason that if we are upset with someone they must have done something wrong, right? Otherwise, why would we have become upset with them? The answer is that we can become upset with someone else for reasons that have nothing at all to do with that person.

My client Suzanne becomes very angry whenever her husband turns the television up too loud. "I don't know how many times I've asked him to turn it down. All that noise drives me crazy! Sometimes I think he turns it up just to get to me."

When Suzanne and I explored what was really going on in this situation it turned out that Suzanne's father used to turn the television up really loud whenever he got drunk. Now, whenever the television gets a little loud, like during a commercial, Suzanne becomes triggered, remembering her father.

You need to take responsibility for your own feelings and reactions. In Suzanne's case, she needed to connect with what had triggered her reaction and separate the present from the past. She also needed to share the reason for her upset with her partner and stop blaming him for her reaction.

Unless you complete your unfinished business from the past (i.e., acknowledge and release your anger toward those who abused you) all the anger, fear, guilt, shame, and pain you once felt and still feel toward those people who harmed you in the past will be put onto innocent people in your life today, people who either remind you of these original abusers or people who inadvertently push your buttons by behaving in similar ways. In part four, "Long-Term Recovery Strategies," we will focus on ways for you to resolve your unfinished business with your parents and other significant caretakers and abusers, but for now begin by taking more responsibility for your reactions.

You also need to take responsibility for your projections. The act of projection is to attribute to others those feelings and reactions that we ourselves are having but do not want to acknowledge, or in some cases, feelings that we fear we may have or have had in the past. Projection is an unconscious defense mechanism and so generally we are not aware that we are doing it. It occurs whenever an unrecognized and rejected trait or characteristic of our own personality is observed in someone else. In other words, we see and react negatively to the behavior or personality characteristic of someone else because we fail to see the very same behavior or characteristic in ourselves.

Work on Developing Your Empathy Skills

One of the after-effects of having been neglected or abused as a child is that your ability to have empathy for others is compromised. Those with a history of neglect or abuse often have difficulty being able to put themselves in another person's place or to imagine how someone else might feel. This lack of empathy can therefore give them permission to be neglectful toward their children or abusive toward their partner, their children, or their coworkers.

The following exercise will strengthen your empathetic abilities.

EXERCISE: *Imaginary Letters*

In this exercise you are going to write several letters. These letters will be to yourself, from your partner and children.

- One by one imagine what your partner and each of your children would like to say to you about the way they feel when you are at your worst. For example, put yourself in your partner's place when you lose your temper and go off on him. Write down all the things you imagine your partner might be feeling and how you imagine it makes your partner feel about himself.

- Once you have completed one letter, put it aside and begin working on another letter from a different person. You may choose to write all your letters at one sitting or to spread them out, possibly writing one letter a day. If you have children, write a letter from each one of them describing how you imagine that child feels when you are too busy to spend time with him, when you become impatient, or when you are too demanding.

- When you have completed all your letters begin reading them to yourself, one by one. Imagine that each letter was actually written by this person and allow your heart to open to their words. When it becomes difficult to take in, take a deep breath and remember your commitment to yourself to break the cycle. Try to avoid becoming defensive or slipping into denial.

Agree to Disagree and Take Time-Outs

Those who become abusive with their partner tend to believe that their partner needs to agree with them in order to be loving and supportive. But this belief encourages both abusive and victimlike behavior. In order to have an emotionally healthy relationship, there must be space in your relationship for disagreements without one or both partners feeling unloved or unloving. You do not need to force your partner to see things your way, nor do you need to struggle to change your views or perceptions as a sign that you love your partner. You each have a right to your own opinions. Agreeing to disagree means that when you have reached an impasse, it is far more productive to simply say, "We are not going to agree on this, so let's drop it," than to keep hammering away at each other in the hopes that one of you will change your mind.

There are also times when the most constructive thing you can do is to walk away. If you are so angry that you can't stop calling your partner names or berating her behavior, the best thing to do is to leave the room or the home, if necessary. After you have cooled off, you may want to sit down and discuss your problem rationally, but until then, it is best to stay away from each other. The same holds true if you are on the receiving end of your partner's wrath. You don't have to sit there and take it because he is dishing it out, in fact you shouldn't. Get up and leave, for your sake and for the sake of the relationship.

Learn Effective Conflict Resolution Skills and Fair Fighting Techniques

Few of us learned effective conflict resolution skills when we were growing up. In fact, those who come from dysfunctional homes learn unhealthy ways of resolving conflict. The following questions will help you explore what lessons you learned about solving conflicts from your parents.

QUESTIONNAIRE: *How Did Your Parents Deal with Conflict?*

1. Did your parents discuss problems rationally or did they tend to blow up at one another?

2. Did they express emotions easily or did they hold in their feelings?

3. Did your parents tend to blame one another for their problems?

4. Did your parents argue often?

5. Did your parents give one another the silent treatment?

6. Did your parents yell at one another?

7. Did your parents punish one another?

8. Did your parents emotionally abuse one another?

An Internal Process for Handling Conflicts

Since most of us didn't learn effective conflict resolution skills, we need to be taught. The following is an effective process for handling conflicts that will not actually involve dealing with your partner directly. It is highly effective in avoiding arguments and in preparing you to discuss your issues with your partner in a rational way.

Step 1. Make sure you are in the present, dealing with the present situation and the person who is right in front of you. If you are being triggered by an old memory you are no longer perceiving the present situation accurately and you shouldn't try to resolve the conflict directly with your partner at this time.

Step 2. Do a feelings inventory. Am I feeling: hurt, angry, guilty, afraid, rejected, abandoned?

Step 3. Take responsibility for your feelings. Instead of blaming your partner for your feelings remember:

- Your partner didn't *make* you feel this.
- Your upset was caused by your reaction to the situation and the meaning you attached to it.

Step 4. Assume the best about your partner unless he or she shows you otherwise. Few people deliberately set out to hurt you. In fact, most people are rather oblivious to how their behavior and actions affect others until they are informed about this.

Step 5. Either change your perception about the experience or communicate your needs/feelings to your partner.

The way to resolve most upsets with your partner is to either change the way you are looking at things or to change the way you are communicating. When we change the way we look at things we examine how we perceived the situation (bring yourself into the present, assume the other person did not intend to hurt you). When we change the way we are communicating we examine whether we have been clear about our needs and expectations.

Learn How to Fight Fairly

Sometimes we just need to hash things out with one another. Each person needs to have an opportunity to voice his or her feelings and to know that his or her partner has really heard their point of view. The following are instructions for having a fair fight, one that does not escalate into emotional abuse or physical violence.

1. Make sure you will not be interrupted (turn off the phone, turn off the TV, wait until the kids are asleep).

2. Don't have a fight if either of you have been drinking or taking drugs.

3. Know what it is you are fighting about.

4. Stick to one issue at a time.

5. Clearly describe the problem behavior. Do not attack the other person.

6. Describe how the problem affects you, or your feelings.

7. Do not bring up past problems, stay in the present.

8. Don't tell the other person how he or she thinks or feels or how they should think or feel.

9. Don't threaten or bribe.

10. Ask for feedback.

11. Don't bring in third parties.

12. No name calling, insults, or other forms of verbal abuse.

13. Humor is okay but don't ridicule the other person.

14. Don't destroy things, especially things that are meaningful to the other person.

15. There is never an excuse for hitting, slapping, or any other form of physical abuse.

16. Take a time-out if tension is mounting.

17. Balance the negative with positive. Say positive things about the problem or the other person.

18. Try to settle things, at least temporarily, in thirty minutes.

19. Work out a flexible solution or compromise.

20. Realize that the decision is not permanent. You can renegotiate.

21. Commit to follow through.

22. Actively work toward a solution.

23. Seek counseling if you're unable to resolve the conflict.

Recognize Signs of Abuse in Its Early Stages

You don't have to wait until you or your partner begin to verbally or physically abuse one another before you realize you are in an unhealthy relationship. There are certain behaviors that are both indicators of emotional abuse and warning signs that more serious forms of emotional or even physical abuse could occur in the future if something is not done to change the dynamics in the relationship.

1. Do you or your partner tend to embarrass or make fun of one another in front of your friends, family, or in-laws?

2. Do you tend to put down one another's accomplishments and goals?

3. Do you frequently question one another's decisions or ability to make decisions?

4. Does your partner always tend to take the opposite view of whatever you say? Do you do this to your partner?

5. When you try to discuss an issue with your partner does he generally get angry or cut you down by saying he doesn't know what you're talking about? Do you do this with your partner?

6. Do you ever use intimidation or threats to get one another to do as you wish?

7. Has your partner ever said or implied that you are nothing without him or that you were nothing until he came along or have you been guilty of saying such things?

8. Do you ever treat each other roughly when you are upset, such as pushing or shoving each other?

9. Does your partner call you several times a night or show up to make sure you are where you said you would be? Are you guilty of this kind of possessive behavior?

10. Do either or both of you use alcohol or drugs to excess?

11. Do you tend to get into arguments when you drink?

12. Does one or both of you tend to blame the other for everything that goes wrong in your lives?

13. Does your partner pressure you sexually—either for things you are not ready for or to have sex more often than you would like? Do you ever pressure your partner in this way?

14. Have either one of you ever insinuated that there is no way out of the relationship—meaning that you or your partner will not let the other one go?

15. Does your partner prevent you from doing things you want to do—like spending time with your friends or family members? Are you guilty of doing this to your partner?

16. Have either one of you ever tried to keep the other one from leaving during a fight?

17. Have either one of you ever abandoned the other somewhere during a fight to teach the other a lesson?

18. Have you ever been afraid of how your partner was acting or what he was capable of doing? Have you ever been afraid of how you were acting or what you might be capable of doing?

19. Do you feel like no matter what you do, or how hard you try, your partner is never happy with you? Do you think your partner would say this about you?

20. Do you always feel like you are walking on eggshells, trying to avoid a conflict or make your partner angry? Has your partner ever said that this is how she feels?

If you answered yes to many of these questions your relationship is either emotionally abusive or it is heading in the direction of becoming either emotionally or physically abusive. Emotional abuse is an insidious form of abuse that tends to sneak up on people and often precedes physical abuse. In a healthy relationship these kinds of interactions do not occur on a regular basis. Instead, as we have already discussed, both partners feel supported and respected by one another as opposed to feeling threatened, embarrassed, or criticized. Both partners allow each other the space and freedom necessary to maintain their separate sense of self. And instead of feeling threatened by the other's successes, they feel genuinely happy for them.

Are You a Victim of Domestic Abuse?

Your partner doesn't have to hit you for you to be a victim of domestic abuse. Answer the following questions as honestly as possible to determine if you are a victim of domestic abuse.

1. Has your partner ever threatened to hurt you?

2. Are you afraid of your partner?

3. When drinking, does your partner get rough or violent?

4. Does your partner always blame others for his problems?

5. Does your partner frequently explode in a rage?

6. Does your partner throw objects or break things when he or she is angry?

7. Has your partner ever deliberately hurt a pet?

8. Does your partner have a Dr. Jekyll and Mr. Hyde personality?

9. Do you usually give in when you argue because you are afraid of your partner?

10. Are your children afraid when your partner is angry?

11. Are you afraid to have friends or family come over for fear of your partner exploding?

12. Does your partner listen in on your phone calls?

13. Does your partner constantly accuse you of doing things behind his back?

14. Does your partner insist on going everywhere with you?

15. Is your partner suspicious of your every move?

16. Has your partner ever forced you to have sex even though you did not want to?

17. Have you ever called, or thought of calling, the police because an argument was getting out of control?

18. Does your partner ever threaten to take the kids away if you leave her or him?

These are all warning signs of potential physical violence and should be taken seriously. If these things regularly take place you are already being emotionally abused, even if the physical violence has not started.

CHAPTER 10

How to Prevent Child Abuse

*The experiences of childhood directly, consciously or
unconsciously, affect our parenting styles, the character
of our children and the direction of societies.*

—MICHAEL LERNER, *Parenting and Its Distortions*

"I'm afraid to have children. I'm afraid I'll treat my kids like my parents treated me and I don't want that. How do you know whether you will be a good parent or if you will become abusive like your parents were?"

I'm often asked this question by clients who are working on recovering from abusive or neglectful childhoods. Some are already aware of certain shortcomings that they fear might get in their way of being good parents, such as a lack of patience, a tendency to be selfish or preoccupied, a tendency to be overly critical, or a problem with their anger. Some are afraid they will repeat the cycle of emotional, physical, or sexual abuse that has been passed down in their families for generations. This was the case with my client Dwayne:

"My dad beat me because his dad beat him. I've even found some evidence that my grandfather's dad beat him. I don't want to pass on this family legacy, but I have a temper and I know how these things work. My wife wants a child very badly, but I'm afraid to take the chance. How can I be sure I won't end up doing the same things that were done to me?"

Since we know that those who were abused and/or neglected as children are at high risk of passing on this abuse or neglect to their own children, what is the solution? Should those with such a history avoid becoming parents altogether? Or is there a way to prevent becoming abusive or neglectful even if you suffered such a background? Is there really a way to break the cycle and not pass on a legacy of abuse and neglect to one's children?

All the steps you have taken so far will provide you significant help in avoiding becoming an abusive parent, as will the long-term steps later on in this book. But this chapter will offer those of you who are parents and would-be parents more specific information and strategies that you can call upon to strengthen your resolve to break the cycle. Although there are certainly no guarantees, I strongly believe that for most of you, following the recommendations and guidelines in this chapter will help you avoid making the same mistakes your parents made. You do not have to treat your children the way you were treated. You do not have to repeat your family's patterns of neglect and abuse. You can, in fact, be the first person in your family to break the cycle.

Unfortunately for some of you, the only way to break the cycle will be for you to wait to have children until you have healed more from your abusive childhood. This was the case with me. I realized that I was not a good candidate to be a parent because I would have been far too critical of my children.

Those of you who are already parents will be presented with various suggestions on how to nurture your children with attentive, nonviolent child-rearing practices. These strategies can be the key to the prevention of violence and hostility.

The Risk Factors for Child Abuse

It is my strong belief that the unconscious reenactment of trauma for the purposes of ridding ourselves of the shame and fear attached to child maltreatment and neglect, and our attempts to master unresolved issues with our parents and other caretakers is at the heart of all forms of child abuse. It is also my belief that child neglect is primarily caused by a parent's inability to emotionally bond with his or her child, again a direct reaction to having oneself been neglected as a child. But there are also many other reasons why adults hurt children, including the following:

- They don't know how to manage their anger and frustration.

- They become triggered by memories of their own childhood.

- They take their anger and frustration out on someone weaker than themselves.

- They don't know how to discipline a child.

- They expect behavior that is unrealistic for a child's age and ability.

- They lose control when they use alcohol or drugs.

- They are stressed by financial or other problems.

Attitudes and Beliefs as Predictors of Child Abuse

There are also certain types of attitudes and beliefs that tend to perpetuate the cycle of violence. For example, the following are predictors of child abuse:

- Negative perceptions of one's children. This is one of the most significant predictors of child abuse. According to one study of 181 low-income families involved with the Oregon Healthy Start program, researchers found that parents who felt their kids were difficult or deserved punishment were more likely to abuse their offspring. Other indicators of a negative view of the youngster included unrealistic expectations by parents, and a perceived lack of bonding between parent and child.

- Taking things too personally. Parents need to understand that their child isn't deliberately trying to anger them or embarrass them by making a mistake. For example, their crying baby isn't trying to purposely anger them or to keep them from watching television. He or she is probably hungry, or hot, or needs a new diaper.

- Belief in the value of spanking. Advocates for corporal punishment argue that it is the most effective way of teaching children to respect their elders and to learn important lessons. But what a beaten child really learns is to fear his parents, to play down his own pain, and to feel guilty. In the long run, it has been found that the exertion of force merely serves to reinforce aggressive behavior on the part of children and adolescents.

- An assumption that their child intentionally misbehaves or that their child is bad. This belief is at the heart of many forms of child abuse. Parents who basically can't trust their children or who assume their children are bad end up emotionally abusing them in one of the most devastating ways—by damaging their basic trust and belief in themselves.

- Having unreasonable expectations of your child. This includes expecting a child to act more mature than he is capable of, performing at a higher level than he is capable of, and being good all the time.

Do You Have What It Takes to Be a Good Parent?

Research shows that the long-term effects of trauma (such as abuse in childhood) tend to be most obvious and prominent when people are stressed, in new situations, or in situations that remind them of the circumstances of their trauma. Unfortunately, becoming a parent creates all three of these circumstances. First time parenthood is stressful, new, and almost always triggers memories of our own childhood traumas. This sets the stage for child abuse.

Although there isn't a parent personality, there are certain personality characteristics that predispose one to parenting, certain traits that most good parents have in common. These traits are:

- Patience

- Flexibility

- Tolerance for intrusion

- The ability to put oneself aside for prolonged periods of time without experiencing deep resentment or anger

Patience

Some of us are more patient than others. Those who are patient don't mind waiting in a grocery checkout line or getting stuck on the freeway quite as much as those who are impatient. It's not that these people don't feel inconvenienced or even frustrated; it's just that they are able to take it in stride more than those who tend to be impatient.

Impatient people, on the other hand, have little tolerance for waiting. They tend to be goal-oriented and some tend to be a bit controlling, resenting anything that gets in the way of achieving their goals. Instead of begrudgingly accepting a delay, their tension increases every minute they have to wait.

Parenting requires a lot of patience. Children do things slowly. They dawdle and daydream and do things the wrong way. They make messes that take time to clean up. They seem to have the uncanny ability to create a delay of some kind whenever their parents are in a hurry.

It is impatient, goal-oriented parents who tend to become the most frustrated with their children. This frustration can, in turn, cause parents to become controlling and even abusive. The following scenario is a good example of how a parent's impatience can lead to controlling, demeaning, and frightening behavior:

Margo is bent on getting to the department store when the doors open in order to take advantage of an annual sale. She got up extra early, allowing herself plenty of time to get her four-year-old son David dressed and fed before getting dressed herself. Once she finished getting dressed, she called to David to get his coat on and to meet her at the front door. Glancing at the clock, she assures herself she has plenty of time, takes a deep breath, and walks downstairs. Expecting to see David at the door, she impatiently calls upstairs for him. There is no answer. She huffs up the stairs to find him. When she walks into his room, she finds David in his underwear, quietly and calmly sorting through his dresser drawers.

Mortified, she screeches, "What are you doing? Why are you undressed?"

"I want to wear my red shirt."

"Fine," she says, pushing him aside in her haste to find the shirt. "But why did you have to take off your pants? Put them back on this instant!"

A dejected David slowly starts to put on his pants while Margo jerks open another drawer, scattering clothes in her desperate search for David's red shirt. Finally, she finds it at the bottom of a drawer.

"Here it is. Now put it on!" she commands as she turns to find David sitting on the edge of his bed, one leg in a pant leg, the other out.

"Would you hurry up! What's taking you so long!"

Totally exasperated, Margo looks at her watch. She swoops over to David, stuffs him into his pants, and pulls his red shirt over his head. "Now come on!" she says as she pulls him down the stairs and pushes him out the door. Hurt and upset, David starts to cry.

As you can imagine, Margo and David are in for a stressful day. Had she been a more patient person, Margo would have taken the shirt and pants incident in stride, tried to understand her son's need to change clothes, and quietly helped him to do so. Since she'd allowed herself enough time, she would have realized that the few minutes' delay wasn't going to make that much of a difference. And she would have been able to remind herself that, after all, her son was far more important than getting herself to the store early for the sale. Consequently, she would have saved herself a lot of hassle and had a far more pleasant day. She would have also saved David the pain of experiencing his mother's anger and disapproval.

The point here is that children are unpredictable, often stubborn, often difficult, and hardly ever cooperative when it comes to a timetable. To try to force them into a schedule without recognizing that there will be inevitable delays is only inviting frustration and may create an abusive situation. Although some parents learn this lesson and eventually learn to be patient, most who are impatient never learn it or learn it the hard way—after they have become dictatorial or abusive toward their children.

Flexibility

In addition to patience, parents need to be flexible. It simply isn't possible for parents to plan or exert the same control over their lives once they have a child. Learning and practicing flexibility simply makes life easier.

Flexible people have an easier time choosing which battles are worth fighting and which are not. This goes a long way in parenting. For example, in the previous example, had Margo been a bit more flexible, she could have saved herself and her son a lot of grief. A more flexible parent would have taken a few deep breaths when she found her son undressed and let go of her insistence on getting to the store as the doors opened. Parents who are flexible find it easier to give their children choices in regard to small things, which then makes it easier for them to accept unilateral decisions when they occur. Overall, this makes for greater parent-child cooperation. And of course, raising a child is an unpredictable endeavor in the long run and this presents difficulties for those who like to be in charge.

Tolerance for Intrusion

Becoming a parent also means giving up your physical and emotional space. This can be especially difficult for those who were neglected or abused as children. Children are by nature intrusive, climbing all over you, interrupting your conversations and your work, insisting on your attention. And the greatest intrusion of all, the noise that children inevitably and quite naturally make, epitomizes the feeling of being intruded upon. The decibel level of life automatically rises around even the best-behaved child. Parents must learn to endure a cacophony of sound ranging from ear-piercing crying and yelling to the irritating beeps and crashes of video games and the repetitious singing of *Sesame Street* songs. As my client Naomi told me, "I know I can't have kids. I can't even stand to be around them for very long—all the noise drives me crazy."

For some, the idea of sharing their physical and emotional space with a child on a full-time basis creates a feeling of claustrophobia. The truth is, some people have temperaments and histories that make them super-sensitive to intrusion. If you are one of the people who require privacy and uninterrupted time for your well-being, parenting is likely to be far too stressful for you. In addition, some parents end up feeling emotionally smothered by their children and this can mirror the experience they had with their parents.

The Ability to Put Oneself Aside

Parenthood requires sacrifices both great and small. On a daily basis, parents must put their own needs and desires aside for the safety of their children. Some people are able to make meeting their child's needs their top priority and are happy to do so. For these people, gratification far outweighs any feelings of frustration, deprivation, anger, or resentment.

Others, however, have problems with such extreme self-sacrifice. This is especially true for those who did not get their own emotional needs met as a child. For these people, the idea of sacrificing themselves to their children can bring up a great deal of pain and resentment toward their own parents. If these people choose to have children, they risk projecting that resentment onto their children.

Some simply cannot put their own needs aside to raise a child because their own needs are too great. Some were so deprived or neglected as children that they find it difficult to respond to other people's needs, as was the situation with my client Lupe:

"I have too many needs myself. I still long to be nurtured and held the way I should have been as a child. I'm still looking for a mother."

EXERCISE: *Your Score As a Potential Parent*

1. On a scale of 1 to 10, ten being the highest, rank yourself for each of the following qualities: patience, flexibility, tolerance for intrusion, ability to put oneself aside.

2. Take a close look at how you ranked yourself. If you ranked yourself low (below a 6) on many of the items, it does not mean you are defective in some way but it does mean that you are lacking qualities necessary for parenthood. This ranking will give you a good idea of not only your overall penchant for parenthood, but will pinpoint the areas where you need work.

The Key Skills of Good Parenting

Other traits and abilities necessary in order to be a good parent include:

- The ability to emotionally bond with your child

- The ability to handle stress in a positive way

- The ability to find appropriate outlets for your negative emotions

- The ability to get your own needs met by the adults in your life instead of expecting your child to meet them

- Reasonable expectations of your child

- The ability to love your child unconditionally (to dislike his behavior but love the child)

- The willingness and ability to devote a great deal of time and energy taking care of your child's needs without taking your anger out on your child or inducing guilt in your child

- The ability to feel protective of your child

- The capability to allow your child the space and encouragement to grow into his or her own unique person

If you do not have many of these traits, you may choose to wait for parenthood until you have worked on yourself further. If you already have children, I would strongly suggest you work on obtaining these important traits.

Key Skills and Information You Should Know to Prevent Child Abuse

Immaturity and the absence of parenting preparation and skills, coupled with the lack of knowledge of child development and appropriate discipline techniques also contribute to the incidence of abuse. By making a point of learning these skills and information you will take a significant step toward preventing yourself from abusing your children. I have broken this information down into the following categories:

- Attachment

- Understanding child development

- Discipline

- Anger management

- Stress management

Attachment

According to the American Academy of Pediatrics (AAP), the attachment process that occurs during the first three to five years of life is the primary focus of early brain and child development. This is the critical period when the foundation is laid in the human psyche for trust, empathy, dependency, and optimism. It is the attachment to one consistent, warm, loving, and encouraging caregiver that also ensures the development of conscience.

By just nine months of age, babies have formed a specific attachment to one or more caregivers. Studies show that a child who does not experience this attachment process is at great risk of experiencing difficulty connecting with other people. According to many experts, including James Garbarino, the author of *Lost Boys: Why Our Sons Turn Violent and How We Can Save Them*, the majority of violent juveniles share this early childhood problem. The first years of their lives are marked with inconsistent care, abandonment, and parental absence.

Secure attachments early in life have long-lasting effects, not only on temperament and cognitive capacities but also on the degree of empathy they are capable of having. The degree of attachment is highly dependent upon the degree of parental acceptance or rejection of the child.

According to Ronald P. Rohner, Ph.D., the founder of the Center for the Study of Parental Acceptance and Rejection (CSPAR) at the University of Connecticut, "The extent to which children experience or fail to experience parental acceptance and rejection may have a greater influence on them than any other single experience. Parental acceptance and rejection have been shown in the United States and in cross-cultural research, to affect the emotional, behavioral, and social-cognitive development of children, as well as their psychological functioning and well-being as adults."

Understanding Child Development

Learning about child development helps parents be realistic about what to expect of children at different ages. In order to avoid becoming abusive and to be successful in teaching children positive nonviolent behaviors, adults need to take action based on what children are capable of understanding and doing at different ages and stages of development. Expecting behavior that is beyond a child's capacity leads to frustration and anger for both parents and children. Adults are less likely to become frustrated or anxious about their child's behavior when they understand child development because they will only ask children to do things they are capable of doing.

Adults are also more effective in teaching positive behaviors and in responding to children if they know how children of different ages might think and act. For example, if you understand that a two-year-old has a very short attention span, you will not expect him or her to stay seated quietly for a long church service.

The American Psychological Association (APA) and the National Association for the Education of Young Children (NAEYC) developed a brochure outlining important information, based on decades of research, about children's abilities and behaviors at various ages until age eight. Instead of taking up time and space here, I recommend you download the brochure by visiting the ACT (Adults and Children Together Against Violence) Web site at www.actagainstviolence.org.

Discipline

Discipline does not mean punishment. It actually means teaching children about what behavior will help them get along and be successful in the world. It is about changing behavior and developing self-control, not blaming or finding fault with the child who is not behaving.

Physical force should never be used to discipline a child. Physical discipline does not work and is experienced by the child as abuse. The exertion of force only serves to reinforce aggressive behavior on the part of children and adolescents. The only thing a beaten child learns is to fear its parents and that those more powerful have a right to dominate those who are weaker than themselves.

Results of a recent study found important links between parenting style and children's prosocial development. The results suggest that mothers who are overly strict and harshly punitive, who do not tend to reason or establish reasonable and consistent rules, and who strongly show their anger or disappointment in their children, are likely to impede their children's prosocial development. This relationship was true for both children with and without behavior problems. Conversely, children had greater concern for others when mothers were warm, used reasoning and set appropriate guidelines, and avoided the use of harsh punishments. One explanation for this pattern is that angry, authoritarian parenting could be interpreted by the children as a lack of care or concern on the part of their parents.

Prevention of bad behavior is the best tool a parent can use to discipline a child. The best ways to help your child behave are to:

- Reward good behavior. Parents often forget to compliment their child on a job well done.

- Ignore the little things. Concentrate on what you really want changed.

- Set a few simple, clear rules and reinforce them consistently. Children listen better when they have some input into the rule making.

- Redirect the behavior you do not like. Get the child interested in positive activities or change the setting so they don't get into trouble.

- Keep a positive attitude. Your sense of humor can go a long way in helping your child to be cooperative and positive.

- Set a good example for your child to follow. Children learn what they live.

- Get the child's attention. Say his name, touch him, and look him in the eye before you give him instructions.

- Spend time with your children. Kids need individual, personal attention from their parents.

It has been found that using positive consequence methods of discipline such as effective praise (praising a child when he or she behaves in positive ways) and offering special incentives (such as rewards for outstanding performance) work much better than negative feedback.

Effective praise works as follows:

1. Look at the child in the eyes.

2. Move close to the child physically.

3. Smile.

4. Say lots of nice things about the child such as, "My, you certainly have been working hard on your homework. I'm so proud of you. I'm sure you're doing a great job."

5. Praise the behavior, not the child.

6. Show physical affection (put your hand on his shoulder, gently touch his face, tousle his hair, give him a kiss).

To exhibit mild social disapproval:

- Look at the child

- Move closer physically

- Make a disapproving face or give a disapproving look.

- Make a brief statement about the behavior (not about the child).

- Use a calm and serious voice.

- Do not linger, show your disapproval and move on.

The point system works as follows:

- The child earns points for doing specific required tasks (putting toys away, brushing teeth, and putting cap back on toothpaste).

- Encourage child to make a chart (with or without your help) to keep track of points earned.

- Agree on reward for points earned (spend them on being able to go to a particular place, get a weekend off from chores, etc.).

Your techniques for disciplining your child will change as your child grows and matures.

Anger Management

If you wish to break the cycle of violence it is vitally important that you learn to manage your anger. Certainly you want to avoid becoming physically or emotionally abusive toward your children but there are other reasons as well. Children whose parents are aggressive are more likely to be aggressive and violent themselves in adolescence and young adulthood. As stated earlier, children who witness their parents frequently fighting or being physically abusive to one another are far more likely to become either victims or abusers themselves when they enter adult relationships.

The relationship between domestic violence and child abuse is well-known. For years, it has been generally accepted that if couples are engaged in domestic abuse, their kids are more likely to be abused than those whose parents don't hit each other. Experts differ on the reasons why. Some suggest that it is a learned behavior. If the father hits the mother, she is more likely to hit the children, or the father will extend his abuse to the child as well as his spouse. Others have suggested that the youngsters get blamed for the problems between the parents.

If you have a problem with anger, enroll in an anger management course or a parenting course, or seek counseling. The following stress reduction techniques will also help.

Stress Management

In chapters 8 and 9, I provided you some stress management techniques. It is vitally important that you learn and practice these techniques in order to manage the inevitable stress that comes with child rearing. Practicing stress reduction techniques will reduce the likelihood that you will blow up or lose it with your child. Highly stressed parents tend to assume that their children intentionally misbehave instead of being able to step back and see the broader picture.

When you find yourself losing your temper with your child, try some of the following techniques to calm yourself down.

- Focus on a word or image that will relax you. For example, say the word calm to yourself over and over. Visualize a scene that is relaxing to you (the ocean, the mountains).

- Get involved with a creative activity—especially one that involves using your hands.

- Learn and practice meditation or yoga.

- Practice deep breathing.

- Get a massage or give yourself a head and neck massage. (Gently massage your head by moving the flats of your fingers in small circles against the skin. Start with your scalp, then move to your ears, your face, your forehead, and temples. Continue the circular movements on the sides and back of your neck, and then on both shoulders. An alternative way to massage is to simply press your fingertips deeply into the skin.)

EXERCISE: *Reducing Your Stress through Relaxation and Visualization*

1. Lie down or sit in a comfortable chair. Relax and close your eyes. Begin to breathe deeply and evenly.

2. Deeply relax all your muscles, beginning at your feet and progressing up to your face, by first tensing them as hard as you can, and then letting go and relaxing them.

3. Now visualize a beautiful scene in nature, such as a brook or a meadow or whatever comes to mind. Immerse yourself in this scene. Notice all the details of the scenery and imagine you are actually there. Enjoy the beautiful world you have created.

Specific Strategies to Help You Avoid Becoming Abusive to Your Children

The following are some specific strategies to help you avoid abusing your children.

1. Have reasonable expectations of your children. In order to avoid becoming emotionally or physically abusive to your children it is important that you do not have unreasonable expectations of them. Expecting children to act in ways that are beyond their emotional or physical maturity, expecting children to never make mistakes, and demanding absolute obedience are primary examples of unreasonable expectations that parents can have.

2. Practice alternative discipline and problem solving strategies in order to make discipline decisions less reactive and harsh. Those parents who do not have these skills readily available to them tend to resort to spanking or even harsher forms of punishment.

3. State clear family rules and reasons for expected behaviors. This includes "dos" and "don'ts"—for example, what are respectful behaviors and what are disrespectful behaviors. Make sure your child is clear what the rules and expectations are and be consistent about them.

4. Learn from your parents' mistakes. Let your parents' mistakes be a constant reminder of how *not* to be.

EXERCISE: *Avoiding Your Parents' Mistakes*

- Make a list of your parents' mistakes/behaviors that you don't want to repeat with your children.

- Create a plan for how you are going to accomplish this.

- Notice any resistance/negative beliefs you have that might prevent you from accomplishing your plan. Make a list of these negative, limiting beliefs.

- Challenge these old negative beliefs by creating new ones that will empower you toward your goal. List the positive steps you've already taken toward your goal—your accomplishments.

- Don't expect perfection. Learn from your mistakes instead of allowing them to sabotage your progress.

The general information you have read thus far applies to the prevention of all forms of child abuse. In the following section we'll focus on preventing specific types of abuse.

How to Avoid Emotionally Abusing Your Child

If you were emotionally abused as a child it is going to be extremely difficult for you to avoid repeating the kind of behavior that you experienced. For this reason, it is crucially important that you identify the types of emotional abuse you experienced and that you be on the lookout for them in yourself. For example, if one or both of your parents were extremely critical or demanding of you, you will have a tendency to be the same way with your children. The same is true if your parents were emotionally distant or emotionally smothering.

EXERCISE: *The Types of Emotional Abuse You Experienced*

- Make a list of the types of emotional abuse you experienced (verbal abuse, emotional distancing, extreme criticism).

- Spend some time thinking about the way you treat your children. If you are completely honest, have you noticed some of these same tendencies in yourself?

The following questionnaire will help you decide.

QUESTIONNAIRE: *Have You Been Guilty of Emotional Abuse?*

1. Have you ever called your child demeaning names like stupid or loser or lazy?

2. Have you ever sworn at your child or called your child a swear name?

3. Have you ever made fun of your child's looks, intelligence, or other characteristics that he or she feels particularly sensitive about?

4. Have you ever threatened to kick your child out of the house or send him away (to live with a relative, a boarding school, or foster care)?

5. Have you ever threatened to hit or spank your child but didn't do it?

6. Have you ever threatened to hurt your child's pet but didn't do it?

7. Have you ever blamed your child for an adult's drinking or mental health problem or blamed her for marital or family problems?

8. Have you ever ignored your child's request for help when she was crying, hurt, or frightened?

9. Have you ever failed to show your child needed/desired affection (hugs, kisses, holding)?

10. Do you sometimes make no attempt to monitor your child's whereabouts?

11. Do you feel you have demonstrated little or no interest in or love for your child?

12. Have you ever used extreme or humiliating forms of punishment (e.g., making her wear a sign reading "slut" or shaving his head).

13. Have you ever made fun of your child's feelings about something of importance to him or her?

14. Have you ever deliberately tried to terrify your child?

15. Have you ever threatened to withdraw love from your child?

16. Have you ever placed your child in a position where he or she had to play a parental role?

If you are guilty of some or many of these types of behavior, you need to seek professional counseling in order to work through your own abuse experiences.

How to Avoid Physically Abusing Your Children

If you were physically abused as a child or if you are a battered spouse, the most important things you must do to avoid physically abusing your children are:

1. Determine that you will never use any form of physical discipline on your children. It has been proven that physical discipline such as spanking or beating does not work, so there is no reason for you to use this form of discipline other than as an unconscious way of reenacting your own abuse. Although your conscious intention may be to simply teach your child a lesson, your anger at having been physically abused yourself can take over at any time and trigger a deep rage inside of you, a rage that can cause you to seriously injure your child—both physically and emotionally.

2. Develop alternative ways of disciplining your children that are fair and consistent. Treat each child equally and never discipline a child when you are angry.

3. Find constructive ways of releasing your anger.

4. Practice stress reduction techniques to help you stay calm around your children.

5. Make it a practice of taking time-outs when you are feeling out of control or highly emotional because you are overstressed or because you have been reminded of your own past trauma. This includes letting someone else take care of your children until you are certain they can be safe around you.

6. Do not be ashamed of needing time away from your children in order to cool off. Remind yourself that it is the best thing you can do for them under the circumstances and that when you return you will be in a better position to give them what they need.

How to Avoid Sexually Abusing Your Own or Other People's Children

Many of you who were sexually abused as a child are no doubt afraid that you might continue the cycle of abuse by doing to your child what was done to you. Others of you may be horrified that I would even suggest that you would do such a thing. Even if you have no fears in this area, you need to read this section because no one who has been sexually abused themselves is immune. The shame surrounding child sexual abuse—both the shame that you no doubt carry and the shame the perpetrator projected onto you—can sometimes overwhelm you to the point that you feel compelled to reenact your own abuse. These feelings can be triggered by other incidents in which you feel shamed, such as when you feel rejected or ridiculed or when you are chastised for making a mistake.

Having close physical contact with a child, especially with your own child, can cause memories of your own childhood and your own abuse to come flooding back. In those moments you won't be exactly clear about what is the present and what is the past. Everything may become very hazy, and you may have intense feelings that you do not know what to do with. You may suddenly feel like a child again, or you may not be able to distinguish between your own feelings and that of your child. Clients have described themselves feeling dizzy, disoriented, and having trouble breathing. Some experience something that can only be likened to a drug-induced hallucination. For example, several parents I worked with who molested their children became convinced that their child wanted them to touch him or her in a certain way and they were convinced that to do so would bring their child pleasure. Even though on some level they knew that this kind of touching was inappropriate, in that moment it was as if they were hypnotized, unable to use their logical mind but instead were compelled to continue.

These kinds of feelings can be very intense and very overwhelming. Don't fool yourself. Even the most determined person can have difficulty resisting such powerful urges. That is why it is so important that you continue to work on your recovery. It takes a lot more than integrity or will power to resist such powerful forces. It takes the support of a therapist or the support of others who have also been molested. It takes continual work on ridding yourself of the shame you took on, the overwhelming pain you felt and the rage that you experienced about being violated and betrayed.

If you were sexually abused you need to receive specialized therapy for survivors of child sexual abuse. Otherwise you are at risk of either sexually abusing your own children or bringing a child molester into your children's lives. If you don't get the help you need your own denial may prevent you from seeing the evidence that your child is being abused—even if it is happening right under your nose. Your denial will cause you to disbelieve your children if they tell you they are being abused. And if your child is abused you won't be able to offer the kind of support he or she needs because you will be so caught up in your own pain.

What If It Is Too Late?

For those who have already begun to abuse their children it is important to realize that it is never too late to change. In the next chapter I provide specific strategies that abusive parents can use to short-circuit their abusive tendencies. By apologizing to your children for the way you have treated them in the past you will be helping your children to heal. By making it clear to your children that it is your problem, not your children's, you will help remove the shame attached to child abuse and help raise your children's self-esteem.

Protect Your Children from Others

In addition to avoiding becoming abusive toward your children you also need to protect your children from the abuse of others. This includes being careful about the people you bring into your children's lives. Those who were abused as children tend to be attracted to romantic partners who either abuse them or their children. Research shows that female survivors of child sexual abuse often become involved with men who molest their children. David Finkelhor, in his book *Child Sexual Abuse,* found that stepfathers were five times more likely to sexually victimize a daughter than was a natural father. In fact, child molesters often become involved with a woman in order to have easy access to her children. Diana Russell found that one out of six women who had a stepfather was sexually abused by him.

By following the suggestions in the previous chapter—especially by going slowly in your romantic relationships and being on the lookout for abusive behavior—and listening to and believing your child you can protect your children from the fate you experienced. Refer to the recommended reading list in the back of this book for further help in this area.

You also need to protect your children from other children. Children who have been abused tend to act out their anger and shame with other children. Children who have been sexually abused tend to pass on the abuse to other kids. Sibling abuse is one of the most damaging forms of child abuse. Here are some suggestions that will help you protect your children:

1. Do not leave your children alone to play with other kids without checking on them periodically. This is especially true of very young children.

2. If your child complains to you that another child, including a sibling, is physically hurting him, do not pass it off as rough-housing or child's play. This is especially true if your child tends to be passive and the other child tends to be aggressive or hostile.

3. If you know that another child has been or is being physically or sexually abused, do not leave your child alone with this child. While your heart may go out to the child, do not expose your child to the possibility that the abused child will pass on the abuse to your child.

4. Do not expect your older child to babysit for a younger one. Older children usually resent this and can take out their anger on their younger sibling.

5. If your child is acting aggressively with other children, get him the help he needs.

CHAPTER 11

If You Have Already Become Abusive

Our greatest glory consists, not in never falling,
but in rising every time we fall.

OLIVER GOLDSMITH

If you've already become abusive to your partner, your children, or to others in your life it doesn't mean that there is no hope. Although it certainly would have been better if you would have been able to begin your changes before you became abusive, it is never too late to change. By following the steps outlined in this chapter you can still have a chance to turn things around and to be the one to break the cycle in your family.

Step 1: Admit the Truth

If there is any hope for real change you will need to admit to yourself and to others that you have become abusive. No one wants to have to face the fact that he or she has lost control to such an extent that he or she has become abusive. And certainly no one wants to have to face the fact that his or her actions and/or words have caused those they love emotional or physical damage. It would be much easier to continue to justify or rationalize your behavior by telling yourself that your partner forced you into becoming abusive or that your children deserved the way you treated them. But if you have abused your partner or your children, the only way you are going to save them from further harm, save the relationship, and save yourself is to stop making excuses and admit the truth.

Those who admit they are responsible for abusing their partners or their children, who realize that they did something wrong and want to change, have the best chance of successfully turning their lives around.

Step 2: Seek Help

If you have already become abusive you need more help than this book can provide. You need the help of a professional therapist, a batterer's treatment program, an anger management program, or a program to help abusive parents. The fact that you are reading this book attests to the fact that you are committed to change, but you can't do it all alone. If it was just a matter of the desire to change and having discipline there wouldn't be the epidemic of child abuse and spousal abuse that we have today. You can have all the motivation possible and an iron will and still lose control and become abusive. Those professionals who specialize in working with child abuse and domestic violence can offer you the missing keys necessary to break the cycle.

If You Have Physically Abused Your Child

If you have physically abused your child I strongly urge you to seek individual psychotherapy. You need the support and knowledge of a trained professional to help you work through your issues from childhood. If you cannot afford psychotherapy I suggest you find a Parents Anonymous group in your area. Parents who have abused their children meet together in a group setting with trained therapists free of charge. There are also groups available for your children while you are at your meeting. To find a group in your area go online to www.parentsanonymous.org or look up Parents Anonymous in your local phone directory.

If You Have Physically Abused Your Partner

There are many programs available to help men and women prevent the recurrence of domestic violence, including groups for abusers. The group setting allows participants to see that they are not alone, that other people have suffered from similar fear, confusion, and lack of comfort in their intimate relationships. Although participants are always required to take responsibility for their actions, they are also recognized as human beings who have potential to change if they are committed to doing so. They are helped to heal and learn how to deal with anger in healthy ways and have healthy relationships based on equality and respect.

Groups for battering men seek to counter the fact that many men are taught that violence is an acceptable, manly response to anger.

Many boys are taught they must act like a man, which means being tough, domineering, and in control. They are expected to fight to solve problems. Many men's groups discuss these roles and expectations and the effect they have on men. Most batterer programs are open to any man who seeks to enroll. Most are either free of charge or charge on a sliding scale, according to income. Some of the leading men's programs in the country are listed in the resources section.

If you do not wish to go to group, private therapy is also available. Low-cost counseling is offered by many community health organizations, churches, and other sources. State domestic violence coalitions and local organizations can provide referrals.

The earlier you seek treatment, the better chance you have of changing your behavior. But you must be patient. Domestic violence is a learned behavior that took you years to learn—most likely from spending years in a violent home where your father (or mother) controlled other family members through intimidation and abuse. Not surprisingly, it can take time to unlearn such ingrained behavior and replace it with positive relationship skills. Many people are asked to commit to a six-month counseling program but for many, it takes up to two years.

Many batterer programs cover subjects such as developing better communication and coping skills, building self-esteem, stress management, setting boundaries, anger management, and parenting skills— many of the topics we have covered in this book. If you have a substance abuse problem you need to seek treatment for this in addition to treating your violence problem. Some programs are beginning to use peer sponsorship, similar to that used by Alcoholics Anonymous.

Step 3: Work on Repairing the Harm

The third step is for you to begin to repair the harm you have caused to your children, your partner, or others. This will be important for several reasons:

- It will help those you have neglected or abused to stop blaming themselves and to begin to heal.

- It will provide an opportunity for those who have been harmed to vent their anger directly toward you instead of reenacting the abuse with innocent people.

- It will make it clear to children (and some adults) exactly what is appropriate and what is not appropriate behavior.

- It will help remove the shame you feel about your actions. You need to take responsibility but overwhelming shame can cause you to re-abuse.

The process of repairing harm will include the following steps:

1. Acknowledge the harm. Go to those you have harmed and admit what you have done to hurt them. It is important that you tell those you have harmed that they have a right to their anger and that you encourage them to voice their anger directly to you. Make certain, however, that you do not allow anyone to verbally abuse you or to shame you.

2. Apologize for your actions or inaction. You must feel and express genuine regret for what you did, show empathy for those you harmed, and take complete responsibility for your actions. This means you make no excuses and that you don't blame anyone else. For more information on how to give a meaningful apology, refer to my book *The Power of Apology*.

3. Make amends. Making amends may include paying for any damage you may have caused or paying for therapy for those you have harmed.

4. Make a commitment to change. Make a verbal commitment to not repeat your damaging behavior backed up by a plan of action. Words alone aren't enough. Show that you mean business by entering therapy or enrolling in a treatment program.

Sometimes repairing the harm involves helping those we have abused or neglected to get the help they need. Most victims of abuse need professional help in order to heal from the damage caused by betrayal and damage to their self-esteem. This may also include confronting your adult children about their abusive or neglectful behavior toward their partner or their children. As my client Pamela shared with me at our first session, "I see how I've damaged my own kids and now I'm seeing how they are passing it on. I want to know how I can help them without shaming them or making them defensive."

Step 4: Create a Plan of Action

Part of your commitment to change is to develop a specific plan as to how you will avoid repeating your past abusive or neglectful behaviors. For example, your plan of action may include: (1) entering therapy or a treatment program; (2) asking others to call you on negative or damaging behavior; (3) recognizing signs that you may be about to repeat damaging behavior; and (4) finding ways to take time-outs in order to avoid abusive actions.

Wendy's Plan

My client Wendy came to realize that she had become very much like her controlling mother. Although her intentions were good, her fear of her boys getting hurt or failing in life compelled her to be too protective and demanding of them. Her oldest son rebelled against her tendency to be controlling by constantly arguing with her and eventually running away from home. Her youngest son withdrew and started failing in school. Through therapy Wendy was able to work on her issues with her mother—including being able to vent her anger. This helped her to realize that much of the anger she expressed toward her sons was actually misdirected anger toward her mother. She also faced the truth about how much she was damaging her sons and decided she was going to work toward repairing the harm. Together we created a plan of action that included:

1. Acknowledging to her sons that she had a problem.

2. Apologizing to them for being controlling and verbally abusive.

3. Promising to be less controlling and to stop criticizing them.

4. Inviting her oldest son back into the home with new ground rules.

5. Becoming less rigid and more flexible (i.e., allowing them to stay out later at night, not insisting that the boys keep their rooms clean at all times).

6. Taking responsibility for her triggers and not projecting onto her sons (i.e., realizing that just because her sons were wasting time by watching TV, it didn't mean they were going to fail in life).

Six months after her oldest son's return the climate in the household had turned from constant upheaval and chaos to one of harmony and calmness. "I can't believe it, my sons actually invite their friends over now," Wendy recently shared with me.

Her oldest son is less abrasive toward her and much more respectful. In the past he would walk out of a room when she entered. "Now we can actually sit down together and watch TV. That would have never happened in the past."

Her younger son is doing better in school now that she isn't constantly on him about his homework. "I couldn't trust my boys to do the right thing because my mother never trusted me," Wendy explained. "Now I give my boys healthy boundaries but I'm not always breathing down their neck and expecting them to fail."

Step 5: Continue to Work on Your Anger and Your Aggression

If you have become physically or emotionally abusive to either your children or your partner you have a problem with your anger. The truth is, your problem is not that you *get* angry, it is that you *are* angry. Unless you discover the root cause of your anger you will not be able to let go of your abusive tendencies. Unless you learn to control your anger you will continue to hurt others.

You also need to own your anger. You probably get angry a lot and hang onto your angry feelings too long because you believe that the solution to your anger lies outside of yourself and is caused by the actions of others. You probably believe that if other people would only act differently you wouldn't get angry. But the cause of your anger is not outside yourself. Instead of blaming other people for making you angry, you need to begin to focus on your own emotional response. You must stop getting stuck in the if onlys—If only your wife had picked up the cleaning like you asked, if only your employee had done the job right—you wouldn't have gotten so angry. The cause of your anger doesn't lie in the actions of others. It lies within you—in your own biological and psychological makeup and reactions. Instead of focusing on what others are doing that makes you angry you should be focusing on why you get angry at what others are doing.

You will never eliminate unhealthy anger from your life until you stop trying to change how other people treat you instead of focusing on changing your own behavior. As long as you externalize your anger—that is, viewing the cause of your anger as outside yourself—you will remain irritated, upset, and stressed. As long as you continue to believe that the reason you are so often angry is because other people are inappropriate, disrespectful, or incompetent, you will continue to have problems with your anger. Forget how others are treating you. Focus instead on what is happening inside of you.

Step 6: Work on Your Unfinished Business from the Past

In order for you to change your abusive pattern you will also need to continue to work on your unfinished business. The following is a brief overview of what completing your unfinished business will entail:

1. Acknowledge the anger, pain, fear, and shame that you feel as a result of the neglect or abuse you experienced as a child. Those who become aggressive or abusive as a way of coping are particularly prone to becoming desensitized to their feelings. For this reason it may be difficult for you to recapture these lost feelings and make them your own. But if you are to recover from your childhood and put an end to your aggressive behavior this is exactly what you must do.

2. The first emotion you need to access is your anger. Whereas you may have no difficulty becoming enraged with those who are in your life today, your anger toward your original abuser or abusers may be buried deep inside you. Fortunately, you can use your current anger to help you access your repressed and suppressed anger. Although you may not associate your tendency to be angry with what happened to you as a child, you will need to work on making these all-important connections.

EXERCISE: *Making the Connection*

The next time you become overly aggressive with your partner, child, or friend think of a time when one or both of your parents (or other caretakers) treated you in a similar way.

• How do you feel when you remember this incident? Angry? Ashamed? Afraid?

- Write in your journal about the emotions that you are feeling now and the feelings that you felt as a child. Don't hold back— let it all out—all the rage, all the shame, all the fear.

3. After you have acknowledged your anger about what was done or not done to you as a child, you will need to realize that underneath your anger lies pain. This may be even more difficult than getting in touch with your anger. You have probably built up a wall to protect yourself from these more vulnerable feelings and it will take safety and patience to bring these walls down. This may mean that you will need to seek the help of a trained professional therapist who will work with you to bring down the walls in a safe, supportive environment. Find safe, constructive ways to release your anger and pain concerning your childhood neglect or abuse. Writing in your journal is a very effective tool, as is expressing your emotions through poetry, painting, collage, or sculpting.

4. Confront your abuser or abusers with your anger. Refer to chapter 15 for information on how to go about doing this.

5. Resolve your relationships with your abusers in some way. This may involve forgiveness, reconciliation, or temporary separation. We'll discuss this further in chapters 15 and 16.

If You Have Already Sexually Abused Someone

If you have already sexually abused a child you need to immediately take the following actions:

1. Report the abuse to your local child protection agency, your doctor, or a therapist. This is the best thing to do for all concerned: the child, yourself, and, if it was a family member, your family. Research and legal records prove that offenders rarely stop on their own. In fact, many report feeling relieved when they are caught. Making the report yourself will show authorities that you really care about your child and that you want help to stop your urges. The degree of risk of additional abuse to the child is of first concern to the authorities. In some cases, the offender or the entire family may be required to

attend a treatment program, in other cases, the offender may face criminal charges. Doing jail time can actually be beneficial for the victim as well as the offender because in this way both feel that there have been consequences for the crime (and Fthe child will likely feel safer knowing you won't be able to get to them again).

You need professional assistance to help you find ways to resist your urges to molest children. Long-term therapy will help you work through your shame and anger and pain concerning your own experiences of sexual and other forms of abuse. You did not do this act because you are a bad person, you did it because you are out of control. You did it because you are overwhelmed with shame and rage and pain and fear. You owe it to the children you are around and to yourself to get the help you need. If you aren't prepared to turn yourself in to the authorities, at least seek professional help. If you aren't ready to seek professional help, at least contact an organization called Parents United, a nonprofit organization dedicated to breaking the cycle of sexually abusing children. It has more than ninety chapters throughout the United States, Canada, and Mexico and offers group therapy for each family member, led by professionally trained therapists. For more information, see the resources list at the back of the book.

2. If you can't turn yourself in, get as far away from your victim as you possibly can. You must protect this child from your impulses and right now you cannot trust yourself. This child needs to be safe and that means she or he needs to be away from you. If it is your own child this will mean you will need to leave the home and have no unsupervised contact with your child. If you can't tell your spouse why you need to leave, make up some excuse, but by all means, get out of there. You are not a monster, you are a person who was unable to control his or her urge to molest your child. But if you willingly continue to expose your child to your urges then you are a selfish, self-absorbed individual who deserves to be locked up.

If you are in a position of authority over children or have a job where you are frequently exposed to children, you need to ask for a leave of absence or quit your job. You cannot trust your impulses and this is not about will power. You simply cannot continue to be exposed to children. If you care about these children the way you say you do, protect them from yourself.

3. Get help for the child you molested. You were no doubt molested yourself as a child so you know first hand how much sexual abuse damages a child. The child you molested needs professional help immediately. If it is your child you molested put your own needs aside and get her or him into therapy immediately. Yes, you risk being arrested and possibly being put into jail, but aren't your child's needs more important? Coming forward and getting your child the help he or she needs will show the authorities that you care about your child and are serious about getting better. It may make the difference between keeping your family together and tearing it apart if you continue to deny and hide from the truth. When children who were abused by a parent are asked what the worst part of their sexual abuse was they say it was losing a parent. They want them to take responsibility, get help and come home. According to Parents United, approximately 30 percent to 50 percent of families want to reunite and ninety percent of families that reunite stay together.

4. If the child told someone that you molested her or him, admit the truth. Back up the child's story instead of making things worse by confusing the child and saying it didn't happen, or worse yet, calling the child a liar.

5. Take complete responsibility for what happened. It doesn't matter whether you were drinking or sober—you are still responsible for your actions. Children do not want to have sex with adults. Even so-called seductive teenagers are not mature enough to make a responsible decision. You are the adult; you are responsible for what happened and you are responsible for stopping it.

CHAPTER 12

If You Have Already Been Abused or Established a Victim Pattern

*If you have made a mistake . . . there is always another chance for
you. . . . You may have a fresh start any moment you choose, for this
thing we call "failure" is not the falling down, but the staying down.*

MARY PICKFORD

If you have been either emotionally or physically abused by a partner
or have already established a pattern of victimization it is important to
know that there is hope and that there is help available. This chapter
will point you in the right direction in terms of what you need to focus
on and in terms of seeking further help. It will also offer you strategies and exercises that will help empower you and give you the
courage and strength to make the changes that will be necessary to
break out of your victim pattern.

If You Have Been Physically Abused

If you have been physically assaulted by your partner you need outside help. Even if he or she has only hit you once, statistics show us
that the probability is extremely high that he or she will do so again,
and that next time it will be worse. Don't fool yourself into thinking
that just because he or she is sorry and promises to never do it again
that you are safe. Women who have been hit once are particularly at
risk. Women die by the thousands every year at the hands of men who
have promised to never hit them again.

Even if you are not ready to leave your relationship at this time,
reach out for help. Many shelters offer battered women's support
groups and you don't have to be living in the shelter to qualify. Some
shelters are now offering help to battered men. There are also groups

212

available through private and public counseling programs such as community mental health providers, churches, and hospitals. Some of the groups are formally structured and led by professionals, while others use trained interns or volunteers.

Individual therapy can also be very beneficial if you can afford it. Just don't allow a therapist to do what is commonly referred to as blaming the victim by insinuating that you somehow asked to be abused or that you are a masochist. It is best to look for someone who specializes in working with abuse victims. Individual psychotherapy can be especially beneficial to those who have a history of abuse. It can help you to raise your self-esteem, deal with the tapes inside your head telling you that you are weak, not good enough, that you need to please others first and that you deserve to be treated poorly. It can help you to replace these negative learned thought patterns with more positive ones and offer you the nurturing and positive regard you may have never received from your parents.

Don't Pretend It Isn't Affecting Your Children

Growing up in an atmosphere of domestic violence does tremendous harm to children. As discussed earlier, research strongly suggests that children (especially boys) who witness violence frequently are more likely to adopt violent behaviors. The vast majority of children whose mothers were abused actually witness violence and its aftermath in their family, in contrast to many parents' estimates that they have protected their children from the experience. Children witness abuse in many ways, including screams, threats, or glass breaking, or seeing the aftermath of the abuse (bruises, black eyes). Children who witness their mother's victimization suffer from both short-term and long-term adjustment problems. According to the Bureau of Justice Statistics: Executive Summary (1996), subtle symptoms of children who witness violence include the following:

- They learn that violence is an acceptable way to resolve interpersonal conflict.

- They learn various rationalizations for the use of violence in order to maintain power and control in relationships.

- They feel some degree of responsibility for the violence.

- They may have conflicts and skill deficits regarding how to handle emergencies.

According to a report by the National Center for Education Statistics (1994) children are often the unintended victims of battering. The risk of child abuse is significantly higher when partner assault has taken place. Nearly half of men who abuse their female partners also abuse their children. Children in violent homes face dual threats—the threat of witnessing traumatic events and the threat of physical assault. Additionally, this report found that children who are abused might:

- Be injured during an incident of parental violence

- Be traumatized by the fear from their parent or guardian or helplessness in protecting their parent or guardian

- Blame themselves for not preventing the violence or for causing it

- Be abused or neglected themselves

In another study, Cellini (1995), one-third of the families reporting a violent incident between the parents also reported the presence of child abuse. Also found in this study was that women being battered are less able to care for their children. Eight times as many women report using physical discipline on their children while living with their batterers than those who live alone or with a nonbattering partner. Recent research also shows that men who batter their wives may also sexually abuse their daughters.

If you aren't ready to leave the relationship, talk to your children. They probably already know what is going on—children are smarter than you think. Make sure they understand that the violence is not their fault.

Recognize That You Have Choices

People who are being physically abused often feel they have no choices. But there are always some options available, even if you are not currently aware of them. The following is a list of options experts in the field suggest considering. Not all these choices may be right for you and not all may be available to you but at least some are worth considering. While some people escape all at once, others need time to plan. Advance planning can make leaving both easier and safer.

The idea of changing your whole life—moving to a new area, finding another place to live, finding a way to support yourself and your children—can be overwhelming. Add the psychological damage, terror, and uncertainty that come from constantly living in a dangerous setting and the situation can be almost paralyzing. Yet you can accomplish a great deal by taking small steps toward freedom. The following list includes recommendations from the National Coalition Against Domestic Violence, *The Domestic Violence Sourcebook* by Dawn Bradley Berry, and other sources.

1. Get information. Books on domestic violence are recommended in the back of this book. Learn about your situation and what options you have. Gather up the telephone numbers of all the people and agencies you can call upon for help in an emergency and afterward: hotlines, the police, shelters, friends, the sheriff, the YWCA, the Salvation Army, state and local domestic violence coalitions, and general crisis or self-help lines.

2. Call the local crisis line, hotline, or shelter for help and information. Even if you don't want to leave the relationship now, even if you truly believe it will never happen again, it is important to find out what services are available in your community. Ask about crisis accommodations for you, your children, and even your pets. Be aware that shelters often provide counseling, group sessions, and referrals to women not living in the shelter as well.

3. Pack a bag with emergency supplies (a change of clothing for yourself and your children, a toothbrush, some cash, canned and nonperishable food, and telephone numbers of friends, the local shelter, and taxis). Leave the bag at the home of a trusted friend or family member who lives nearby. If you have no one you can trust completely, consider a locker at a bus or train station or the airport.

4. Talk to a legal adviser. Find out about restraining orders, divorce, and other legal concerns. Many communities have legal advocates, lawyer hotlines, or legal aid groups that can provide free advice and referrals to lawyers.

5. Many professionals recommend self-defense training to help you build self-reliance and emotional strength. Don't rely on such training alone to make you safe, however. Many women can still be overpowered by an enraged man and can even end up being more seriously injured if they try to fight back. Note that most authorities warn against bringing weapons into the house because far too often they are used against the victim or end up in the hands of children.

6. Get important documents together, such as birth certificates for you and your children, insurance papers, passports, social security cards, school records, investment records, titles to your car or other property, savings account books, tax returns, and medical records. If you are worried that moving or removing these things will cause suspicion, make photocopies.

7. Start putting as much money aside as you can. Save money out of the grocery fund or any separate funds you receive. Get a credit card in your own name and have the statements sent to your workplace or to a friend's address. Make sure you keep enough money with you to pay for a cab to a safe place or for a few nights at a hotel.

8. Learn the signs of impending violence. Work on sharpening your observation skills by noticing changes in his behavior before he goes into a violent rage—his tone of voice, what he says, his habits, his behavior toward you and the children. Pay particular attention to whether these changes take place weeks or merely hours or minutes before the violence.

9. When you see the signs coming, or preferably before, get out. Go to a trusted friend's or relative's house. Be careful not to go back too soon—he may be hanging on to the rage until you return. Stay away until you can be sure the rage is spent. Use a third party to speak to your partner periodically so you can avoid being talked into returning too soon.

10. If the rage builds up at night, plan to have a reason to go outside. Start to do the laundry, walk the dog or throw out the garbage at night. If need be, once outside the door, just keep going. Get in the car and drive away as quickly and quietly as possible. If you don't have a car, get a bicycle or go on foot.

11. If you have children make sure you take them. They are probably terrified of the current or coming violence and they will
be less frightened at getting up and being rushed away from a
threatening person than finding out in the morning that you
have disappeared without saying goodbye. Even if the abuser
has never battered the children, you can't be sure he won't
start now, especially when he discovers you have left the
house.

12. Begin thinking about what it will be like to live indepen-
dently. If you are employed, consider whether or not you
want to change jobs. If you are unemployed, think about what
kind of work you are qualified to do. Acquire new job skills
or look into job training programs or classes in your community. Teach yourself to use a computer, learn about community college courses.

EXERCISE: *Reasons for Leaving*

The following exercise will help you stay focused even when you
become confused or overwhelmed with doubts and fears about
whether you will have the courage and strength to actually leave
your abuser.

• Write about the worst experience of violence you can remember. Include all the details—the terror you felt at the time, the
physical damage he or she caused you.

• Make a list of all the reasons why you want and need to leave.
Include the effect it is having on your children, your fear about
the violence getting worse, and so on.

If You Are Currently Being Emotionally Abused

If you are currently being emotionally abused your first step is to
admit to yourself just how much damage your partner's behavior has
caused you. One of the best ways to accomplish this is to put it down
on paper; writing tends to make things more real and harder to deny
later on.

Exercise: *Your Abuse Journal*

1. Write down every incident of emotional abuse that you can remember. Take whatever time is necessary, but write down all the details, including what abusive tactic your partner used and how it made you feel. If there has been a great deal of abuse and you have been with your partner for a long time, this may take quite some time. *But every hour that you spend writing about your experiences is an hour of healing.* You need to face what has happened to you, and you need to allow yourself to feel all the emotions you've suppressed and repressed. Of course, you won't be able to remember every single incident, but try to recall the major incidents and the feelings you had because of them.

2. Review what you have written and using your feelings as your guide, make a list of all the ways the abuse has damaged you (i.e., lowered your self-esteem, caused you to doubt your perceptions, made you feel stupid).

Once you have begun to come out of denial about how much damage you are experiencing in your relationship you will need to ask yourself what you are willing to do to stop the abuse. Are you willing and able to confront your partner about his or her abusive behavior? Are you willing and able to establish clearer boundaries with your partner? If you are not able to do either of these things are you willing to end a relationship that is clearly a destructive one to you and your children?

If you are confused as to what emotional abuse looks like in adult relationships, refer to my books *The Emotionally Abusive Relationship* or *The Emotionally Abused Woman*. These books will also offer you help in how to confront abusive behavior and how to leave an abusive relationship.

Resist Your Tendency to Blame Yourself

You have allowed emotional abuse to take place because you were raised with certain beliefs, because you were neglected or abused as a child, and because you have fears that prevent you from standing up for yourself. This does not mean that you want to be abused or that you deserve to be abused. The abuse is not your fault. Neither is the way you have learned to respond to abusive behavior. Nor are you alone. There are many, many people, men as well as women, who are in abusive relationships. All experience similar reactions to the abuse. Understanding these common reactions will help you to stop blaming yourself for the abuse.

During abuse, victims tend to dissociate emotionally with a sense of disbelief that the incident is actually occurring. This is followed by the typical posttraumatic response of numbing and constriction, resulting in inactivity, depression, self-blame, and feelings of helplessness. Lenore Walker, author of *The Battered Woman,* describes the process as follows: tension gradually builds (phase one), an explosive battering incident occurs (phase two), and a calm, loving respite follows (phase three). The violence allows intense emotional engagement and restores the fantasy of fusion and symbiosis. Hence, there are two powerful sources of reinforcement: the arousal-jag or excitement before the violence and the peace of surrender afterwards. Both of these responses, placed at appropriate intervals, reinforce the traumatic bond between victim and abuser.

Begin to Stand Up for Yourself

Those who were victimized as a child tend to suffer from learned helplessness, which we discussed in chapter 3. Learned helplessness is the belief that you cannot control the outcome of any situation through your own actions. Those with this mind-set believe that nothing can be gained by standing up for one's rights or protecting oneself from harm. Therefore, even though you may feel angry about the way someone is treating you, if you have this mind-set you might think to yourself, "What good will it do to tell him how I feel? It won't change anything."

There is also a strong likelihood that the reason why you have difficulty standing up for yourself is that you are afraid. In order for you to begin to overcome this fear it is important to understand the specific reasons for it. These include:

The fear of retaliation. This is a very real fear if you were punished when you were a child every time you got angry or if you have been abused as an adult when you stood up to your partner.

The fear of rejection. This is also a very real fear for those who have experienced rejection when they dared stand up for themselves.

The fear of hurting another person. This fear is especially strong in those who have had the experience of hurting someone when they stood up for themselves.

The fear of becoming like those who abused you. If you were emotionally, physically, or sexually abused as a child or adolescent your primary reason for not standing up for yourself or getting angry with those who mistreat you may be your fear that you will become an abuser yourself. This is a very real concern. But if you fear continuing the cycle of abuse there is even more reason for you to begin to communicate openly about your angry feelings. If you continue to hold in your anger it is likely that you may one day explode in a rage. And it is very likely that you are already taking your anger out on your loved ones in a negative way (belittling or berating, punishing with silence, unreasonable expectations). Your old anger toward your original abusers needs to be released in constructive ways and your current anger needs to be spoken. Then you can be assured that you will not become like those who abused you.

The fear of losing control. To you, expressing or communicating your anger may seem like you are losing control. You may be afraid that once you begin to express your anger you will go crazy and hurt others or yourself. Ironically, it is usually the person who represses his or her anger who is most likely to become destructive or to have rage erupt in inappropriate ways and at inappropriate times. You will not go crazy if you allow yourself to feel and express your anger. If you learn to consistently allow yourself to express your anger instead of holding it in you will find that you will actually feel more in control of your emotions and yourself, not less.

The fear of becoming irrational. Far from making you irrational, anger can often cause you to think and see things more clearly. It can also empower you to make needed changes in your life. This is especially true if you don't allow your anger to build up to the point where you lose it and begin to yell, act irrationally, or lash out at someone.

PART FOUR

Long-Term Strategies to Help You Break the Cycle

CHAPTER 13

Emotionally Separating
from Your Parents

*Real development is not leaving things behind, as on a road,
but drawing life from them, as from a root.*

G. K. CHESTERTON

One of the primary reasons many people repeat the cycle of abuse and
neglect is that they have not completed the individuation process.
Individuation is the act of becoming a separate person from one's parents and one's family. Those who have a history of neglect or abuse
tend to remain enmeshed with their family of origin out of the desperate desire to get what they did not get when they were children. In
order to break out of this enmeshment you need to accept that you
have to grow up, even if you don't feel equipped to do so.

Even though you may have worked hard to be different from your
parents, even though you may have been on your own for quite some
time, it doesn't mean that you have completed the individuation
process. This takes more than just getting older. It takes emotional
maturity and conscious effort on your part.

In healthy families, emotional separation takes place naturally and
gradually, accelerating as we reach our teens. Adolescence is a time
when we have one foot in childhood and the other in adulthood. During
this typically tumultuous time most adolescents are extremely rebellious, insisting on doing things their own way and rejecting their parents' suggestions, values and sometimes, rules. They are inexplicably
angry with their parents, blaming them for anything and everything that
goes wrong in their life. This is actually healthy, since anger helps adolescents to separate from their parents and discover their own identity.

Unfortunately, those who were neglected or abused often do not
go through adolescence in a healthy way. They are often too afraid to

become angry with their parents or to rebel against their parents' values. And they are often too caught up in trying to gain their parents' approval and love to work on developing a separate identity from them. Abusive parents often do not want their children to separate or lack the skills to help them separate in a healthy way. Young adults from abusive families often leave home with a great deal of emotional baggage because a natural separation did not take place.

In this chapter we will focus on helping you to emotionally separate from your parents and to complete the individuation process. This will include expressing the anger you have been afraid to express, acknowledging your unmet needs and facing the fact that the time for getting those needs met by your parents is over. It will also include grieving for all the pain, rejection, abandonment, and betrayal you experienced at the hands of your parents or other caretakers.

Individuation also involves resolving your relationship with your parents in a conscious way as opposed to constantly reenacting the relationship with others, namely your spouse and children. One of the ways those who were abused or neglected create a false sense of connection with their parents is by unconsciously repeating their life. If they repeat what their parents did, they do not have to feel separate from them. It is as if they are living their parent's life instead of their own. In this way they never have to become a separate person and take responsibility for their own life.

Enmeshment

Many survivors have a very difficult time acknowledging the abuse or neglect they suffered at the hands of their parents and an especially difficult time becoming angry with their parents, partly because they don't want to have to face the truth and come out of denial, but also because they are too enmeshed with their parents. Enmeshment is a psychological term used to describe an unhealthy dependence with another person. In order for some people to admit what was done to them they need to develop their own identity separate from their parents (or other abuser).

My Pain or Yours?

Janice was so enmeshed with her mother that she was unable to feel her own pain about how her mother was emotionally unavailable to her when she was a child. Each time she spoke with me about her mother and started to connect with her pain, she thought about her mother's pain. She thought about what she had learned about her mother's childhood—how she was also deprived of emotional support from her mother. I explained to Janice that although it is good to have empathy for our parents and what they went through as children, we can't allow this empathy to block the process of dealing with our own pain.

But Janice was so enmeshed with her mother that she couldn't separate her mother's pain from her own. In addition, she felt guilty and disloyal for feeling angry with her mother. I assured Janice that admitting her anger toward her mother didn't mean she loved her less, it just meant she would have more of herself.

Finally, Janice was able to speak out loud about how she really felt: "I am angry with my mother. There were so many times when I felt I needed her but she wasn't there for me. I needed someone to talk truthful to me. Someone who cared deeply about me."

As we continued to explore her feelings Janice was able to come to the conclusion that her mother was simply incapable of supporting her in the way she needed. "She just didn't have the capacity for it," she finally concluded one day. "She still doesn't. I know she loves me but she just can't be there for me in that way." With this awareness, Janice started to sob. Her body looked as if it had crumbled. She looked very small and broken. Not only was Janice allowing herself to face the truth about how she was neglected but she was facing the fact that she would never have the mother she wanted and needed. She was experiencing a profound sense of loss. Janice had taken a giant step toward individuation.

We remain enmeshed with our parents in the following ways:

- Continuing to stay in denial about how they treated us

- Withholding our anger concerning their neglectful or abusive treatment

- Completely taking on their values and beliefs without any analysis or questioning

- Replicating their behavior and becoming just like them

- Trying to be the exact opposite of them

- Working hard to never anger them or otherwise risk their rejection

- Deliberately doing things that will make them angry or creating conflict with them

- Not setting healthy limits and boundaries with our parents

The following information and suggestions will help you counter the ways you have remained enmeshed.

Declare Your Independence

Individuation requires us to step away from our parents (and from the rest of the world) and to declare your independence. You began to do this when you started to face the truth about your parents and other family members and the negative role their behavior has had on your life. When you began to give voice to this recognition by expressing your righteous anger the emotional separation process accelerated. Vowing to break the cycle and not repeat your parents' behavior furthered the individuation process. Standing up to your parents and saying no to them (perhaps for the first time) are other ways of declaring your independence. Declaring your independence from your parents and their ways of doing things can be empowering and exhilarating. It allows you to see how different you are from the people you identified with as a child.

Your Mother, Your Father, Your Self

Declaring your independence does not involve denying the emotional impact your parents have had on you, however. By denying your parents' role in shaping your personality you risk denying a part of yourself. It is inevitable that you will take on many of your parents' characteristics. After all, their influence on you, both genetically and environmentally, is the most profound influence you will ever experience.

Separation includes acknowledging how you are similar to your parents as well as how you are different. Many of the traits that you have inherited from your parents are no doubt very positive ones indeed—your mother's beautiful smile, her musical talent, her patience; your father's physical strength, his wizardry at math.

Some people spend most of their lives trying desperately to become different from one or both of their parents. Ironically, those who work hard to become different from one or both parents are actually just as emotionally tied to that parent as those who attempt to emulate a parent. Their focus on being different from their parent can actually prevent them from becoming themselves. By focusing too much energy on being different from your parent you take away energy from discovering who you really are. Your parents' voices will remain in your psyche long after they are dead and gone. Your parents are your connection to all the ancestors who had a part in making you who you are today. By acknowledging their role, you reclaim part of your self and part of your heritage.

It is inevitable that you will possess some of your parents' traits—both good and bad. We simply cannot escape the inevitable—we are and will remain to be more like our parents than we probably care to be. But one thing that you can change is your tendency to take on your parents' abuser or victim pattern.

EXERCISE: *The Good and the Bad*

1. List all the ways you feel you are similar to your parents.

2. List all the ways you feel you are different from your parents.

3. List the ways you have avoided taking on your parents' abusive or victim patterns.

4. List the ways that you have taken on your parents' abusive or victim patterns.

If you find that you are acting like an abusive or victimlike parent think of it as having a Mother attack or Father attack. This is a way of acknowledging your parents' influence and externalizing it at the same time. The more times you catch yourself acting like your parents, the more control you will have over extinguishing the behavior.

Question Your Parents' Values and Beliefs

You do not have to automatically take on your parents' or your families' values and beliefs, especially if they are ones that encourage neglect or abuse. In fact, you can be the first one in your family to question values and beliefs that up until now have been taken for granted to be true. The following exercise will help you begin:

EXERCISE: *Your Parents' Beliefs/Your Beliefs*

1. Make a list of your parents' beliefs and values that you agree with.

2. Make a list of their values and beliefs you disagree with.

3. Consider which of your parents' beliefs and values are con-ducive to the neglect and/or abuse of children.

4. Consider which of their beliefs and values are conducive to domestic violence or the domination of one spouse over another.

5. Which of the values and beliefs from items #3 and #4 have you taken on as your own?

Set Healthy Limits and Boundaries

If you have continued to be controlled or manipulated by your parents or if you have remained too dependent on them you will need to set boundaries and limits in order to individuate from them and in order to break the cycle. It can be painful to see your parents' pain and dis-appointment when you begin to tell them no—no, you aren't going to do as they suggest, no, you aren't coming over now; no, you aren't going to become what they wanted you to become. You may be afraid they will say, "In that case, to hell with you" in response to your show of autonomy. Your parents may, in fact, initially become quite angry when you first begin to set limits and boundaries with them. They may even become insulting, bitter, or threatening when you stand up to them and tell them you are going to run your life your way. But do not allow these reactions to take you off your course. There will be more on setting limits and boundaries in chapter 16.

Complete Your Unfinished Business

Completing your unfinished business with your parents or other abusers can include any or all of the following: expressing and getting past your anger, confronting your abusers, resolving your relation-ship, and forgiveness.

Getting Past Your Anger

Resentment is the most frequent kind of unfinished business. Al-though it is natural and normal for you to feel resentment (which translates into *anger*) toward your parents, you will need to get past your anger if you are to emotionally separate from them. When we remain angry with someone we stay emotionally tied to them in a very negative way. We continue to feel victimized by them, and we continue to invest a tremendous amount of energy in blaming them. While anger is a natural, healthy emotion when ventilated properly, blame is a wasted and negative experience. The difference between anger and blame is that blaming keeps you caught up in the problem, whereas anger constructively allows you to work through the problem.

If you have not successfully worked through your anger toward your abuser(s), refer back to chapter 7 for help on constructively releasing your anger toward them.

Confrontations

Confronting your parents or other abusers has many benefits. It can help you emotionally disconnect from those with whom you continue to have an unhealthy emotional connection and help you resolve or bring closure to the relationships that plague you most (your parents, your siblings, or other abusers).

When you confront you break the cycle of victimization. Confronting those who hurt you enables you to take back your power, proving to yourself that you are no longer going to allow anyone to frighten, control, or mistreat you. It provides an opportunity to set the record straight, to communicate what you need from now on. It gives the other person another chance to make amends and to treat you better now. Most important, if you don't confront those who hurt you in the past you will tend to be attracted to people who are similar to them in an attempt to resolve your unfinished business or you will attribute characteristics to others that are not really theirs.

A confrontation is a way of declaring the truth, standing up to those who have hurt you, telling them how they hurt you, and how you feel about them. It is not an attack and it is not meant to alienate the person. It is also not an argument. Its purpose is not to change the other person or to force someone to admit that they were wrong in the way they treated you.

Confronting is different from releasing your anger. Although your confrontation may include expressing your anger along with your other feelings, it is generally important that you have released a great deal of your anger in constructive ways before you confront because you will be better able to communicate your feelings in a strong, clear, self-assured manner. You will also be less likely to explode or lose control. It is strongly recommended that you write an anger letter before you do your confronting. From this letter you can glean the material for your confrontation.

Practice your confrontation by writing it down, speaking into a tape recorder, or just talking out loud. You can practice with a friend or with a therapist. Using the following format as a guide, you may then pick and choose which points you wish to include in your actual confrontation.

- List the neglectful or abusive behaviors this person inflicted upon you.

- Explain how you felt as a result of these behaviors.

- List the effects these behaviors had on you, both as a child and as an adult and how your life has been affected.

- List everything you would have wanted from this person at the time.

- List what you want from this person now.

There are several ways to conduct your confrontation: face-to-face, via telephone, or by letter or email. Face-to-face confrontations are the most advantageous but sometimes this is not possible because of distance constraints or because you are not prepared to see someone in person. Choose the method that suits your needs and trust that whichever one you choose will work out.

Before you choose to actually confront someone in person, consider the following:

- Decide whether you would like to have someone come with you for support. If you are apprehensive about violence or loss of control, you may need to have a third party present—even if it is your own rage or loss of control that you fear.

- Set some ground rules for the confrontation and determine how you will express these to the person. Here are some examples: I want you to hear me out before you respond; I don't want you to interrupt me or stop me until I am finished; I don't want you to defend, justify, or rationalize, just listen. You'll get your chance to respond later.

- Even if the person does agree to your ground rules, be prepared for any of the following, both during and after your confrontation:

    Denial ("I don't remember," "That never happened," "You're exaggerating," "You're lying.").

    Blame ("You were such a demanding child," "I had to do something to control you," "You wanted it—you came on to me," "Why didn't you tell me?").

    Rationalizations ("I did the best I could," "Things were really tough," "I tried to stop drinking but I couldn't," "I was afraid to leave your father—how were we going to make it?").

    Self-pity ("I have enough problems without this," "You just don't understand how hard it was for me," "I'm too old [or sick] to take this.").

    Guilt ("This is what we get after all we did for you?" "Nothing was ever enough for you," "How could you do this to me?").

- Make sure you have supportive people to talk to before and after the confrontation.

- Be prepared to end the confrontation whenever you feel it is no longer effective, beneficial, or safe, i.e., if you feel threatened or fear you are losing control; if the person is too busy defending himself to really hear you; or if the confrontation has turned into a shouting match.

Don't set yourself up with the false hope that your parent or other family member will suddenly see the error of his ways and apologize profusely. In fact, you can expect him to deny, claim to have forgotten, project the blame back onto you, or get very angry. Give the person time to think about what you have said. Don't assume that just because she didn't apologize on the spot that she didn't take what you said seriously and might not apologize in some way later on.

No matter how the confrontation turns out, consider it successful simply because you have had the courage to do it. This confrontation symbolizes the beginning of a change in the balance of power in your relationship and is a significant act of individuation on your part.

Resolve Your Relationships with Your Parents and Other Abusers

Unresolved relationships will continue to bother you and negatively affect your life until you get things out in the open, giving room for healing. Resolving a relationship with a parent or other abusers may involve any or all of the following: forgiveness, reconciliation, temporary separation, or divorce.

Forgiveness

There is no doubt about the fact that forgiveness frees us. Forgiveness has the power to heal our bodies, our minds, and our spirits—our very lives. But we need to make sure we aren't forgiving just because we think it is the right thing to do or because we are giving in to pressure from others. And we need to make sure that we are not just using forgiveness as another form of denial.

True forgiveness only occurs when we allow ourselves to face the truth and to feel and release our emotions, including our anger, about what was done to us. It is completely premature to forgive if you haven't even acknowledged that you were harmed. Alice Miller notes that when children are asked to forgive abusive parents without first experiencing their emotions and their personal pain, the forgiveness process becomes another weapon of silencing. The same is true of adults who rush to forgiveness. Many people have been brainwashed into submission by those who insist that they are less than human if they don't forgive.

Many people think that forgiving someone who hurt them is the same as saying that what happened to them was okay or that it didn't hurt them. But forgiveness doesn't mean that what happened was okay. It simply means that we are no longer willing to allow that experience to adversely affect our lives. Ultimately, forgiveness is something we do for ourselves. The information in the next chapter will further help you to forgive your parents.

Reconciliation

Even though you may have forgiven those who abused you, you may not feel safe around them. Many survivors of childhood abuse have stopped seeing their parents or other family members in order to protect themselves from further abuse. This is especially true of those who confronted their abusers in the past but did not achieve positive results. If your abuser is not open to looking at what he has done to damage you, continues to abuse you in the same way he did when you were a child, or presents a threat to your children, you may need to continue your separation from him or even divorce him. (For more information on this, refer to my book *Divorcing a Parent*.)

On the other hand, if your abuser has shown some capacity for understanding your pain and some willingness to take responsibility for her actions—however small that capacity and willingness may seem—there may be hope for the relationship. This is also the case if you have noticed that your abuser has been open to your attempts at setting limits and boundaries.

Before you reconcile, ask yourself the following questions:

1. Am I strong enough to be around this person without losing ground in my recovery?

2. Can I maintain a sense of emotional separation from this person when I am in her presence?

3. Am I strong enough to set appropriate limits and boundaries so that I do not allow myself to be abused again?

4. Am I being pressured into reconciliation (by other family members, by my spouse, by guilt, or by my religious beliefs) before I am actually ready?

5. Is this person ready to reconcile with me? Is she still angry with me for being angry with her, for not having seen her for awhile, or for bringing the abuse out in the open? (If so, she may need more time to heal and forgive, no matter how forgiving you might feel.)

If you can't answer yes to items 1, 2, 3, and 5 and no to item 4, you may need to wait a while before attempting a reconciliation.

Facing the Pain and Confusion of Emotional Separation

Emotional separation often involves emotional pain. It can be painful to face the truth about your parents, to question their beliefs and the lessons they taught you, to stand up to your parents, or to disagree with them today. Separation brings losses and even though they are necessary losses they are still painful. You may have to give up the false hope that your parents will one day be the kind of parents you have longed for and deserve. This can be especially painful.

Emotional separation can also create internal conflict. You may realize that taking care of yourself and being true to yourself will necessitate going against your parents' wishes and beliefs. This may cause you to feel you are being disloyal to your parents. You may vacillate between such conflicting emotions as wanting to recapture a real or imagined sense of family closeness and a desire for revenge or compensation from your parents. At one moment you may feel like you want nothing to do with your parents or other abusive family member and at another you may worry that your parents may disown you. It is especially challenging to distinguish between the negative internalized messages of your parents and the healthy messages of your true voice.

Emotional separation involves the ability to hold the tension of two opposites. While it is important to face the truth about your parents' mistreatment of you and allow yourself to be angry with them it is also important to realize that your parents were themselves mistreated. And although it is important to understand that you didn't deserve the way you were mistreated, neither did your parents. Whereas your parents were not responsible for what happened to them as children, they are responsible for what they did to you.

You will find that you will continue to grieve over the losses of your childhood throughout the separation process and this will be a significant part of your healing. Your parents no doubt experienced losses in their childhood but were not able to grieve over them. This contributed to their repeating what was done to them. By facing your grief you reduce your own need to abuse others.

While emotional separation often takes time and the support of others, such as supportive friends, family members, therapists or self-help groups, those who have been able to complete these steps report feeling like they have finally taken the reins in their life.

CHAPTER 14

Facing the Truth about Your Family Legacy

*We respect our ancestor's achievements by standing
on their shoulders and seeing further, not by crouching
in their shadows and seeing less. . . .*

DONALD CREIGHTON

*We must let ourselves feel all the painful destructiveness we
want to forgive rather than swallow it in denial. If we do not
face it, we cannot choose to forgive it.*

KENNETH MCNOLL, *Healing the Family Tree*

At the beginning of this book we discussed how the legacy of abuse
and neglect gets passed down from generation to generation. In order
to truly break the cycle you must learn as much about your family
legacy as possible because only by being clear about what you are
dealing with can you truly overcome it. Knowing your family legacy
will provide you the wisdom you will need in order to avoid repeating
the same mistakes your ancestors did. It will also help you spot any of
the family tendencies in your own children so you can offer them the
help they will need.

The other reason why it is important to know your family legacy
is that it will provide you the necessary empathy you will need to forgive yourself and your ancestors for the harm you and they have done
to others. This is especially true of the harm your parents have done to
you and the harm you have done to your own children. Once you have
put your own pattern into the context of your family history you will
be able to take on an entirely different perspective and this new perspective can be nothing less than life-transforming.

Determining your family history can sometimes be a difficult matter, especially in dysfunctional families where secrecy, denial, and rationalization are prevalent. Although you may have heard many stories about the escapades or hardships of various family members, eliciting information relevant to the history of abuse in the family will undoubtedly be harder to come by.

My Family Legacy

I found this to be especially true in my family. My mother was extremely proud and secretive and believed strongly in keeping things to herself. Whenever I asked her questions about our family she was very elusive. She always cried whenever I asked her about my grandmother (who had died before I was born) and so I stopped asking about her. The only things she told me was that my grandmother had suggested my name, that she died when she was hit by a car and that she was a wonderful, gregarious woman that everyone loved. Whenever I asked about my father she was even more elusive and I soon learned to stop asking about him as well. Even so, throughout the years I was able to piece together enough information to give me a fairly good picture of our family legacy.

My mother's parents had five children: three boys and one girl. My grandfather was a carpenter who designed beautiful hand-crafted furniture, so the family was fairly well off. My grandmother was a social butterfly who loved to entertain. That was before the Depression came. When the Depression hit my grandfather had to go out of town to work. He sent a check home once a month with the warning to my grandmother that the money had to last all month. But my grandmother didn't heed the warning. As soon as she got the check she went right out and bought liquor for herself and her friends and chocolate-covered cherries for the kids. Then she had her friends over for a party. By the last week of the month the family had to live on boiled potatoes.

As the Depression dragged on my grandfather was finding it harder and harder to find work and to feed his family. My mother's oldest sister decided to get married at sixteen, which helped the family out considerably. But there were still four kids to worry about. My uncle Forrest went to work at fourteen, and they decided to send the youngest son, my uncle Kay, to California to be with relatives. My uncle Kay never got over this abandonment by his family. He became a lifelong alcoholic. My uncle Frank also suffered an enormous disappointment. A very talented artist, he had been accepted to a prestigious art school just before the Depression. Unable to pursue his lifelong dream, he eventually became an alcoholic as well.

The five children were devastated by the Depression, and although my uncle Forrest tried to keep them together, they were never close again. My mother and my aunt Natalla stayed in Missouri, but the boys eventually all went to California. Frank died in his forties of alcoholism and a broken heart. He never married. Throughout his life he continued to paint but always regretted not attending art school. Kay lived a long life, in spite of his alcoholism. He was married once, in his early twenties, but abandoned his wife and newborn baby (as he had been abandoned).

Aside from the alcoholism, the other thing that Kay and Frank had in common was the fact that they were selfish and narcissistic. This can, of course, be partly explained by the fact that they probably became stuck in their adolescence—an adolescence that was taken from them so abruptly. But it can also be explained by the fact that narcissism runs in my family. Forrest and my mother also suffered from it.

So where did the alcoholism and the narcissism start? Even though my mother had always spoken of my grandmother in glowing terms, just before she died I learned that my grandmother was an alcoholic. It wasn't until then that I learned the whole truth about her death. She had been drinking the night she was killed. She was drunk and had decided to walk down the street to see some friends. She evidently was in the middle of the street when the car hit her.

As far as the narcissism is concerned, this disorder is not necessarily caused by spoiling a child, which is often the belief, but by emotional deprivation. Certainly my mother's siblings were all deprived of love and emotional security.

And the criticalness? I saw one picture of my grandfather, who looked very cold and rigid-looking. I can imagine him being very critical. And even though my mother had always spoken of my grandmother in glowing terms, after my mother died I learned from my cousin (Forrest's daughter) that my grandmother was actually a very stern, critical, almost caustic woman. She had visited them several times and was very critical of my cousin's children.

From what I was able to piece together both from the little I learned about my family and from my mother's behavior, my mother and her siblings were raised by a selfish, critical mother who was also an alcoholic. My mother in turn became highly critical of me and was too wrapped up in herself to pay much attention to me. My mother also abused alcohol and when she drank she became very verbally abusive to me.

Learning more about my mother's family helped me to gain a great deal of empathy for both my mother and myself. I too abused alcohol in my younger days and became verbally abusive when I drank. Once I understood more about our family legacy, I was able to understand myself better, and this helped me to forgive both my mother and myself.

While discovering the truth about your family legacy can be difficult, do not be discouraged. Keep in mind that every perpetrator of abuse was himself abused. Every abuser is someone's child, sibling, spouse, parent, friend, or neighbor. Ask questions, keep digging, and you will find the answers you are looking for.

The Legacy of Child Sexual Abuse

In her book *Because I Love You: The Silent Shadow of Child Sexual Abuse*, Joyce Allan tells the story of child abuse which spans five generations. Her father was a pedophile who molested her throughout her childhood. Years later, he abused her own children. He sexually violated dozens of children throughout his life.

It took Joyce seven years to research and write her book. She used her father's hospital records and letters from and to him, and interviewed more than one hundred fifty people who knew him and their family throughout his life: relatives, childhood friends, neighbors, coworkers, and mental health and legal professionals. She also had the sad opportunity to identify over two dozen of her father's victims and to interview many of them as adults.

During her research Joyce learned a great deal about her father. She learned that he had been abandoned by his father and that he grew up with his mother and two sisters in impoverished circumstances. But it wasn't until she spoke with his second wife, Irene, that she found out what she had really been searching for—the reason why he had become a pedophile. Irene told Joyce that her father had been sodomized by an uncle. "When he was telling me about it, he held his buttocks and said, 'ouch.' He tried to make his own abuse an understatement. I think he tried to bury that memory, and I'm not sure it was the only incident," Irene explained.

Joyce sat stunned at this revelation. As she wrote in her book, "For the first time, I had actually glimpsed the wounded and terrorized and silenced little boy who grew up to be my father." She thought about the fact that her father, suffering from tuberculosis, had been sent to spend summers on his uncle's farm from the age of four until he finished high school and wondered how many times he had endured anal rape over those long years. As an indication that that sodomy continued, in her father's own assaults on children, he showed a preference for children age four through sixteen, the ages he was probably assaulted. There were other parallels between Uncle Ralph and her father. Both committed suicide.

Discovering Family Patterns

Sometimes when we delve into our family history we discover more than the fact that a certain type of neglect, abuse, or other unhealthy behavior such as alcoholism runs in our family. We discover that we are actually repeating a family pattern. This was the case with my client Lena.

Lena discovered quite a lot about her family history, information that shocked her but at the same time helped her to make sense of circumstances that were profoundly perplexing and upsetting. Lena was sexually abused by a man her mother was having an affair with—a man who actually lived in the same home as Lena, her parents, and the rest of her siblings. Not only did the affair go on right under her father's nose but so did the molestation. Even more astonishing, Lena's mother had two children with this man who we will call George. Not only did Lena have to grow up with the devastation and pain that comes with sexual abuse but she later on discovered that her very own mother had had an affair with her abuser and that two of her siblings were actually the children of her abuser.

If there was ever proof that abuse and neglect get passed down generation after generation it is found in the history of Lena's family. When Lena's grandmother (her mother's mother) was growing up there was a man who took a liking to her. Even though he was old enough to be her father, he started walking her home after school, buying her gifts and paying a lot of attention to her. Today this kind of unhealthy interest in a child warns others that such a man is seducing the child, but in those days it probably was not seen in that way, as evidenced by the fact that this story was passed down as part of the family history. The man then arranged for his son to marry Lena's grandmother, no doubt for the purpose of continuing to have access to her. Once married and with kids, Lena's grandmother either started or continued to have an affair with her now father-in-law and they had a child together.

After Lena's mother died she learned from her aunt (her mother's sister) that her mother had also been sexually abused by her own father, Lena's grandfather.

Although Lena did not continue the same strange legacy as her mother and grandmother of having an affair with a child molester, she did marry a sex addict. He was so sexually demanding that he would get up and get dressed to go out to find another woman to have sex with him if she didn't give in to his demands.

After Lena put together her family history and discovered the pattern that existed with her grandmother and mother, Lena divorced her husband. As she explained to me, "I may or may not have married a child molester, I don't know. But he was forcing himself on me, and in many ways, because of my abuse, I'm still a child."

CHAPTER 15

Breaking into the Dysfunctional Family System

Life can only be understood backwards, but it must be lived forwards.

SOREN KIERKEGAARD

If you are truly going to break the cycle you will need to confront the dysfunctional family system that created your family legacy. You do not want to expose your own children to the same abuse or neglect that damaged you and you do not want to have to continually ward off damaging remarks or abusive or neglectful treatment that will threaten to damage your self-esteem. Although we can have control over who we bring into our lives and our children's lives today, we can't choose our family of origin. Therefore, if you are going to continue to relate to family members who were or still are abusive or neglectful you will need strategies that will help you to cope and to begin to change the family system.

In this chapter I will offer suggestions and strategies that will help you break into the dysfunctional family system and confront the neglect or abuse that has been passed down for generations. I offer strategies for how to break the silence with family members and how to deal with family members who insist on staying in denial. I use the phrase "breaking into the family system" because in many cases it will feel like you are having to break into a fortress in order to make any significant changes in your family. Dysfunctional families build up huge walls to keep secrets in and to keep others out and these walls are difficult to topple.

Breaking into the family system can include all the following:

1. Confronting an abusive or neglectful family member.

2. Telling other family members about your experience of being neglected or abused.

3. Sharing the family legacy with other members of the family.

4. Calling an abusive family member on his or her current behavior.

5. Breaking dysfunctional patterns of relating.

6. Teaching and modeling healthy behavior.

Confronting an Abusive or Neglectful Family Member

If you haven't already done so, you will need to confront those members of your family who neglected or abused you in order to begin the process of changing the dysfunctional family system. Confronting a neglectful or abusive family member will enable you to take back your power. It is a way of declaring to the other person and to yourself that you are no longer going to allow him or her to frighten, control, or mistreat you again. By facing a family member with the truth and with your feelings, no matter how frightened you are, you are breaking the cycle of victimization and are no longer being impotent, passive, and ineffectual, allowing things to happen to you. Refer to chapter 13 for details on how to go about preparing and conducting your confrontation. There are, of course, some people who are unsafe to confront. If this is the case, consider whether this person is safe to be around, and particularly, for your children to be around.

Telling Other Family Members About Your Experience of Being Neglected or Abused

While it will eventually be important for your entire family to know about your personal experience with abuse and your family legacy, most survivors of neglect or abuse decide to deal with family members one-on-one as opposed to facing the entire family all at once. Many survivors choose to break the silence with the family member they feel closest to or the one they expect will support them the most.

Whether you choose to tell individual family members or the entire family all at once, it is important that you set the stage for your disclosure. Otherwise family members can react too intensely or too defensively. Call or write the family member ahead of time and tell him or her that you have something important to talk about. Set a time for the meeting when you and the other family member can talk privately without interference. Make certain that you set aside enough time to process the feelings that will undoubtedly emerge after you have revealed the abuse.

After you tell, recognize that your relative will need time to absorb the information and process his or her feelings. Just because a family member doesn't respond in the way you would like them to in the moment doesn't mean he or she isn't capable of doing so at a later time. It is unrealistic for you to expect your relative to do any of the following at this first meeting: state that he or she believes you, choose you over the abuser, ask your forgiveness for not protecting you, admit that he or she abused you. Your relative is going to have to revise his or her perceptions of the abuser, of you, of themselves, and of the entire family and this will take time. If you handle this first meeting properly, this will be the first of many conversations about the abuse.

Sharing Your Family Legacy with Other Family Members

In chapter 14, I told you the story of Janice, my client who had difficulty individuating from her mother because she was too enmeshed. When Janice explored her family history, especially the history of all the women on her mother's side of the family, she discovered an interesting and for her, heartbreaking fact. All the women on her mother's side of the family, as far back as her great-grandmother, had been raised by mothers who had not been there for them emotionally.

Once Janice learned that all her female ancestors had suffered a similar fate she felt even more understanding and forgiving of her mother and even more determined to break the family pattern and be the kind of mother that her daughter, and every young woman, deserves. This strengthened her determination to work even harder in therapy to recover from her own wounding so that she could be there for her daughter emotionally as well as physically.

Janice's family legacy is actually a fairly common one. I cannot tell you how many clients I've had throughout the years who have a similar story. The mother-daughter wounding is, in my opinion and in the opinion of many experts, the most devastating wounding that can occur. When a daughter is emotionally neglected by her mother she suffers a wound so deep that it affects every aspect of her life—her self-esteem, her sense of safety and security in the world, her ability to emotionally bond with a partner, and most importantly, her ability to emotionally bond with her own children. A woman who was herself emotionally neglected or abandoned by her mother will either experience difficulties feeling emotionally connected to her children, tend to smother her children, or be what is considered a disconnected, distant, or inadequate mother, as was the case with Janice's mother. This will in turn, get passed on to her own children and the cycle continues.

Once Janice came to understand all this she felt compelled to have another conversation with her mother. She told her mother about her new-found understanding and explained to her that she had been able to forgive her on an even deeper level than she had before. But this time she was also able to cry with her mother over the fact that she had felt so abandoned by her emotionally. And surprisingly, her mother, who appeared to be less defensive than usual, was able to hold Janice and comfort her. Later they had a wonderful conversation about the women in their family. "Once my mother understood what had happened to her—why she wasn't able to be there for me, it was like a burden was lifted off of her. In some strange way it seemed to free her to actually be there for me," Janice explained to me.

Armed with the information on your family's legacy of neglect and/or abuse and softened by the empathy that comes from realizing why your relatives have acted as they have done, you are in the unique and powerful position to not only heal yourself but other members of your family. By sharing your family history with other members of your family you can promote real understanding and real change in the family.

You can choose to go about this in several ways. Some have chosen to call a family meeting, feeling that since it is a family problem, it might as well be talked about with the entire family present. If you are in therapy, you may feel more comfortable having the family meet in your therapist's office where you will have the added support of your therapist.

Confronting Family Members
Who Continue to Be Abusive

Sometimes having empathy and talking to a family member in an understanding way doesn't do any good. He or she just continues to act the way he or she always did, seemingly oblivious to the way it affects you and others. With the exception of sexual abuse, in these cases it will be far more appropriate for you to confront the family member each time his or her behavior becomes inappropriate, offensive, or abusive. For example, if a parent continues to be emotionally abusive I suggest you say something like: "I don't want you to criticize me anymore. You may not be aware when you are doing it, so each time you criticize me I'm going to say, 'Ouch!' If you continue to criticize me I'm going to immediately remove myself from your presence."

Another suggestion is to limit your time with a parent or other family member who continues to be abusive. For example, being in the presence of an emotionally abusive parent can be very damaging to self-esteem. It can also cause you to begin to doubt your perceptions and your reality. For this reason, spending only a few hours at a time with such a person can limit the amount of damage they can do.

In some cases, the only way to truly break the cycle is to temporarily separate or divorce oneself from one's parents or other family members. This is a radical step but unfortunately, a necessary one when a parent or other relative continues to be abusive. This is especially true when family members pose a threat to the safety of one's children but it can also be true if the way your parent treats you negatively affects how you treat yourself or others. My mother continued to be extremely critical of me even after I became an adult. It got so bad that I couldn't visit her without becoming physically ill. Finally, I decided that if I was going to recover I needed to stop seeing her altogether.

Fortunately, this break with my mother acted as a wake-up call for her. I wrote about my experience in my book *The Power of Apology* if you want to read the whole story but suffice it to say that my mother finally apologized for her abusive behavior. This was a turning point not only in my life but in hers as well. During the few years we had together before her death she worked hard to not be critical of me.

I told my mother that I forgave her and asked her to forgive herself. She had a harder time doing that but I encouraged her to realize that she was only doing what had been done to her. She continued to deny that she had ever been mistreated but finally, before her death, she acknowledged that her mother had been quite critical.

Breaking Dysfunctional Patterns
of Relating in the Family

There are certain types of interactions found in all abusive families. These include: denial, lack of clear boundaries, inconsistency and unpredictability, role reversal, a closed family system, incongruent communication, extremes in conflict, and lack of empathy. In order to break the cycle of abuse it is crucially important you and your family work on changing these negative ways of interacting.

Counteract Denial

In dysfunctional families there is a consistent tendency to deny feelings and deny the truth. Parents constantly tell their children that they were wrong about what they saw and what they heard. This causes the children to doubt their own perceptions. Parents lie to their children and themselves so often that everyone ends up believing the lies. This mass denial, like mass hysteria, is so compelling and so contagious that it feeds off itself. The more one member in the family denies the truth about what is really happening in the family, the more it encourages other members of the family to do the same. At first it just feels better not to have to face the pain of the truth, but eventually each grows to doubt his own perceptions. Everyone begins thinking that if other members of the family act as if nothing happened, then maybe nothing did. Maybe they were imagining it all along.

Keeping secrets is another destructive aspect of a dysfunctional family. Secrets create an atmosphere of shame. In fact, secrets are so destructive that in Alcoholics Anonymous there is a saying, "You are only as sick as your secrets." Secrets also divide family members since secret keeping is based on collusion and exclusion, making certain family members feel special and connected whereas others feel less important and left out. Keeping secrets is what allows child abuse and domestic violence to continue.

Do your part in breaking the cycle in your family by refusing to continue keeping the secrets any longer. Stop denying and minimizing the truth. Stop pretending that things are better than they are. Acknowledge that your family is dysfunctional and that there are serious problems in your family. Encourage other family members to come out of denial as well and to tell the truth about the family. Be a support to other family members as they come forward with their own stories of abuse and neglect. Don't contribute to the denial by mini-mizing their pain or by making excuses for their abusers. Give them your undivided attention, even when what they tell you hurts you as well. Let them know that it is worth it to tell the truth and face their pain and that there is someone there to support them.

Set Clear Boundaries

In a healthy, functional family, there are discernable (recognizable as distinct) boundaries between the individuals in the family, whereas in dysfunctional families, the boundaries between family members are unclear. A dysfunctional family can be likened to a large, sticky mass. Everyone in the family is emotionally stuck to everyone else. There is no psychological or emotional separation between one individual and another. Individual identities are lost. This situation of enmeshment is often experienced as closeness when in reality, it is a jail sentence locking individuals into a life of false masks, pretense, and an inabil-ity to experience fulfillment in personal relationships.

Respect for privacy is essential for personal development. With-out it, children find it difficult to differentiate between themselves and the rest of the family. But privacy is seldom afforded children in a dysfunctional home. Parents enter the bathrooms and bedrooms with-out knocking, read mail addressed to their children, and listen to their children's private conversations. In dysfunctional families, parents take showers with their children, older brothers are allowed to sleep with younger sisters, and parents walk around nude in front of their children.

In dysfunctional families, children are not taught that they have any rights. In fact, their experience teaches them that adults have the right to have easy access to them. Whenever parents want, they can reach out and hit them, grab them, or sexually abuse them. They are told to hug and kiss visitors whether they want to or not and made to feel bad if they try to refuse. Their belongings are given away, sold, or thrown away without their knowledge or permission.

For all of these reasons it is important for you and other family members to develop clear boundaries between each other. This includes respecting each other's right to personal space and privacy. Knock before entering the bathroom or a family member's bedroom and lock the bathroom door when you enter. Only read mail that is addressed to you personally and do not read other family members' diaries or journals. Teach your children to do the same. Teach your children to say no to anyone who tries to touch them when they do not want to be touched. This includes saying no to relatives who want to kiss them or hold them on their lap. Teach your children that they have rights, too.

Practice Consistency and Predictability

Dysfunctional families, rather than serving as a source of stability and safety, become sources of turbulence, chaos, and danger. Rules are often unclear and are often broken. Parental behavior fluctuates daily, even hourly. Children often have to guess at what their parents will do next, and they find it impossible to predict with any certainty whether their parents will be there for them at all, either physically or emotionally. Parents forget to pick their children up at the movies, don't come home when they are expected, and are not available to comfort their child in need.

In order to counter this pattern of chaos and instability, it is important that you provide consistency and predictability for your own children. Encourage your family to sit down together and decide on some basic family rules. These rules should represent the needs of each individual in the family as well as the family as a group. For example, "No drunkenness around the children," "No talking behind each other's back," and "No telling dirty jokes around other family members," might be good rules for your family to consider.

Instead of family rules, you may want to talk about what is most important in the family and make some agreements as to how you as a family can go about achieving these goals. For example, if what is most important is that the children in the family are protected (as they should be), you may agree as a family that a family member who has been abusive to children in the past, either verbally, physically, or sexually, will never be left alone with the children. You may also decide as a family that a certain family member needs to seek professional help in order to remain in the family.

Reverse Role Reversal

The appropriate role for parents in a healthy family is to provide for their child's physical and emotional needs, to protect their children, to provide guidance and support, and to set limits when needed. In a dysfunctional family, the roles are often reversed. Parents turn to their children to meet their needs, whether they be for support, advice, affection, or even sex. Children in these families often become little adults capable of running a household, taking care of younger siblings, even earning money for the family. These pseudo adults are expected to behave like adults and are often punished when they act like normal children. They grow up never having a childhood and never having a chance to develop emotionally.

If you grew up in a family where you were expected to take care of your parents' needs, you may have a tendency to treat your own children in the same way. Make certain that you break the cycle by not turning to your children to meet your needs. Allow your children to be children instead of expecting them to be little adults. Encourage other family members to do the same. If you catch one of your parents or siblings treating your child as if he or she were an adult, remind them that he or she is only a child and should not be expected to take care of their adult needs.

You may also need to reverse the role reversal that may still exist between you and your parents. Although it is no longer your parents' responsibility to take care of your needs or to protect you, neither is it your responsibility to meet their needs. For example, it is not your job to take care of your mother, even if your father does beat her up, or to pick your father up at the bar because he can't drive, or to undress him and put him to bed. By continuing to rescue your parents you are actually enabling them to continue their dysfunctional behavior. Certainly this does not include caring for elderly or sick parents.

Open Up the Family System

A dysfunctional family system is a closed one. Parents tend to maintain few ties outside the family. They don't tend to share their home with friends or neighbors, nor are children encouraged or allowed to bring friends over. There is a pervasive sense of isolation both because of parental reluctance to allow children to socialize and because of children's embarrassment concerning the family. There are secrets to be kept. Parents do not want their children to have ties with the outside world for fear of exposing physical or sexual abuse and children do not want to risk the embarrassment of their friends seeing their parent drunk, yelling at them in front of their friends, or other evidence of the general dysfunction of the home, such as a messy house.

Begin to counter the isolation you may have experienced growing up and which may still exist within your family. Establish friendships outside the family and encourage your children to do the same. Do not depend only on family members to be your support. Reach out to others for solace and guidance.

Practice Open and Clear Communication

In dysfunctional families, parents often say one thing while their body language shows something entirely different. This makes it difficult for their children to decipher their parents' real message. Children are often confronted with mixed messages, making them have to guess at what the actual message was. Confused by mixed messages, children learn not to trust what was said and instead be alert to how it was said. They become acutely aware of all the nonverbal messages their parents send, finding them to be far more reliable than words.

Work at communicating clearly instead of giving mixed messages. Say what you mean and mean what you say. Counter the incongruent messages you received as a child by being very clear and consistent with your children. When other family members give you mixed messages, ask them to clarify what they mean.

Learn Conflict Resolution

In a dysfunctional family, there is either too much or too little conflict. When there is too much conflict, there is often emotional or physical abuse. The atmosphere is tense, and the children never know when the next explosion will occur. Fighting becomes a way of life. Children become hypervigilant anticipating the next attack.

When there is too little conflict, everything is kept hidden. Problems and issues are never fully discussed, and no one ever fights. Problems that are never directly handled tend to fester. When people avoid conflict, the tension between them builds.

As you improve your communication skills, you may also need to teach your family how to settle conflicts peacefully and to everyone's satisfaction. This will be one of your biggest challenges. Although everyone has some conflict in his or her family, not all people express their conflicting feelings openly. Some erupt in a rage, others silently seethe, refusing to even acknowledge conflict.

Most people react to conflict by thinking, "If only you loved me, you'd agree with me." But we can't simply wish conflict away. This kind of immature and wishful thinking tends to escalate conflicts instead of resolving them. This attitude denies another person's right to differ from you, essentially sending the message, "If you really love me, you have to think, feel, and be exactly like me." It places all responsibility for resolving disagreements—and all power to change— in the hands of the other person.

You can be the one to model conflict resolution in your family. Start by acknowledging its existence. Recognize that conflict is essential to each person's growth and to the growth of the family and that each relationship inevitably involves a clash of needs, opinions, and feelings.

The next step is to recognize that, contrary to what you may have learned growing up, not all differences are irreconcilable, and not all conflicts are unsolvable. In fact, most conflicts can be resolved amicably if both people are willing to communicate and work toward that end. If you keep these things in mind, you won't be afraid to disagree with another family member.

Encourage your family to agree to work out your disagreements together. If those in conflict stubbornly try to force the other person to change or to prove that one is right and the other is wrong, reconciliation becomes impossible. But if you approach conflict with the goal of coming together, resolution is not only possible but probable. This will require that family members let go of the kind of black-and-white thinking that causes us to see only right or wrong possibilities in arguments. It will also require family members to commit to working out problems instead of falling back on old standbys such as: taking sides in an argument, gossiping and backbiting, name calling, storming off in anger, or silently seething in anger and refusing to talk to one another. If you are a positive role model for more constructive problem solving, you will have a positive impact on the family. The next section will help.

Learn and Practice Empathy

Empathy is the ability to put yourself in another person's shoes and to imagine what she or he is feeling. It is the ability to be sensitive and responsive to another's feelings and needs. Often members of dysfunctional families are unable to do this and this adds to the distance and misunderstandings between them. It is important that family members learn not just to listen to one another but to listen empathetically. As you each listen to one another, imagine yourself in the other person's situation. What do you think she or he is feeling?

Parents in dysfunctional families do not know how to empathize with their children because their parents did not empathize with them. They have difficulty relating to the feelings and needs of their children because their own needs were denied or discounted when they were growing up. Because of this lack of empathy, these parents tend to punish their children too often and too severely. If this is part of your family legacy you will need to work on developing empathy so that you do not pass on this pattern to your children.

CHAPTER 16

Continue to Heal

We move ahead by going deeper.

JENNIFER JAMES

Asking for help does not mean we are weak or incompetent. It usually indicates an advanced level of honesty and intelligence.

ANNE WILSON SCHAEF

Of course the most significant thing you can do in your efforts to break the cycle is to continue to work on your own recovery. You must heal the wounds of your own childhood. This can be a long and arduous task but it is extremely worthwhile. The more your own wounds are healed the less likely you will be to reenact your abuse and inflict those same wounds onto someone else. The more you heal your shame the less need you will have to shame others, to abuse yourself or to allow others to misuse, degrade, or abuse you.

As we discussed at the beginning of this book, you experienced certain emotional reactions to the neglect and/or abuse you suffered as a child. These emotions included fear, shame, guilt, sadness, and anger. In order to avoid passing on the neglect or abuse you experienced you will need to make certain that you have cleared these old emotions from the past—that you have found ways to express them in safe, constructive ways so that you do not transfer them to your partner, your children, or other people in your life who do not deserve to be the recipient of them.

If you haven't already entered individual psychotherapy I encourage you to do so. Support groups or group therapy is also an invaluable healing tool. A group can recreate a sense of belonging to counter the isolating effects of child abuse. As Judith Herman so eloquently wrote in her masterpiece *Trauma and Recovery*, "The solidarity of a group provides the strongest antidote to traumatic experience. Trauma isolates; the group re-creates a sense of belonging. Trauma shames and stigmatizes; the group bears witness and affirms. Trauma degrades the victim; the group exalts her. Trauma dehumanizes the victim; the group restores her humanity."

The group experience is especially profound for those who have felt isolated by shameful secrets. Survivor's groups provide a degree of support and understanding that is simply not available anywhere else. When you join a survivor's group you discover that you are not alone. Learning that others have experienced the same or similar feelings and challenges helps take away the feelings of isolation, shame, and stigma that have plagued you for years.

When a group develops cohesion and intimacy, a complex mirroring process occurs. As participants extend themselves to others, they become more capable of receiving from others. The compassion, tolerance, and love you give to other group members will be returned to you. Group acceptance increases each member's self-esteem, and each member in turn becomes more accepting of others.

Groups also provide collective empowerment. Since it nurtures the strengths of each member the group has the capacity to bear and integrate traumatic experience that is greater than that of any individual member.

Recommended Therapies

There are many types of therapies available to help you heal from an abusive childhood. Whichever type you choose I suggest you find someone who specializes in the treatment of abuse survivors and has several years' experience working with this population.

Supportive Therapy

Earlier in the book I discussed the importance of having a compassionate witness who will listen to your story in a caring, concerned way. Psychotherapy with a supportive, caring therapist has proven to be more effective than analytical, insight-based therapies for the treatment of childhood abuse. Although this kind of therapy may be interesting, reassuring, and helpful in understanding your childhood, it is unlikely to provide real healing, to provide you with what you missed out on in childhood, or to restructure your personality. But four to six years of a loving relationship with a therapist who provides you with unconditional regard can supply the repeated contact with a responsive environment (also known as re-parenting) that can provide real healing.

Cognitive-Behavioral Therapy (CBT)

Not everyone has the financial means for the long-term, intensive treatment that is often needed to help heal an abusive childhood. With a cognitive-behavioral approach the therapist focuses on teaching you new behaviors versus attempting to make deeper changes. The therapist uses your ability to think to help you control your behavior and focuses both on observable behavior and on the thinking or beliefs that accompany the behavior. This type of therapy is especially effective for those who have exhibited self-destructive or abusive behavior. According to the cognitive-behavioral model, since violence is a learned behavior, nonviolence can similarly be learned.

The Interactional Model

The goal of interaction therapy is for each partner in a relationship to identify and change how he or she contributes to the problems in the relationship. The problem with most couples counseling is that those who are being abused usually are unable to speak up for themselves or adequately explain how their partner's behavior is affecting them. Also, those who are abusive tend to be experts on making themselves look good and on clouding the real issues.

I have created a way of working with couples called *synchronistic healing,* in which the focus is on healing each partner's past so they do not continue to act out or project their unfinished business onto each other. I use this method primarily with couples where one or both are emotionally abusive. Abusive behavior is addressed but in a nonblaming manner. It is viewed as a symptom of an abusive childhood or a reenactment of previous trauma, not something that one intentionally does. The abusive partner is taught how to have empathy for his or her partner, ways to contain his or her anger, and ways to identify and cope with his pain and shame. The abused partner is taught assertiveness techniques, encouraged to put her own needs and the needs of her children ahead of her partner's needs, and taught to communicate limits and boundaries. Both partners are encouraged to focus on healing their abusive childhood instead of focusing so much on their partner.

Treatment of Posttraumatic Stress Disorder

Therapeutic approaches commonly used to treat PTSD include:

- Cognitive-behavioral therapy (CBT)
- Eye movement desensitization and reprocessing (EMDR)
- Pharmacotherapy (medication)
- Group Treatment
- Brief psychodynamic psychotherapy

COGNITIVE-BEHAVIORAL THERAPY (CBT)

Increasingly used in the treatment of dissociative disorders (DID) and borderline pesonality disorder (BPD), dysfunctional or maladaptive behaviors, thoughts, and beliefs are replaced by more adaptive ones. *Exposure therapy* is one form of CBT unique to trauma treatment which uses careful, repeated, detailed imagining of the trauma (exposure) in a safe, controlled context, to help the survivor face and gain control of the fear and distress that was overwhelming in the trauma. Along with exposure, CBT for trauma includes learning skills for coping with anxiety (such as breathing retraining or biofeedback) and negative thoughts (cognitive restructuring), managing anger, preparing for stress reactions (stress inoculation), handling future trauma symptoms, as well as addressing urges to use alcohol or drugs when they occur (relapse prevention), and communicating and relating effectively with people (social skills or marital therapy).

EMDR (EYE MOVEMENT DESENSITIZATION AND REPROCESSING)

A procedure that produces rapid eye movements in a client while a traumatic memory is recalled and processed. This technique seems to lessen the amount of therapeutic time needed to process and resolve traumatic memories. Developed by Francine Shapiro, this technique requires training and following of specific protocols for appropriate use. For more information contact:

EMDR Centers
P.O. Box 141743
Austin, TX 78714-1743
(512) 451-6944 (to obtain a referral in your area).

Treatment for Borderline Personality Disorder

DBT (Dialectic Behavioral Therapy)

Though the term borderline personality disorder is sometimes considered pejorative, there is no question that people (mostly women) who carry this label are highly distressed and in a great deal of emotional and often physical pain. Regardless of what you believe about the label borderline, the skills developed by Marsha Linehan to treat this disorder are highly effective. The people who commit to doing the skills training offered in Dialectic Behavioral Therapy (DBT) groups get better. Most mental health centers now offer DBT groups. Refer to Marsha Linehan's *Skills Training Manual for Treating Borderline Personality Disorder* (Guilford Press, New York, 1993) for more information on this form of therapy.

Epilogue

You and I have been on quite a journey together throughout this book. I've shared more about myself than I have in any other book in the hope that you would not feel alone in your struggle to break the cycle. My deepest hope is that you do not stop working on breaking the cycle when you put down this book. It will take continued diligence on your part to catch yourself in the act when you begin to repeat your parents' or an abuser's abusive or neglectful behavior. It will take continual courage on your part to stand up to those who try to dominate or control you and to walk away from abusive relationships that are replicas of those you experienced in your childhood. But you must remain strong. Breaking the cycle of abuse or neglect is probably the most important thing you will ever do in your lifetime—for yourself, for your partner, for your children, and for your children's children. It is also the most significant contribution you can make to society. By not passing on the abuse and neglect you experienced as a child you are contributing to the betterment of our world, as opposed to simply creating more problems.

I value your feedback and would appreciate hearing about how this book has affected you. I am also available for lectures and workshops. You can e-mail me at Beverly@beverlyengel.com or write to me at P.O. Box 6412, Los Osos, CA 93412-6412.

Resources

HOTLINES

National Child Abuse Hotline: A twenty-four-hour child abuse hotline. Trained crisis counselors provide crisis intervention, information and referrals. (800) 4-A-CHILD

RAINN: Rape, Abuse and Incest National Network. National hotline linked to rape crisis centers; refers callers to survivor resources for support.

(800) 656-HOPE (4673)

National Domestic Violence Hotline. Staffed twenty-four hours a day by trained counselors. (800) 799-SAFE (7233)

PREVENTION OF CHILD ABUSE

Organizations

CALM (National Committee to Prevent Child Abuse). Good prevention resources, conferences, and newsletter.
332 S. Michigan Avenue,
Suite 1600
Chicago, IL 60604

Center for Improvement of Child Caring, Effective Black Parenting Program
1-800-325-CICC
www.ciccparenting.org
Childhelp USA is dedicated to meeting the physical, emotional, educational, and spiritual needs of abused and neglected children. Founded in 1959, Childhelp USA is one of the largest and oldest national nonprofits dedicated to the prevention and treatment of child abuse and neglect. Its comprehensive programs and services include the Childhelp USA National Child Abuse Hotline, 1-800-4-A-CHILD®; residential treatment facilities (villages) for severely abused children; child advocacy centers that reduce the trauma of child abuse victims during the interview and examination process; group homes; foster family selection, training and certification; child abuse prevention programs; and community outreach.

Internet Resources

International Society for the Prevention of Child Abuse and Neglect. www.ispcan.org
www.prevent-abuse-now.com

Generation Five, whose goal is to end child sexual abuse within five generations. Provides resources. www.generationfive.org

The Safer Society Foundation, a nonprofit organization that maintains a treatment provider database and referral for residential and outpatient treatment programs in North America. It also specializes in sexual abuse prevention and treatment publications. www.safersociety.org

Stop It Now, a nonprofit organization dedicated to the prevention of child abuse through public health approaches, including effective treatment. www.stopitnow.com

CHILD ABUSE RESOURCES

National Council on Child Abuse and Family Violence. Provides information and referrals on spouse, child, and elder abuse through their toll-free help line operated 8:00 A.M. to 5 P.M. PST, Monday through Friday.
(800) 422-4453 (calls on child abuse)
(800) 537-2238 (spouse or partner abuse)
(800) 879-6682 (elder abuse)
(800) 221-2681 (counseling referrals)

DOMESTIC VIOLENCE RESOURCES

National Coalition Against Domestic Violence (NCADV).
This Web site provides many links to other organizations against domestic violence, including those assisting victims with special issues, such as rural residents, gays and lesbians, and immigrants. www.ncadv.org (303) 839-1852

American Indian Women's Circle Against Domestic Violence
1929 S. 5th St.
Minneapolis, MN 55454
(612) 340-0470

Asian Task Force Against Domestic Violence
P.O. Box 120108
Boston, MA 02112
(617) 338-2350

Black Battered Women's Project
2616 Nicollet Ave. South
Minneapolis, MN 55408

National Gay and Lesbian Domestic Violence Victims' Network
3506 S. Ouray Circle
Aurora, CO 80013
(303) 266-3477

BATTERER'S RESOURCE AGENCIES

EMERGE
2380 Massachusetts Ave.
Cambridge, MA 02140
(617) 422-1550

National Training Project
206 W. Fourth St.
Duluth, MN 55806
(218) 722-2781

The Oakland Men's Project
1203 Preservation Parkway, Suite 200
Oakland, CA 94612
(510) 835-2433

POSTTRAUMATIC STRESS DISORDER

National Center for PTSD: www.ncptsd.org.
The Sidran Foundation, the only nonprofit, charitable organization specifically devoted to providing mental health information, resources, publications, and education to survivors of psychological trauma, their supportive family members and mental health care service providers. The Sidran Press publishes books and educational materials on traumatic stress and dissociative conditions. www.sidran.org.

SURVIVORS OF CHILDHOOD SEXUAL ABUSE

American Coalition for Abuse Awareness/One Voice, a national organization that operates a phone line offering legal referrals and research information. Provides press kits on sexual abuse and memory. Maintains online resource lists, with the latest legal, research, public policy, and media articles regarding childhood sexual abuse and adult survivors.
P.O. Box 27958
Washington, D.C. 20038-7958
(202) 667-1160
ACAADC@aol.com

VOICES in Action, Inc. A national network of incest survivors and supporters. Includes over a hundred special interest support groups.

P.O. Box 14830
Chicago, IL 60614
(312) 327-1500

The Linkup. A national organization of survivors of clergy abuse.
1412 West Argyle
#2
Chicago, IL 60640
(773) 334-2296
www.ilikeup.org

IF YOU HAVE SEXUALLY ABUSED A CHILD OR YOUR SPOUSE HAS SEXUALLY ABUSED YOUR CHILD

Parents United International, an organization that provides individual and group therapy as well as a guided self-help component. Treatment is available for offenders, nonoffending parents, and survivors.
232 Gish Road
San Jose, CA 95112
(408) 453-7616, ext. 124

Stop It Now! Focuses on ending sexual abuse through nonpunitive (recuperative) accountability for offenders.
1-888-PREVENT
www.stopitnow.org

Association for the Treatment of Sexual Abusers, the primary organization of professionals who evaluate, treat, or supervise adolescent and adult sex abusers and it also has links to other sites that may be helpful. www.atsa.com.

References

CHAPTER 2. ASSESSING YOUR RISK FACTORS

American Psychological Association President's Task Force on Violence and the Family, 1994.

Judith Herman, M.D., *Trauma and Recovery* (New York: Basic Books, 1997).

National Center on Child Abuse and Neglect, U.S. Department of Health and Human Services, "Caregivers of Young Chidren: Preventing and Responding to Child Maltreatment" (1992).

Prevent Child Abuse America, "Total Estimated Cost of Child Abuse and Neglect in the United States" (2001).

————. "The Relationship between Parental Alcohol or Other Drug Problems and Child Maltreatment" (1996).

H. N. Snyder and M. Sickmund, *Juvenile Offenders and Victims.* A national report. Washington, DC: OSSDP, U.S. Dept. of Justice (1995).

"Links to Child Abuse," Oregon State University Study, *USA Today,* December 2001, p. 6 (1).

CHAPTER 3. WHY WE DO TO OTHERS (AND TO OURSELVES) WHAT WAS DONE TO US

E. H. Carmen, et al., "Victims of Violence and Psychiatric Illness," *American Journal of Psychiatry,* 141 (1984): 378–383.

Rebecca Coffey, *Unspeakable Truths and Happy Endings* (Lutherville, Maryland: Sidran Press, 1998).

Lloyd deMause, *Journal of Psychohistory,* 25 (Winter 1998).

R. C. Kessler, et al. "Past-year use of outpatient services for psychiatric problems in the National Comorbidity Survey." *American Journal of Psychiatry,* 156 (1991): 115–123.

Alice Miller, *For Your Own Good: Hidden Cruelty in Child-Rearing and the Roots of Violence* (New York: Farrar, Straus, Giroux, 1984).

CHAPTER 4: COMING OUT OF DENIAL

Judith Herman, M.D., *Trauma and Recovery.*

CHAPTER 5: LEARN TO IDENTIFY AND MANAGE YOUR EMOTIONS

Marti Loring, *Emotional Abuse: The Trauma and the Treatment* (San Francisco: Jossey-Bass, 1994).

CHAPTER 6: HOW TO IDENTIFY AND MANAGE YOUR SHAME

Judith Herman, M.D., *Trauma and Recovery.*

Gershen Kaufman, *Shame: The Power of Caring* (Cambridge, Mass: Schenkman Publishing Co., 1980).

H. B. Lewis, *Shame and Guilt in Neurosis* (New York: International Universities Press, 1971).

Lewis B. Smedes, *Shame and Grace: Healing the Shame We Don't Deserve* (San Francisco: HarperSanFrancisco, 1993).

Lenore Terr, M.D., *Too Scared to Cry: How Trauma Affects Children . . . and Ultimately Us All* (New York: Basic Books, 1990).

Herbert E. Thomas, M.D., *The Shame Response to Rejection.* (New York: Alband Publishing, 1997).

CHAPTER 7: MANAGING YOUR ANGER

Beverly Engel, *Honor Your Anger: How Transforming Your Anger Style Can Change Your Life* (New York: John Wiley and Sons, 2003).

Lenore Terr, M.D., *Too Scared to Cry.*

CHAPTER 8: COPING WITH FEAR

Judith Herman, M.D., *Trauma and Recovery*

CHAPTER 9: HOW TO PREVENT PARTNER ABUSE

Beverly Engel, *Loving Him without Losing You* (New York: John Wiley and Sons, 2000).

Judith Herman, M.D., *Trauma and Recovery*

CHAPTER 10: HOW TO PREVENT CHILD ABUSE

Beverly Engel, *The Parenthood Decision* (New York: Doubleday, 1998).

David Finkelhor, *Child Sexual Abuse: New Theory and Research* (New York: The Free Press, 1984).

James Garbarino, *Lost Boys: Why Our Sons Turn Violent and How We Can Save Them* (New York: Anchor, 2000).

Diana Russell, *The Secret Trauma: Incest in the Lives of Girls and Women* (New York: Basic Books, 1986).

Chapter 12: If You Have Already Been Abused

Dawn Bradley Berry, J.D., *Domestic Violence Sourcebook* (Los Angeles: Lowell House, 2000).

Lenore Walker, *The Battered Woman* (New York: Harper and Row, 1982).

Chapter 14: Face the Truth about Your Family Legacy

Joyce Allan, *Because I Love You: The Silent Shadow of Child Sex Abuse* (Virginia, Virginia Foundation for the Humanities Press, 2002).

Chapter 16: Continue to Heal

Judith Herman, M.D., *Trauma and Recovery.*

Marsha Linehan, *Skills Training Manual for Treating Borderline Personality Disorder* (New York: Guilford, Press, 1993).

Recommended Reading

ANGER

Engel, Beverly. *Honor Your Anger: How Transforming Your Anger Style Can Change Your Life* (New York: John Wiley and Sons, 2003).

Harbin, Thomas J. *Beyond Anger: A Guide for Men* (New York: Marlowe and Company, 2000).

Lerner, Harriet Goldhor. *The Dance of Anger: A Woman's Guide to Changing the Patterns of Intimate Relationships* (New York: Harper and Row, 1985).

Williams, Redford, and Virginia Williams. *Anger Kills: 17 Strategies for Controlling the Hostility That Can Harm Your Health* (New York: Harper Paperbacks, 1993).

ANGER, VIOLENCE, AND CHILDREN/ADOLESCENCE

Fried, Suellen. *Bullies and Victims: Helping Your Child Survive the Schoolyard Battlefield* (New York: M. Evans and Co., 1998).

Garbarino, James. *Lost Boys: Why Our Sons Turn Violent and How We Can Save Them* (New York: Anchor, 2000).

Levy, Barrie. *In Love and in Danger: A Teen's Guide to Breaking Free of Abusive Relationships* (Seattle: Seal Press, 1993).

APOLOGY AND EMPATHY

Ciaramicoli, Arthur, and Katherine Ketcham. *The Power of Empathy: A Practical Guide to Creating Intimacy, Self-Understanding, and Lasting Love* (New York: Dutton, 2000).

Engel, Beverly. *The Power of Apology: Healing Steps to Transform All Your Relationships* (New York: John Wiley and Sons, 2001).

BREAKING THE CYCLE

Engel, Beverly. *The Parenthood Decision* (New York: Doubleday, 1998).

Miedzian, M. *Boys Will Be Boys: Breaking the Link Between Masculinity and Violence* (New York: Anchor Books, 1991).

Pipher, Mary. *Saving the Selves of Adolescent Girls* (New York: Ballantine, 1995).

Schwartz, Pepper. *Peer Marriage: How Love Between Equals Really Works* (New York: Free Press, 1994).

DOMESTIC AND PARTNER VIOLENCE

Barnett, O.W., and A.D. LaViolette. *It Could Happen to Anyone: Why Battered Women Stay* (Newbury Park, Calif.: Sage Publications, 1993).

Berry, Dawn Bradley. *The Domestic Violence Sourcebook* (Los Angeles: Lowell House, 2000).

Hegstrom, Paul. *Angry Men and the Women Who Love Them: Breaking the Cycle of Physical and Emotional Abuse* (New York: Beacon Hill Press, 1999).

Ni Carthy, Ginny. *Getting Free: You Can End the Abuse and Take Back Your Life* (Seattle: Seal Press, 1986).

Paymar, Michael. *Violent No More: Helping Men End Domestic Abuse* (Alameda, CA: Hunter House, 1993).

Walker, Lenore. *The Battered Woman* (New York: Harper and Row, 1982).

Wilson, K. J. *When Violence Begins at Home* (Alameda, CA: Hunter House, 1997).

EMOTIONAL ABUSE

Engel, Beverly. *The Emotionally Abused Woman* (New York: Ballantine, 1990).

———. *The Emotionally Abusive Relationship* (New York: John Wiley & Sons, 2002).

FORGIVENESS

Enright, Robert D. *Exploring Forgiveness* (Madison, Wisc.: University of Wisconsin Press, 1998).

Klein, Charles. *How to Forgive When You Can't Forget: Healing Our Personal Relationships* (New York: Berkley Publishing Group, 1997).

McCullough, Michael E., Steven J. Sandage, and Everett L. Worthington. *To Forgive is Human: How to Put Your Past in the Past* (Illinois: InterVarsity Press, 1997).

Safer, Jeanne. *Forgiving and Not Forgiving: A New Approach to Resolving Intimate Betrayal* (New York: Avon, 1999).

Smedes, Lewis B. *Forgive and Forget: Healing the Hurts We Don't Deserve* (San Francisco: Harper and Row, 1984).

HEALING CHILDHOOD ABUSE

Banerott, Lundy. *When Dad Hurts Mom: Helping Your Children Heal the Wounds of Witnessing Abuse* (New York: Penguin, 2004).

Farmer, Steven. *Adult Children of Abusive Parents* (New York: Ballantine Books, 1989).

Forward, Susan. *Toxic Parents* (New York: Bantam, 1989).

Golumb, Elan. *Trapped in the Mirror: Adult Children of Narcissists in Their Struggle for Self* (New York: William Morrow, 1992).

Miller, Alice. *The Drama of the Gifted Child*, rev.ed. (New York: Basic Books, 1994).

———. *For Your Own Good*, 3rd ed. (New York: Noonday Press, 1990).

Sahiraldi, Glenn. *Post-Traumatic Stress Disorder Sourcebook* (New York: McGraw Hill, 2000).

HEALING CHILD SEXUAL ABUSE

Bass, Ellen, and Laura Davis. *The Courage to Heal.* (New York: HarperCollins, 1988).

Blume, E. Sue. *Secret Survivors* (New York: Ballantine, 1991).

Engel, Beverly. *The Right to Innocence: Healing the Trauma of Childhood Sexual Abuse* (New York: Ballantine Books, 1989).

———. *Families in Recovery: Healing the Damage of Childhood Sexual Abuse* (McGraw Hill, 2000).

Hagans, Kathryn. *When Your Child Has Been Molested* (San Francisco: Jossey-Bass, 1997).

Lew, Mike. *Victims No Longer* (New York: William Morrow, 1992).

Love, Patricia. *The Emotional Incest Syndrome* (New York: Bantam, 1991).

PREVENTION OF CHILD ABUSE

de Becker, Gavin. *The Gift of Fear: Survival Signals that Protect Us from Violence.* (New York, Little Brown, 1997).

———. *Protecting the Gift: Keeping Children & Teenagers Safe.* (New York: Dell, 2000).

Monteleone, James, M.D. *A Parent's and Teacher's Handbook on Identifying and Preventing Child Abuse* (New York: G. W. Medical Publishing, 1998). Available from the Safer Society Press.

Salter, Anna. *Predators: Pedaphiles, Rapists and Other Sex Offeners: Who They Are, How They Operate, and How We Can Protect Ourselves and Our Children* (New York: Basic Books, 2003).

RECONCILIATION

Davis, Laura. *I Thought We'd Never Speak Again* (New York: HarperCollins, 2002).

SHAME

Kaufman, Gershen. *Shame: The Power of Caring* (Cambridge, Mass: Schenkman Publishing Co., 1980).

Smedes, Lewis B. *Shame and Grace: Healing the Shame We Don't Deserve* (San Francisco: HarperSanFrancisco, 1993).

Thomas, Herbert E., M.D. *The Shame Response to Rejection* (New York: Albanel Publishing, 1997).

STRESS REDUCTION

Davis, Martha, Matthew McKay, and Elizabeth Eshelman. *The Relaxation and Stress Reduction Workbook* (Oakland: New Harbinger, 2000).

Epstein, Robert. *The Big Book of Stress Relief Games* (New York: McGraw-Hill, 2000).

Kabat-Zinn, Jon. *Wherever You Go, There You Are: Mindfulness Meditations for Everyday Life* (New York: Hyperion, 1995).

Miller, Fred, and Mark Bryan. *How to Calm Down* (New York: Warner Books, 2003).

YOUR FAMILY LEGACY AND HEALING FAMILY CONFLICTS

Allan, Joyce. *Because I Love You: The Silent Shadow of Child Sex Abuse* (Virginia: Virginia Foundation for the Humanities Press, 2002).

Bloomfield, Harold. *Making Peace with Your Parents* (New York: Ballantine Books, 1983).

Engel, Beverly. *Families in Recovery: Working Together to Heal the Damage of Childhood Sexual Abuse* (New York: Contemporary Books, 2000).

———. *Divorcing A Parent* (New York: Ballantine Books, 1991).

McGoldrick, Monica. *You Can Go Home Again* (New York: W.W. Norton, 1995).

Secunda, Victoria. *When You and Your Mother Can't Be Friends* (New York: Dell Publishing, 1990).

Index